For William,

From Belfast to Bosnia, and beyond....
Who would have thought
it?

With best wishes,
much appreciation,
and warm regards.

Chris

April 2013

COURTS AND CONSOCIATIONS

COURTS
AND
CONSOCIATIONS

HUMAN RIGHTS VERSUS
POWER-SHARING

CHRISTOPHER McCRUDDEN

AND

BRENDAN O'LEARY

OXFORD

UNIVERSITY PRESS

OXFORD
UNIVERSITY PRESS

Great Clarendon Street, Oxford, OX2 6DP,
United Kingdom

Oxford University Press is a department of the University of Oxford.
It furthers the University's objective of excellence in research, scholarship,
and education by publishing worldwide. Oxford is a registered trade mark of
Oxford University Press in the UK and in certain other countries

First Edition published in 2013

Impression: 1

British Library Cataloguing in Publication Data

Data available

ISBN 978-0-19-967684-2

Printed and bound in Great Britain by
CPI Group (UK) Ltd, Croydon CR0 4YY

Christopher McCrudden dedicates this book to his family—Caroline, Joseph, and Kathleen—with love, and with gratitude for the many arguments over the dinner table that helped to sharpen his thoughts and test his conclusions. This book is as much theirs as it is his.

Brendan O'Leary dedicates this book to the women in his family—Lori, Anna, Hana, and Leila. His family is American, English, and Irish, and all four women have dual ethnic origins. They are just, they negotiate peacefully, and they share power. Sometimes, they agree with him.

Preface

A tale from the future and a salutary story of our times

In October 2024, in the last major legislative initiative of his second term, President James ('Jaime') Garcia persuaded the US Senate to ratify the treaty that he had championed since he had first run for office.[1] Under its provisions, the United States acceded to the Pan-American Convention on Human Rights and Freedoms of 2022, which it had helped to draft, and accepted that the new Pan-American Court of Human Rights and Freedoms had the right to hear cases brought by aggrieved US citizens, including cases dismissed by the US Supreme Court. The chief motivation for US accession to the treaty, it was widely agreed, was to secure for US citizens protection against recent excessive incursions on their liberties, and the US had agreed to bring its law into compliance with the Treaty. Exactly ten years later, however, Garcia expressed astonishment on being told the opinion of the Pan-American Court, in its first important case involving a US citizen. Although the US Supreme Court had earlier held the opposite, the Pan-American Court ruled that article II, §1 of the US Constitution violated the right to equal citizenship of Arnold Schwarzenegger, the former Governor of California. The Court also instructed the US authorities to initiate the required amendments to the offending section, which reads:

> No Person except a natural born Citizen, or a Citizen of the United States, at the time of the Adoption of this Constitution, shall be eligible to the Office of President; neither shall any Person be eligible to that Office who shall not have attained to the Age of thirty five Years, and been fourteen Years a Resident within the United States.[2]

1. Garcia was the first Latino to be elected US President.
2. For early twenty-first-century critical commentary on article II of the US Constitution, see Sanford Levenson, *Our Undemocratic Constitution: Where the Constitution Goes Wrong (and How We Can Fix It)* (Oxford: Oxford University Press 2006) chs 2 and 5.

The Court declared the clause 'nativist' because it negatively discriminates against citizens who emigrated to the United States after the adoption of the constitution. It further maintained that, because the provision lacked objective reasons for its defence, it was 'ethnicist' and 'racist'. Lastly, it held that the provision was 'ageist'. Even though Schwarzenegger's lawyer had not raised the question of the age bar, given that it did not affect the rights of his 87-year-old client, the Court declared that the time was ripe for the US government to modify article II to make all adult citizens eligible for the presidency.

Governor Schwarzenegger professed himself delighted. Refusing to answer when asked whether he would ever run for the White House, he calmly pointed out that changing the US Constitution to comply with the verdict would take time and affirmed that he had taken the case solely to ensure that, in future, all US citizens would be fully equal under the constitution. At a hastily summoned news conference, former President Garcia declared that he would not have advocated, or signed, the treaty had he known that such a ruling would emerge: it had never been his intention to allow the Court to strike down provisions in the constitution regarding the presidency or any other core US governmental institutions. He concluded rhetorically: 'What next? Is the Court now going to strike down the principle of having two senators from each state because voters in small states have more power than voters in large states and that violates equal citizenship?' Seventy-three-year-old former President Barack Obama, by contrast, seemed more relaxed about the opinion. Working at home in Chicago on the eighth volume of his memoirs, he was door-stepped by a web-blogging researcher affiliated with Fox News, whom he is reported to have told: 'Well, had this verdict been around and followed before I ran for the presidency, at least I would not have had to worry about the "birthers".'[3]

After the Court's opinion was published, there was silence for a day from the White House. Then, the Attorney General of the US government, Caitlyn Young, issued a brief statement standing beside the President in the Rose Garden. She expressed disappointment that the Court had ruled that the constitutional provision violated citizens' right to equality and made five

---

3. 'Birther' was the US name for those who believed that President Obama had not been a native-born American citizen and called for his 'real' birth certificate to be released: *Global Dictionary of English Slang* (17th edn, Oxford: Oxford University Press 2035) 321.

points. First, the words of article II, §1, show that, in the drafting of the US
Constitution, foreign-born US citizens, at the time the constitution was
ratified, were eligible for the presidency. For example, foreign-born citizens
who had served as soldiers or diplomats during the revolutionary war, in
principle, could have run for this office, provided that they had been
resident for fourteen years. Therefore the full provision did not have the
impugned 'nativist', let alone ethnicist or racist, character suggested by
the Court.

Second, the Court had paid no attention to the historical context in
which the provision had been drafted and which explained its adoption on
objective grounds. As revolutionary republicans, the US founding fathers
were determined to prevent the restoration of monarchical rule. Consequently, they had introduced an age bar to inhibit the likelihood of young,
unknown, and untested 'favourite sons' succeeding to their fathers' roles—
then a common occurrence in aristocratic and monarchical societies, and
indeed in colonial America.[4] All presidents (and vice-presidents) born after
the constitution came into force were required to be native-born precisely
to prevent the possibility that a rich and foreign-born prince, earl, or duke
might become a US citizen and become an instrument for the subversion of
the new republic. The historical record shows that these fears were widespread among Americans in the 1780s and 1790s, and after.[5] Had more open
eligibility rules for the presidency been drafted instead, then they might well
have jeopardized the constitution's prospects of successful ratification.

Third, the Court had failed to respect the democratic character of the
constitution's ratification. It had been ratified in elected state conventions,

---

4. Akhil Reed Amar, *America's Constitution: A Biography* (London: Random House 2005) 160–4.
5. Joseph Story, the most famous early commentator on the US Constitution, argued that the
   rule:

> cuts off all chances for ambitious foreigners, who might otherwise be intriguing for the
> office; and interposes a barrier against those corrupt interferences of foreign governments
> in executive elections, which have inflicted the most serious evils upon the elective
> monarchies of Europe. Germany, Poland, and even the pontificate of Rome, are sad, but
> instructive examples of the enduring mischiefs arising from this source.

> (*Commentaries on the Constitution*, 1833 3: §§1472–73, cited in Philip B. Kurland
> and Ralph Lerner, *The Founders' Constitution, vol. 3*, Chicago,
> IL: University of Chicago Press 1987, 564)

Historians have shown both that such plots were feared and that at least one was started during
the constitutional convention itself: see Amar (n. 4) 165.

expressly convened to deliberate on the merits of the draft constitution, and after which a Bill of Rights was entrenched in the opening amendments of the US Constitution.

Fourth, the Court had failed to treat the subject as within the legitimate margin of discretion to which a sovereign democratic republic should be entitled—especially one with an excellent track record of granting immigrants full citizenship rights and, since 1965, of doing so on a non-discriminatory basis.

Lastly, the Court had failed to exercise restraint. It could have quietly allowed time for the US government to amend its constitution, under its established rules of amendment.

Concluding more in sorrow than in anger, Young said that the ruling had made it less likely that any US government would propose an amendment any time soon. Even if a future US government were to attempt such an enterprise, the Court's opinion had made it less likely that it would succeed. Responding to reporters' questions, the Attorney General, looking at the President, declared that she could not speak for, or bind, future administrations, but she confirmed that, in the remainder of this administration's term, a campaign to amend the constitution to make it compliant with the Court's opinion would not be a priority. More important subjects were on its agenda, including an arms limitation treaty with China, and the planned merger of the dollar and the euro into a single currency.

*   *   *

This story may strike the 2010s reader as a risible tall tale from an unlikely future. Sceptics may respond by insisting that no US government would ever sign such a treaty. Others may argue that no international court would risk losing its credibility by issuing such instructions to the US government. Critics of the tale, we agree, have significant historical evidence to support their scepticism. It is not our intent, however, to suggest that this tall tale predicts the most likely future for relations between powerful democratic states and international courts; rather, it is to emphasize that something resembling this tale has already occurred regarding a small state, in our own times, and that this fact has not been sufficiently noticed.

This true story has many salutary warnings for those who care about democracy, and the making and keeping of peace through power-sharing in particular. An assertive international human rights court, overturning its previous restraint and caution in prior analogous cases, has recently considered itself to have appropriate power and jurisdiction on an extraordinary matter. It has deemed itself fully entitled to determine whether the provisions governing the eligibility for the role of head of state and the senate in the constitution of a democratic country, forged in a peace agreement that settled a bloody civil war, are consistent with international human rights norms. It has found that the relevant country's provisions violate these norms and has instructed the government of the state in question to modify its constitution.

The European Court of Human Rights (ECtHR) has recently done all of this in a landmark decision in a case taken against the sovereign state of Bosnia.[6]

*   *   *

Dervo Sejdić and Jakob Finci are both citizens of Bosnia Herzegovina (BiH, or simply 'Bosnia').[7] They describe themselves as of Roma and Jewish origin, respectively. Mr Sejdić was the Roma monitor of the Bosnian OSCE[8] Mission. He previously served as a member of the highest representative body of the local Roma community in Bosnia, and as a member of the joint body of representatives of the local Roma community and of the relevant government ministries. Mr Finci, by contrast, has served as the ambassador of Bosnia to Switzerland, having previously been president of the Inter-Religious Council of Bosnia and the head of the State Civil Service Agency. For four years, in the late 1990s, he was executive director of the Soros Foundation Open Society Fund for Bosnia. He has been decorated several times. He holds the Grand Cross of the Order of Merit of Germany and is a French Chevalier of the Legion of Honour. Both men are plainly influential people.

---

6. *Sejdić and Finci v. Bosnia and Herzegovina* Application nos 27996/06 and 34836/06, Grand Chamber Judgment, 22 December 2009.
7. We use the informal name 'Bosnia' to refer to the entire state of Bosnia and Herzegovina throughout this book, in conformity with most local and international usage. The state consists of two entities: the Federation of Bosnia and Herzegovina; and the Serb Republic. Calling the state 'Bosnia' is no slur on the state, or on the residents of Herzegovina, and it does not obliterate the Serb Republic. It enables the foreign reader to remember that the Federation of Bosnia and Herzegovina is not territorially coextensive with the (federal) state of the same name, and thereby to differentiate the internal federation from the state as a whole. When quoting others, we have also systematically replaced the abbreviation 'BiH' with 'Bosnia', so that the number of abbreviations is radically reduced. We have kept 'BiH' only where it is used in naming legal cases or in the titles of publications.
8. Organization for Security and Co-operation in Europe.

In the summer of 2006, Sejdić and Finci challenged the Bosnian constitutional provisions that provide that only persons declaring affiliation with one of three 'constituent peoples' in Bosnia are entitled to stand for certain elected posts. In the Preamble to the constitution, Bosniaks,[9] Croats, and Serbs are described as 'constituent peoples'. The constitution makes a distinction between these 'constituent peoples' and 'Others', which would include other minorities, such as Roma and Jews, or Montenegrins or Vlachs, those from 'mixed marriages', and those who chose not to self-identify with any of the 'constituent peoples'.[10] Bosniaks are predominantly Bosnian Muslims by origin or belief; Bosnian Serbs are predominantly Serbian Orthodox by origin or belief; and Bosnian Croats are predominantly Roman Catholic by origin or belief. Since neither Sejdić nor Finci declared an affiliation with any of the three constituent peoples, they were ineligible to stand for election to the presidency (the three-person, collective head of state) and to the House of Peoples, the second chamber of the state Parliament, which may be thought of as the federal senate of Bosnia. They complained to the ECtHR that their ineligibility to stand for election was because of their Roma and Jewish origin.

In its judgment of December 2009, the ECtHR Grand Chamber concluded, by fourteen votes to three, that the applicants' ineligibility to stand for election to the state's House of Peoples of Bosnia *was* because of their ethnic identity, and that it lacked an objective and reasonable justification. Bosnia had therefore breached the prohibition of discrimination in the conduct of elections under the European Convention for the Protection of Human Rights and Fundamental Freedoms (European Convention on Human Rights, or ECHR) Article 14 (the prohibition on discrimination),[11] read in conjunction with Article 3 of Protocol No. 1 (on the right to

---

9. We use 'Bosniak' throughout this text rather than 'Bosniac'; we understand that this choice has no political implications. To avoid ambiguity, all quotations referencing 'Bosniac' or 'Bosniacs' have been converted to 'Bosniak' and 'Bosniaks'.
10. Edin Hodžić and Nenad Stojanović, *New/Old Constitutional Engineering? Challenges and Implications of the European Court of Human Rights Decision in the Case of* Sejdić and Finci v BiH (Sarajevo: Analitika 2011) 55.
11. Article 14 ECHR provides that:

The enjoyment of the rights and freedoms set forth in this Convention shall be secured without discrimination on any ground such as sex, race, colour, language, religion, political or other opinion, national or social origin, association with a national minority, property, birth or other status.

elections).[12] Furthermore, the constitutional provision under which the applicants were ineligible for election to the state presidency was also held to constitute ethnic discrimination more broadly under the relatively recent prohibition against discrimination in Protocol No. 12. It too was said to lack an objective and reasonable justification. Accordingly, the Court concluded, by sixteen votes to one, that there had been a violation of Protocol No. 12.[13]

Although the term is never used in the judgment of the Court, which preferred the expression 'power-sharing', the arrangements that were challenged and found to be in breach of the Convention are classic components of what is now called 'consociation', especially, but not only, in the political science literature. Even more precisely, we will maintain that they are components of a 'corporate consociation'. Understanding the *Sejdić and Finci* case, and its consequences, is of critical importance for an appreciation of the future relationship between consociations and courts in European, and international, human rights law. The case has elicited highly mixed reactions. For one of the dissenting judges, Judge Bonello, the two applications to the Court 'may be the simplest the Court has had to deal with to date, but they may well be, concurrently, among the more *insidious*'.[14] The case raises, directly and dramatically, the role of courts in balancing the desire to end bloody ethnic conflicts with the need to establish an acceptable degree of human rights protections in the longer term in profoundly divided places.

In this book, we consider the use of consociational arrangements to manage ethno-nationalist, ethno-linguistic, and ethno-religious conflicts, and their compatibility with non-discrimination and equality norms, particularly under the ECHR. We show how consociational cases have figured in precedent-establishing ECtHR decisions. Key questions include to what

---

12. Article 3 of Protocol No. 1 provides that: 'The High Contracting Parties undertake to hold free elections at reasonable intervals by secret ballot, under conditions which will ensure the free expression of the opinion of the people in the choice of the legislature.'

13. Article 1 of Protocol No. 12 provides that:

   (1) The enjoyment of any right set forth by law shall be secured without discrimination on any ground such as sex, race, colour, language, religion, political or other opinion, national or social origin, association with a national minority, property, birth or other status.

   (2) No one shall be discriminated against by any public authority on any ground such as those mentioned in paragraph 1.

14. *Sejdić and Finci v. Bosnia* (n. 6) [53].

extent, if any, consociations conflict with the dictates of global justice and
the liberal individualist preferences of international human rights institutions, and to what extent consociational power-sharing may be justified to
preserve peace and the integrity of political settlements. We argue that, in
three critical cases, the ECtHR has considered equality challenges to
important consociational practices: twice in Belgium; and most recently in
Sejdić and Finci, concerning the constitutional arrangements established for
Bosnia under the Dayton Peace Agreement of 1995. We argue that the
Court's recent decision in *Sejdić and Finci* has significantly altered the
approach that it previously took to judicial review of consociational
arrangements. We seek to account for this change and to assess its implications. We identify several problematic aspects of the judgment. Although
the Court's decision indicates one possible trajectory of human rights
courts' reactions to consociations, we believe that trajectory would be
most unfortunate. If that trajectory continues, it will leave future negotiators
in other places riven by bloody ethnic conflicts with considerably less
flexibility in reaching a settlement. It may, therefore, unintentionally contribute to sustaining such conflicts, while making it more likely that legal
advisers to negotiators will recommend that regional and international
courts are excluded from having any standing in the management of
political settlements.

*   *   *

This case is the subject and occasion of this book, but it is not all that this
book is about. The argument developed in the pages that follow is not a
romantic protest on behalf of small states, such as Bosnia, compared with
large and powerful states, such as the United States. We do not complain
that small states are more likely to be targeted by international law and
courts than are powerful states, although we recognize that international law
and courts are sometimes quite uneven in their application. The propos-
itions advanced form no part of a polemic against human rights norms, or
against international courts, or international law. We have no wish to add to
the many screeds in this vein that often have a xenophobic provenance.
One of the authors professes human rights law as his employment and both
authors have promoted human rights provisions in constitutional advisory
work in sites of past conflict. We frequently agree with human rights
advocates in seeking to remedy provisions in constitutions, laws, or policies
that appear, on their face, to be exclusionary in a racist, ethnic, religious,

sectarian, sexist, or homophobic manner. One of the authors helped to draft a section of a law that places a significant equality duty on public author- ities.[15] This author is therefore deeply concerned to promote equality law and good relations amid diversity. The same is true of the other author, who is on record as welcoming the human rights possibilities in the agreement that led to the statute just cited. He maintained that the new human rights order should be made unambiguously compatible with the statute's power- sharing provisions, which, with many others, he had helped to promote.[16] So neither author should be misread as an opponent of human rights: we are friends of human rights. We are not, however, human rights absolutists: when rights clash, some rights may be more important than others. Rights, moreover, should not always 'trump' other claims of policy. Our position, to paraphrase Shakespeare, is that there are more and better things on earth than are dreamt of by some individualist philosophers of human rights. One of these is the set of political arrangements known as 'consociation'. As we shall argue, consociation is often among the best available institutional responses to deep-rooted antagonisms between peoples.

The argument to follow resembles that which we attribute to Attorney General Young in the tall tale with which this preface opened. First, some provisions in constitutions that may appear nativist, ethnicist, or racist in character may not be exactly what they seem to impatient minds. They deserve care in their interpretation.

Second, the historical and political contexts in which the provisions of constitutions and peace agreements are drafted—especially peace agree- ments that are constitutional texts—need to be properly understood, espe- cially by courts. Apparently repugnant provisions may have defensible political origins. They may have been adopted for 'objective reasons'— a phrase that lawyers and judges use to suggest that there were, and are, publicly defensible reasons that led to the drafting of the provisions in question. They were not, in a word, 'arbitrary'. In particular, fears, espe- cially prominent when making political agreements to terminate wars or after the fall of tyrannical regimes, may generate demands for credible and enduring constitutional commitments that deserve due respect from courts.

---

15. Northern Ireland Act 1998, s. 75. See also Christopher McCrudden, 'Mainstreaming Equality in the Governance of Northern Ireland' (1998) 22 Fordham International Law Journal 1696.
16. See Brendan O'Leary, 'The Protection of Human Rights under the Belfast Agreement' (2002) 72 Political Quarterly 353 and 'The Nature of the Agreement' (1999) 22 Fordham Journal of International Law 1628.

Third, in evaluating constitutions or 'organic laws' (that is, laws that have a constitutional purpose and are usually more difficult to pass or amend than other laws), courts need to consider carefully whether these laws have a democratic character. Were they made in a generally inclusive manner? Were all of the affected people(s) in some reasonable sense free to be represented in the negotiations and deliberations? Were these deliberations ratified by democratic means? If they were, then such provisions deserve greater respect from courts than those that were not; higher standards of human rights scrutiny and protection are warranted when such democratic features are absent.

Fourth, even when a constitution or statute appears to conflict with valued human rights, prudent courts are well advised to treat such subjects as within the legitimate margin of appreciation allowed to a sovereign democratic republic, where the relevant constitutional clauses or laws are designed to resolve deep-rooted antagonisms. Courts should be especially mindful of provisions within peace agreements or constitutions that allow for their review and amendment. When contemplating modifying 'ethnic bargains', courts should respect the rules for change embedded within such bargains.

Lastly, wise courts, especially those with a specialist remit, should exercise restraint both in making meta-political judgments and in giving advice to governments. To issue instructions in a manner that makes it more likely that a judgment will not be followed at all, or that it will be complied with only in a grudgingly literal way, is not to be judicious—that quality most sought from courts.

We address here whether and when an international or regional court of human rights should adjudicate on nationally, ethnically, or religiously sensitive clauses in generally democratic constitutions or laws. If it should have such powers, should its scope extend beyond issuing advisory warnings? Should it have the power to unwind constitutional bargains made by the representatives of nationalities, or ethnic or religious groups, who have been in conflict and who may start, or restart, a war with one another? We certainly intend to be read as seeking to defend the wisdom of adopting what we will describe as defensible 'consociational bargains', showing that they provide one valuable and democratic means of bringing national, ethnic, and religious hostilities to a constructive resolution. Our argument, however, is not confined only to such consociational bargains; it may also apply to multinational federations or union-states that protect group-based bargains.[17] There is, of course, variation in such bargains. Some are more liberal and human rights sensitive than others. What we argue against here is a particular form of universalist, or 'difference-blind', international human rights judicial activism. We think that this 'difference-blind' activism is generally well intentioned, but it has the potential to jeopardize peace and human security. It may worsen or delay the better protection of human rights.

We began with a tall tale from the future based on article II, §1, of the US Constitution. One reason why we did so was to suggest that many constitutional bargains that specify the rules governing the formation and allocation of positions within executives and legislatures may look repugnant to the proponent of universal human rights. It may seem unjust that the US presidency, the most powerful executive position on the planet, is reserved for the native-born and older citizens. Yet, on inspection, it can be defensibly argued that republican (anti-monarchical) principles explain why these rules were initially adopted. It may well seem just to modify these rules and to update them now when the fears that initially prompted the rules have generally dissolved. If so, however, it would be best if such rules were changed under the existing provisions for changing the rules. We hypothesize that few believe that a good route to changing such rules is through the judgment of an international court.

A careful and systematic investigation of the constitutions and organic laws governing the formation and composition of executives, legislatures, militaries, and judiciaries throughout the world's governments would turn up many apparently archaic anomalies or rank injustices. Quite a few would be more profoundly obnoxious, from the perspective of human rights standards, than those found in article II, §1, of the US Constitution. Blood ties, religious tests, and sexist eligibility rules for executive and legislative office exist aplenty amid the world's constitutions and laws, often derived from restrictions on citizenship based on racial, ethnic, religious, or patriarchal dogmas. Let us therefore be clear: it is no part of the argument that follows to suggest that such provisions should be immunized against human rights or any other kind of egalitarian or republican criticism. To the contrary. When such criticism is valid, however, the key question is:

---

17. Belgium is an example of a multinational federation. The United Kingdom, Spain, and India are examples of union-states that have made specific territorial settlements with nationalities or peoples other than the dominant group.

'What is to be done?' Our answer is not that international courts should impose abstract rules come what may—especially when they lack context-sensitive expertise or legitimacy, and when they may endanger peace and democratic stability. Better answers are, we think, outlined in our conclusions. Those who want to see how we derive these conclusions will read on...

Christopher McCrudden
Brendan O'Leary

Oxford, and Philadelphia, PA
October 2012

Acknowledgements

Earlier versions of this argument were presented as seminar papers or lectures at: the Harvard Law School; the University of Michigan Law School; the Institute for Advanced Studies in Jerusalem; Cardozo Law School, New York; the School of Law, Queen's University, Belfast; the Hebrew University, Jerusalem; and the 'Workshop on Ethnic Politics and Electoral Democracy', organized by Bernard Grofman and the Center for the Study of Democracy, University of California, Irvine, and University of Zurich, and by Daniel Boschler of the University of Zurich. We would like to thank all of the participants in these events for their responses, as well as many of our respective colleagues. We have tried to learn from all as best we could. We owe special thanks to Clive Baldwin, Christine Bell, Lucy Claridge, Sujit Choudhry, Jon Fraenkel, Robert Hayden, Donald Horowitz, Samuel Issacharoff, John McGarry, Richard Pildes, Steven Ratner, Sheri P. Rosenberg, Wojciech Sadurski, Rogers Smith, and Nenad Stojanović, and to the anonymous referees who commented on an earlier draft. Christopher McCrudden completed the book whilst holding a Leverhulme Major Research Fellowship, without which it could not have been written. We also wish to thank the Registry for the European Court of Human Rights for allowing us access to its files concerning the case of *Pilav v. Bosnia and Herzegovina*.

Contents

List of Abbreviations

ANC	African National Congress
BiH	Bosnia Herzegovina
CIA	(US) Central Intelligence Agency
DG	Directorate-General
DPA	Dayton Peace Agreement 1995
ECHR	European Convention on Human Rights
ECRI	European Commission against Racism and Intolerance
ECtHR	European Court of Human Rights
ERRC	European Roma Rights Centre
EU	European Union
EUPM	European Union Police Mission
FBiH	Federation of Bosnia and Herzegovina
ICCPR	(UN) International Covenant on Civil and Political Rights
ICERD	(UN) International Convention on the Elimination of All Forms of Racial Discrimination
IDC	Research and Documentation Centre (*Istraživačko Dokumentacioni Centar*)
IFOR	Implementation Force (NATO)
IGO	inter-governmental organization
INGO	international non-governmental organization
Inter-Am Ct HR	Inter-American Court of Human Rights
MRG	Minority Rights Group International
NGO	non-governmental organization
OHR	Office of the High Representative
OSCE	Organization for Security and Co-operation in Europe
PR	proportional representation
RS	Serb Republic (*Republika Srpska*)
SAA	stabilization and association agreement

SDA   Party of Democratic Action (*Stranka Demokratske Akcije*)
SFOR   Stabilization Force (NATO)
STV   single transferable vote
UN   United Nations
US   United States

About the Authors

Christopher McCrudden LLB (QUB), LLM (Yale), DPhil (Oxon), LLD (QUB, Hon), FBA, is Professor of Human Rights and Equality Law at Queen's University Belfast, Leverhulme Major Research Fellow (2011–14), William W. Cook Global Professor of Law at University of Michigan Law School, and a practising barrister at Blackstone Chambers, London.

Brendan O'Leary BA (Oxon), MA (UPenn, Hon), PhD (LSE), is Lauder Professor of Political Science at the University of Pennsylvania, Professor of Political Science at Queen's University Belfast (2012–14), and former senior adviser on power-sharing in the Standby Team of the United Nations Mediation Support Unit.

I

Consociations and consociationalism

John Stuart Mill famously argued that democracy was not compatible with a multinational state. 'Free institutions', he wrote in 1861, 'are next to impossible in a country made up of different nationalities.'[1] Political practice has long sought to prove him wrong, with numerous different strategies developed to support democratic government within multiethnic and multinational states. There are, broadly, two grand strategies that democratic states may adopt to deal with such differences.[2] The first aims to *eliminate* differences from public life, either through assimilation or through a 'liberal integrationist' approach, and often relies on a strategy of majority rule and minority rights, endeavouring to produce a sense of common citizenship based on shared values. The second strategy *manages* the differences, through several institutional options, which may, however, be combined. Federalism is one such strategy.[3] Institutions may also be designed to induce politicians to behave moderately, including moderately toward those from other groups, in what Donald Horowitz has termed 'centripetalism'.[4] Consociationalism is an alternative strategy for managing differences. The expression was rediscovered and remade by political scientist Arend Lijphart, who argues that its practices have a long political

---

1. John Stuart Mill, 'Considerations on Representative Government' in H.B. Acton (ed.) *Utilitarianism, On Liberty and Considerations on Representative Government* (London: Dent 1988) 392.
2. Brendan O'Leary and John McGarry, 'The Politics of Accommodation and Integration in Democratic States' in Adrian Guelke and Jean Tournon (eds) *The Study of Politics and Ethnicity: Recent Analytical Developments* (Leverkusen: Barbara Budrich 2012) 79–116.
3. O'Leary and McGarry (n. 2) 98–101. Federal systems, however, may either be 'territorially pluralist', recognizing and accommodating national and ethnic differences, or they may be integrationist or assimilationist (as the United States has been for much of its history).
4. O'Leary and McGarry (n. 2) 89–92.

pedigree, and are not merely associated with, let alone simply the creation of, modern political science.[5] It is a power-sharing approach that addresses the management of places divided by nationality, ethnicity, language, religion, and other powerful non-class cleavages, including ideological cleavages.[6] 'Consociation' is the noun for the precise institutional arrangements that combine principles of parity, proportionality, autonomy, and veto rights, and on which we will shortly elaborate.

Political scientist Rupert Taylor, no enthusiast of consociation, has identified twenty-nine 'strong' consociational settlements across the world that have been discussed in the political science literature, twelve of which remain in effect and ten of which are recent.[7] Rudy Andeweg, another political scientist, suggests that the number of consociational 'sightings' appears to be increasing.[8] Perhaps the most noteworthy fresh 'sighting' is the European Union itself, as part of discussions of European con-federalization, constitutionalization, and interpretations of its past and possible trajectories.[9] Analysts observe that the European Union has a power-sharing executive (in the Council of Ministers and the Commission), in which principles of parity, proportionality, inclusivity, unanimity, and qualified majority voting often apply. The principle of proportionality applies in the representation of member states in the European Parliament (weighted toward the small states) and often in Union expenditures, whereas the principle of parity operates, for example, in the representation of member-state judges in the European Court

5. Lijphart credits David Apter with reviving an expression first used by Althusius: see David Apter, 'Political Religion in the New Nations' in Clifford Geertz (ed.) Old Societies and New States: The Quest for Modernity in Asia and Africa (New York: Free Press 1963); for Althusius, see Johannes Althusius, Politica (tr. Frederick S. Carney, Liberty Classics edn, Indianapolis, IN: Liberty Fund 1995) and Thomas O. Hueglin, Early Modern Concepts for a Late Modern World: Althusius on Community and Federalism (Waterloo, ON: Wilfrid Laurier University Press 1999).
6. See Arend Lijphart, Democracy in Plural Societies: A Comparative Exploration (New Haven, CT: Yale University Press 1977); many of his major articles on consociation are collected in Arend Lijphart, Thinking about Democracy: Power Sharing and Majority Rule in Theory and Practice (London: Routledge 2008).
7. Rupert Taylor, 'Introduction: The Promise of Consociational Theory' in Rupert Taylor (ed.) Consociational Theory: McGarry and O'Leary and the Northern Ireland Conflict (London: Routledge 2009) 1–12.
8. Rudy B. Andeweg, 'Consociational Democracy' (2000) 3 Annual Review of Political Science 509.
9. Dimitris N. Chryssochoou, 'Democracy and Symbiosis in the European Union: Towards a Confederal Consociation?' (1994) 17 West European Politics 1; Paul Taylor, 'The Lessons of the European Community: The Limits of European Integration—The Concepts of Consociation and Symbiosis' in Paul Taylor (ed.) International Organization in the Modern World: the Regional and the Global Process (London: Pinter 1993); Matthijs Bogaards and Markus M.L. Crepaz, 'Consociational Interpretations of the European Union' (2002) 3 European Union Politics 357.

of Justice. The autonomy of member states is respected in matters affecting national, ethnic, and religious identity. The European Union, for example, has no competence over language, religion, or culture. Veto rights and opt-outs are also formally embedded in the Union's decision-making rules and treaties.

The analogy is suggestive. Europe has a bloody past. Straightforward majoritarian decision-making would not be feasible for the multinational, multiethnic, multiracial, multilingual, and multireligious European Union, the constituent peoples of which do not regard themselves as members of a single demos. Its member states are highly sensitive to intrusions on their autonomy. It is difficult, if not impossible, to imagine the European Union functioning with a 'winner takes all' executive and legislature (or judiciary). The European pedigree of consociationalism should therefore not be in any doubt. European states, or regions of states, that have adopted consociational arrangements at various stages since the nineteenth century include Belgium (1918–), the Netherlands (1917–67), Switzerland (which combines consociational and federal principles), Austria (1945–66), Cyprus (1960–63), Macedonia (2000–), Alto Adige/South Tyrol (1972–), and Northern Ireland (1973–74, 1998–).[10] In the last decade, and before its declaration of independence, Kosova arguably had quasi-consociational arrangements imposed on it by the European Union and the United Nations.[11] The distribution of consociational institutions across Europe is not accidental. They have existed amid sites of past or recent national and ethnic and religious conflict (Northern Ireland and Macedonia), ethnic and linguistic disputes (Belgium), religious conflict (the Netherlands),[12] or permutations

---

10. To avoid cluttering the text with lengthy footnotes, a bibliographical guide on each of these cases is supplied at the end of this book.

11. See Alexandra de Renzy Channer, 'Defeat and Resurrection: A Political History of the Pan-Albanian Revolutionary Movement, 1912–2010' (Unpublished PhD thesis, University of Pennsylvania 2012); Alan Taylor, 'Electoral Systems and the Promotion of "Consociationalism" in a Multiethnic Society: The Kosovo Assembly Elections of November 2001' (2005) 24 Electoral Studies 435.

12. An example of an African power-sharing system that attempted to address (partly) religious cleavages is Côte d'Ivoire. It has been criticized by Andreas Mehler, 'Not Always in the People's Interest: Power-Sharing Arrangements in African Peace Agreements' German Institute of Global and Areas Studies (GIGA) Working Papers (Hamburg: GIGA 2008); see also Denis Tull and Andreas Mehler, 'The Hidden Costs of Power-Sharing: Reproducing Insurgent Violence in Africa' (2005) 104 African Affairs 375. We share the view that promoting power-sharing arrangements to resolve disputed elections may give power-sharing a bad name, especially if it provides perverse incentives for incumbent politicians to steal elections: see Brendan O'Leary, 'Power-Sharing in Deeply Divided Places: An Advocate's Conclusion' in Joanne McEvoy and Brendan O'Leary (eds) *Power-Sharing in Deeply Divided Places* (Philadelphia, PA: University of Pennsylvania Press 2013). For one review of such pseudo-power-sharing, see

of racial, national, ethnic, and linguistic conflict (Alto Adige, Cyprus, and Kosova). Bosnia is therefore not only truly European in being consociational, but also its constitution's prescribed institutions resemble those of the European Union far more than those of the stereotypical nation-state.

Recent influential accounts of peace agreements establish that, among the menu of institutional responses available to local and international negotiators responding to bloody conflict, consociation has been one of the options of choice over the past twenty years.[13] Power-sharing, in both consociational and federal forms, is now frequently recommended as best practice by international organizations, both inter-governmental organizations (IGOs)[14] and non-governmental organizations (NGOs).[15] The United Nations now regularly appoints an expert on power-sharing to the Standby Team of the Mediation Support Unit of its Department of Political Affairs[16]—an illustration that consociational and other power-sharing thought has been partly mainstreamed into international responses to civil wars or protracted violent conflicts. Three examples shall suffice. In Bosnia and in Northern Ireland, the adoption of consociational arrangements, among other provisions, was strongly promoted by US envoys. In Cyprus, successive UN diplomats have, so far unsuccessfully, proposed power-sharing arrangements, combining federal and consociational

Nic Cheeseman and Tendi Blessing-Miles, 'Power-Sharing in Comparative Perspective: The Dynamics of "Unity Government" in Kenya and Zimbabwe' (2010) 48 Journal of Modern African Studies 203.

13. Christine Bell, *Peace Agreements and Human Rights* (Oxford: Oxford University Press 2000) and 'Peace Agreements: Their Nature and Legal Status' (2006) 100 American Journal of International Law 373.

14. '[At] the beginning of the twenty-first century, the attitude toward reserved communal seats and special mechanisms has swung to a point where they are considered signs of liberal progressiveness': Andrew Reynolds, 'Reserved Seats in National Legislatures' (2005) 30 Legislative Studies Quarterly 301. Anne Marie Wieman, 'Consociationalism with an External Actor in Bosnia: Blueprint for Success or Instability' (Unpublished MA dissertation, Rijksuniversiteit Groningen 2010) 23, writes that these types of arrangement are a 'preferred method of the international community to end an ethnic conflict or at least to manage conflicts', citing Ulrich Schneckener, 'Making Power-Sharing Work: Lessons from Successes and Failures in Ethnic Conflict Regulation' (2002) 39 Journal of Peace Research 203.

15. See Peter Harris and Benjamin Reilly, *Democracy and Deep-Rooted Conflict: Options for Negotiators* (Stockholm: International Institute for Democracy and Electoral Assistance 1998); Andrew Reynolds and Benjamin Reilly, *The International IDEA Handbook of Electoral Design* (Stockholm: International Institute for Democracy and Electoral Assistance 1997); and Timothy D. Sisk, *Power Sharing and International Mediation in Ethnic Conflicts* (Washington, DC: United States Institute of Peace 1996).

16. O'Leary held this position in 2009–10; the first postholder was John McGarry in 2008–09.

elements, to settle the dispute between Turkish and Greek Cypriots.[17] Political philosopher Will Kymlicka is not alone in highlighting the increased role that the 'international community' has played in promoting strategies of accommodating national and ethnic difference, including consociation.[18] Mona Lena Krook and Diana O'Brien have observed that consociation has been 'taken up and promoted by international actors, such as the Carnegie Corporation, the OSCE [Organization for Security and Co-operation in Europe], and the International Institute for Democracy and Electoral Assistance'.[19]

Although the European Union's external affairs policy on minorities has been ambiguous, consociation has been encouraged in *practice* by the European Union in its accession negotiations with Central, Eastern, and Balkan European applicant or pre-applicant states in order to establish secure and stable inter-ethnic relations.[20] Krook and O'Brien have argued that power-sharing institutions 'may appear especially attractive to parties if [an] agreement offers important side benefits, like foreign aid or international legitimacy, which are jeopardized if a settlement is not reached'.[21] In 2000, the European Commission for Democracy through Law, better known as the 'Venice Commission', the Council of Europe's advisory body on constitutional matters established in 1990, identified

---

17. For the key role of US envoys in promoting power-sharing, see Daniel L. Curran, James K. Sebenius, and Michael Watkins, 'Two Paths to Peace: Contrasting George Mitchell in Northern Ireland with Richard Holbrooke in Bosnia-Herzegovina' (2004) 20 Negotiation Journal 513. For Northern Ireland's 'consociational plus' features, see John McGarry and Brendan O'Leary, 'Consociation and its Critics: Northern Ireland after the Belfast Agreement' in Sujit Choudhry (ed.) *Constitutional Design for Divided Societies: Integration or Accommodation?* (Oxford: Oxford University Press 2008). On Cyprus, see Claire Palley, *An International Relations Debacle: The UN Secretary-General's Mission of Good Offices in Cyprus, 1999–2004* (Oxford: Hart 2005).

18. Will Kymlicka, 'The Internationalization of Minority Rights' in Sujit Choudhry (ed.) *Constitutional Design for Divided Societies: Integration or Accommodation?* (Oxford: Oxford University Press 2008). Elsewhere, Kymlicka has observed that non-territorial autonomy has become strongly preferred as a prescription for managing national minorities by OSCE member states and the High Commissioner on National Minorities: Will Kymlicka, *Multicultural Odysseys: Navigating the New International Politics of Diversity* (Oxford: Oxford University Press 2007) e.g. 236–7. That is because they think that non-territorial autonomy is less likely to provide secessionist opportunities than territorial autonomy. Differently put, a key element of consociational design is seen as a less risky institutional innovation.

19. Mona Lena Krook and Diana Z. O'Brien, 'The Politics of Group Representation: Quotas for Women and Minorities Worldwide' (2010) 42 Comparative Politics 253.

20. Martin Brusis, 'The European Union and Interethnic Power-Sharing Arrangements in Accession Countries' (2003) 1 Journal on Ethnopolitics and Minority Issues in Europe 1.

21. Krook and O'Brien (n. 19).

'power-sharing political arrangements' based on the Northern Ireland model as one method of facilitating the settlement of ethno-political conflicts in Europe.[22] Given that there is almost no credible dissent from the view that the Northern Ireland model is consociational, we may say that the Venice Commission has, on occasion, looked benignly on consociations. As a way of regulating conflicts, consociationalism cannot be classified as idiosyncratic or particularist; it has regularly been reinvented, with or without direct imitation of exemplary models, and it has increasingly been advocated by external agents and internationalized.

A. Defining consociations

What, then, are the key elements that define consociations as distinct institutional arrangements? In democratic consociations, four are commonly identified. The first is *parity through cross-community power-sharing*—that is, arrangements that encourage or oblige communities to make public policy and law *jointly*, through executive, legislative, judicial, policing, and bureaucratic institutions that ensure that the relevant groups are represented adequately in such institutions. 'Power-sharing', so defined, may include: collective presidencies or co-premiers; rules encouraging (or mandating) the formation of inclusive multiparty governments; proportional electoral and allocation rules for the choice of legislators, cabinet members, and judges; and co-decision-making rules, which prevent simple majorities from making law or policy, and which may mandate either concurrent or qualified majorities in decision-making. Examples may include bicameral or tricameral parliaments or assemblies, which deliberately enhance the powers of minorities through co-decision-making, or concurrent or qualified majority rules. Such cross-community power-sharing aims to achieve greater inclusivity, jointness, and parity than 'winner takes all' democracy. Consociation is just one type of such power-sharing. It requires co-decision-making among constitutionally or legally recognized groups, which enjoy political parity as consociational partners. Other forms of

---

22. Council of Europe, *A General Legal Reference Framework to Facilitate the Settlement of Ethno-political conflicts in Europe*, CDL-INF(2000)16 (Strasbourg: Venice Commission 2000) 7. See further Venice Commission, *Report on Dual Voting for Persons Belonging to National Minorities*, CDL-AD(2008)013 (Strasbourg: Venice Commission 2008) para. 50: 'States have a large scope of appreciation in the matter and many different solutions are possible.'

power-sharing are compatible with consociation, and combinable with it, but they are distinct. These include temporary multiparty coalition governments, or federations that create exclusive and shared territorial powers among federal and regional governments, but which may not oblige inter-group power-sharing. In a federation in which powers are shared between federal and regional governments, one nationality, ethnic group, linguistic community, or political party may still dominate all of the federal and regional governments, so although there may be power-sharing among the federated entities, there is not consociational power-sharing.

The second key feature of a consociation is *community autonomy*. Each recognized group in the consociation has a great deal of internal self-government in at least one public function, for example in establishing and controlling its own schools. Equality between the partner communities in these respects is the norm. So community *self*-government accompanies *shared* government. Autonomy is not an accidental feature of consociations. Without some distinct component of autonomy, power-sharing is not consociational. What degree of autonomy is entrenched varies considerably from consociation to consociation, both in the number of policy domains in which autonomy operates and the degree of autonomy recognized. The system of education in Belgium, in which each of its two major linguistic communities has significant autonomy in the running of its schools, is a good illustration of how autonomy can play an important role in consociational arrangements.

Consociation, simply put, obliges jointness in managing some public functions, while shielding other functions from the decision-making of the entire polity. There are, of course, many different types of arrangement that have been described as 'autonomy' arrangements, but we are concerned with only one of these. Henry Steiner, for example, distinguishes three types of 'autonomy' regime.

1. The first 'gives an ethnic minority political control over a certain territory',[23] developing territorial autonomy or federalism to allow ethnic groups concentrated in a particular geographical region a certain degree of self-rule. An example might be the creation of

23. Henry J. Steiner, 'Ideals and Counter-Ideals in the Struggle over Autonomy Regimes for Minorities' (1991) 66 Notre Dame Law Review 1539.

territories over which Native Americans exercise a degree of territorial autonomy.[24]

2. The second 'provides that members of an ethnic community will be
governed by a personal law distinctive to it, usually a law of religious
origin'.[25] The millet system under which religious communities were
governed by separate personal laws, such as those still found in many
countries formerly part of the Ottoman Empire, is an example.[26]

3. The third is the type of 'power-sharing' regime with which we are
concerned here and which Steiner describes, slightly contentiously, as
'carv[ing] up a state's population in ethnic terms to assure one or
several ethnic groups of a particular form of participation in governance or economic opportunities'.[27]

Consociations therefore protect one distinct type of autonomy—namely,
the exercise of rights by a group in one or more functional domains. These
rights are not necessarily to be understood as being exercised through
conventional territorial power, in which a local, provincial, or federal
regional government allocates or distributes political power across the
entirety of a specified territory, affecting all persons. Where a group and a
territory, for practical purposes, coincide, then functional and territorial
autonomy may coincide—for example, in a region that is thoroughly
dominated by one group whose language is in ubiquitous use, and in
which there are no visible minorities. So consociations may make use of
territorial governments to enable groups to exercise autonomy in given

24. Whether Native American reservations are authentic systems of autonomy has long been
controversial. As those sympathetic to Native Americans observe, since Chief Justice Marshall
the American Supreme Court has tellingly defined Native Americans as 'domestic dependent
nations': see e.g. Vine Deloria Jr and Clifford M. Lytle, *The Nations Within: The Past and
Future of American Indian Sovereignty* (New York: Pantheon Books 1984) 16ff. Native American
reservations and 'treaties' between the federal government and Indian nations have not made
the United States a multinational federation in legal theory or practice.
25. Steiner (n. 23) 1542.
26. Benjamin Braude and Bernard Lewis (eds) *Christians and Jews in the Ottoman Empire: The
Functioning of a Plural Society, Vol. II: The Arabic-Speaking Lands* (Teaneck, NJ: Holmes and
Meier 1982). For a critical view of how the millet system operated, see Bat Ye'or, *The
Dhimmi: Jews and Christians under Islam* (trs David Maisel, Paul Fenton, and David Littman,
Madison, NJ: Fairleigh Dickinson University Press 1985). Personal law systems existed under
the Mughal Empire, but also in British India: Ainslie T. Embree, *Utopias in Conflict: Religion
and Nationalism in Modern India* (ed. Mark Juergensmeyer, Berkeley, CA: University of
California Press 1990).
27. Steiner (n. 23) 1540. It is contentious because the 'carving' metaphor presupposes an organic
unity before the carving—precisely what may be at issue.

domains, but it is *functional* autonomy that is distinctively characteristic of consociational government. It is typically exercised through *functional* self-government and administration, for example through community councils, school boards, or broadcasting authorities.

The third feature is *proportionality*—that is, representativeness in shared institutions, and in the allocation of important resources and public offices (such as in the civil service, police, and judiciary), usually by reference to the proportions of the contending groups in the population as a whole or in the labour market. Proportionality may also apply to the allocation of public expenditures (for example, each group receives the same per capita funding for its primary schools). In Northern Ireland, for example, not only do Catholics have a significant degree of autonomy in establishing and controlling their own schools, but these schools now also receive equivalent funding to that which state schools receive.[28]

Fourth, because power-sharing, proportionality, and autonomy may not provide sufficient assurance to particular groups that their interests will not be overridden, explicit *veto rights* may be granted to each of the communities on vital issues. There are numerous variations in the ways in which these veto rights are allocated and legally entrenched. Some may be implicit in the rules of co-decision-making; others may be overtly exercised through legal rights that may be unilaterally invoked.

Each of these four elements is necessary for there to be a classic consociation. In (full) consociations, there is power-sharing, autonomy, proportionality in representation and allocation, and there may also be explicit veto rights. In a semi-consociation, by contrast, some elements of consociations will be present, but not others. Beyond Europe, semi-consociational arrangements have been adopted in Iraq, Fiji (in the past), South Africa (temporarily), and somewhat fuller consociational arrangements in Lebanon.[29] In semi-consociations, there may be proportionality and

28. Christopher McCrudden, 'Religion and Education in Northern Ireland', in Myriam Hunter-Henin (ed.) *Law, Religious Freedom and Education in Europe* (Aldershot: Ashgate 2012).
29. On Iraq, see John McGarry and Brendan O'Leary, 'Iraq's Constitution of 2005: Liberal Consociation as Political Prescription' (2007) 5 International Journal of Constitutional Law 670; on Fiji, Venkat Iyer, ' Enforced Consociationalism and Deeply Divided Societies: Some Reflections on Recent Developments in Fiji' (2007) 3 International Journal of Law in Context 127; on consociation in the Interim Constitution of South Africa, see Heinz Klug, *South Africa's Experience in Constitution-Building*, University of Wisconsin Legal Studies Research Paper No. 1157 (2011). Under the National Pact and the 1989 Ta'if Accord, Lebanon 'currently allocates three of its most important political offices—the presidency, premiership, and speaker of the legislature—to a Christian, Sunni Muslim, and Shi'a Muslim respectively':

autonomy, for example, but no guaranteed long-run power-sharing or fully effective veto rights. This distinction matters because some semi-consociational practices, often known as 'multiculturalism', are not meant to encompass the entire relevant polity; they are related to improving the inclusiveness of otherwise majoritarian liberal democracies[30] and they are generally thought to be *temporary* measures. These, for example, are the premises on which affirmative action practices are often justified (or attacked).[31] Consociational arrangements, by contrast, often attempt to reconstitute relationships on a *durable* basis. Indeed, time-limiting the period during which full consociational arrangements are to operate is likely to defeat one of the major functions that such arrangements serve—namely, to provide a sense of security and stability to the opposing communities, not only for the immediate future, but also for the long term.[32] Full consociational arrangements leave it to the political partners to agree on any modifications or dissolution of the consociation according to previously agreed rules for making laws or constitutional amendments. These are usually intended to prevent the workings of the system from being disturbed by unilateral dissolutions by one of the partners, as well as by outside agents.

B. Opposition to consociationalism

Consociations, such as those in Bosnia and elsewhere, have attracted political support among conservatives, liberals, and socialists, but these three dominant political traditions in the democratic west have also generated sustained criticisms of these arrangements.[33] Heated debate between

McGarry and O'Leary 'Iraq's Constitution'; Theodor Hanf, 'Conflict Regulation and Crises in Multi-Communal States: The Proliferation of Multi-Communal States in the Twentieth Century' in *Coexistence in Wartime Lebanon: Decline of a state and Rise of a Nation* (London: I.B. Tauris & Co 1993).

30. Issacharoff is appropriately tentative in comparing redistricting in the United States to consociational arrangements ensuring proportionality in elections: Samuel Issacharoff, 'Constitutionalizing Democracy in Fractured Societies' (2004) 82 Texas Law Review 1861.

31. Affirmative action is employed for different purposes in different constitutional arrangements. It can be employed in consociations as a policy to secure proportionality, it can be employed as a multicultural strategy, or it can be used as a strategy to achieve integration.

32. Here, we differ from Samuel Issacharoff.

33. For a review of the rhetoric for and against consociation, see Brendan O'Leary, 'Debating Consociational Politics: Normative and Explanatory Arguments' in Sid J.R. Noel (ed.) *From Power-Sharing to Democracy: Post-Conflict Institutions in Ethnically Divided Societies* (Montreal, QC: McGill-Queens University Press 2005).

proponents and opponents of consociation has been long-lasting.[34] Prominent among the current critics are some in the liberal, left, and feminist traditions. Consociational arrangements are regularly alleged to jeopardize important values, principles, and institutions. One prominent critic, Paul Brass, asserts that 'consociational democracy *inevitably* violates the rights of some groups and the rights of some individuals'.[35] For convenience, we shall refer to these critiques of consociationalism as 'liberal', while recognizing that there are several variations of 'liberal', many of which we wish to be associated with and several of which do not share these criticisms of consociation. We also recognize that these criticisms are made by some who do not regard themselves as liberals.

Three specific criticisms recur.[36] First, while consociations are ostensibly directed at protecting ethnic group identities and interests, liberal critics say that they do so by provoking an unacceptable conflict with the value of *non-discrimination* on ethnic grounds. This appears to be a simple criticism on first appearance, but the more it is examined, the more complicated it becomes—in particular because consociation involves a clash between two different understandings of equality, rather than a clash between equality and consociation. An *individualized* conception of equality is undoubtedly put under pressure by consociation, but consociations seek to further equality between the consociated *groups*. Parity (in power-sharing) and proportionality (in representation, institutions, and allocations) may, therefore, conflict with individualized conceptions of equality.

The second criticism arises from the clash between two different conceptions of *political representation*. One conception, as Mona Lena Krook,

34. Rupert Taylor (ed.) *Consociational Theory: McGarry and O'Leary and the Northern Ireland Conflict* (London: Routledge 2009).
35. O'Leary (n. 33) 6 (emphasis original).
36. They interestingly coincide (or at least overlap) with criticisms of the increasing trend to develop quotas for women in legislative and government contexts: Mona Lena Krook, Joni Lovenduski, and Judith Squires, 'Gender Quotas and Models of Political Citizenship' (2009) 39 British Journal of Political Science 781. The phenomenon of women's quotas has striking similarities with some aspects of consociationalism, especially the ideas of *parity* in status (equal partnership in power-sharing) and *proportionality*. Both consociation and women's quotas reconceptualize the nature of political citizenship; neither is seen as simply a temporary fix, but rather as a constitutional device likely to continue significantly into the future. Both, arguably, 'essentialize'. Yet the implications of these similarities are seldom teased out. For some, supporting women's political quotas might, indeed, appear to be the antithesis of consociationalism, but in what sense are ethnic identities less 'progressive' than those based on gender? Why are gender quotas apparently less challenging to equality than consociation? Why are some 'essences' better than others?

Joni Lovenduski, and Judith Squires point out, considers representation 'to be adequate when a representative acts on behalf of and according to the ideas of those who are represented'.[37] Let us call this the 'delegation' model. Alternative conceptions of political representation 'deem the presence of representatives with relevant social or other characteristics to be suffi-cient'.[38] Let us call this the 'politics of presence'.[39] In consociations, the model of political representation is predominantly based on the politics of presence, rather than the politics of delegation. Liberal proponents of delegated representation object to consociation's emphasis on actual, rather than virtual, representation.

The third regular liberal objection is that consociation 'freezes and institutionally privileges (undesirable) collective identities at the expense of more "emancipated" or more "progressive" identities, such as those focused on class or gender'.[40] The critics believe that opportunities for transforming identities are more extensive than is supposed by what they consider to be the unduly pessimistic proponents of consociation. Consoci-ation, it is said, is built on an 'essentialist' view of the nature of the groups involved, which assumes that each group has 'fixed essences given once and for all, with traits that are homogeneously distributed among all the group members'.[41] Such essentialism is rejected as insufficiently sensitive to indi-vidual uniqueness and the personal choice of identity.

In political theory, the debate over the 'liberalism' of consociational arrangements (and their analogues) has become particularly focused on this third criticism. Given that ethnic consociations depend on some idea of the identity group, the issues are how this is to be defined, on the basis of what criteria, and by whom. For Seyla Benhabib, two normative principles beyond simple non-discrimination need to be respected. The first is 'volun-tary self-ascription', meaning that an 'individual must not be automatically assigned to a cultural, religious, or linguistic group by virtue of his or her birth. An individual's group membership must permit the most extensive form of self-ascription and self-identification'. The second is 'freedom of exit and association', meaning that the 'freedom of the individual to exit the

---

37. Krook, Lovenduski, and Squires (n. 36).
38. Krook, Lovenduski, and Squires (n. 36) 789.
39. Anne Phillips, *The Politics of Presence* (Oxford: Oxford University Press 2005).
40. O'Leary (n. 33) 5.
41. Carol C. Gould, 'Diversity and Democracy: Representing Differences' in Seyla Benhabib (ed.) *Democracy and Difference* (Princeton, NJ: Princeton University Press 2005) 182.

ascriptive group must be unrestricted, although exit may be accompanied by the loss of certain formal and informal privileges'.[42]

These criticisms of consociationalism are met with equally robust defences. Prominent defenders of consociation distinguish between 'liberal' and 'corporatist' versions, and prefer the former to the latter, when this is feasible.[43] The main difference between the two primarily addresses the second and third criticisms considered previously. Corporate consociation may accommodate groups according to ascriptive criteria and rest on the assumptions that group identities are fixed, and that groups are both internally homogeneous and externally bounded, while liberal consociation rewards whatever salient political identities emerge in democratic elections, whether these are based on ethnic groups, on subgroups, or on trans-group identities.[44] An important aspect of liberal consociation, then, is the degree to which the arrangements are conceivably transitional, whether the basis of the consociational pact is national, ethnic, racial, religious, or linguistic, or some permutation of such divisions. For liberal consociationalists, accommodation of ethnic identity may be a more successful way of achieving a non-ethnic future. An extensive period of cooperation between rival ethnic groups may be more likely to transform identities in the long run than liberal integrationist approaches to addressing ethnic disputes—or so John McGarry and Brendan O'Leary have argued, developing a line of argument first articulated by Lijphart.[45] The political and legal question to consider is why corporate, rather than liberal, consociational devices may be chosen. Rather than presuming that the demand for corporate consociational arrangements derives from contempt or disregard for individual human rights, it is wiser to consider whether it arises from concerns for durable

---

42. Seyla Benhabib, *The Claims of Culture: Equality and Diversity in the Global Era* (Princeton, NJ: Princeton University Press 2002) 148–9.
43. They are aware that genuine existential anxieties about security will lead to political parties insisting upon corporate rather than liberal arrangements: John McGarry and Brendan O'Leary, *The Northern Ireland Conflict: Consociational Engagements* (Oxford: Oxford University Press 2004) 33.
44. McGarry and O'Leary (n. 29).
45. See Arend Lijphart, 'Self-Determination versus Pre-Determination of Ethnic Minorities in Power-Sharing Systems' in Will Kymlicka (ed.) *The Rights of Minority Cultures* (Oxford: Oxford University Press 1995). It was rarely noted that the second edition of Lijphart's book on the Netherlands described its 'de-pillarization'. Lijphart argued that Dutch consociational arrangements had created sufficient social peace that eventually the system could dissolve without rancour (partly because of secularization): Arend Lijphart, *The Politics of Accommodation: Pluralism and Democracy in the Netherlands* (2nd edn, Berkeley, CA: University of California Press 1975).

and long-run constitutional commitments, and from the potential tension that may exist between recognizing parity among peoples and the merits of the principle of proportionality in voting power.

C. Tensions between parity and proportionality

Power-sharing based on coalition governments that enjoy majority public support among individual voters within a demos is not controversial among democrats, provided that conduct toward those outside the coalition is not nationally, ethnically, linguistically, religiously, or racially discriminatory. Controversy arises, however, when advocates of consociation insist that the relevant political system contains more than one people and that, in these circumstances, an undifferentiated model of equal, or difference-blind, individual citizenship is inappropriate. Advocates of power-sharing may agree that majority rule is a good democratic decision-making rule where there is a unified demos, provided that the decision rule really means majority rule, rather than plurality or factional rule. But where there are multiple peoples in deeply divided places, consociationalists insist that majority rule is not generally appropriate. Such claims challenge the wisdom of institutions based on treating the relevant unit of voting power as one voter with a vote of equal value in the political system as whole. If the premise is granted that there are multiple peoples in the political system, then the inference is drawn that there is a case for parity in voting (or decision-making) power among the relevant peoples, at least on some matters, just as each independent government may count for one in the decisions of some international organizations despite differences in their populations.

The principle of parity and the principle of proportionality imply roughly the same outcome for representation, or for decision-making power, only when the relevant peoples have roughly the same number of valid voters. Imagine that two key peoples in a polity are roughly balanced in size: people A comprises 47 per cent of the electorate; and people B comprises 43 per cent; others (neither As nor Bs) comprise 10 per cent. Imagine further that all voters in each category vote for just one party of their ethnic category under a system of pure proportional representation (PR). In this example, achieving both proportionality, according to equality among individual voters, and parity between the peoples A and B, seems to be not too difficult.[46] In this case, the use of PR to elect legislators, and of a PR system to determine the executive,[47] can be combined with a concurrent majority decision-making rule among the two peoples, A and B, over key matters. Such concurrent majority decision-making can be achieved explicitly through corporate naming (or 'designation') of the peoples, such as: 'A majority of those deputies who represent people A and a majority of those deputies who represent people B as well as a majority in the parliament shall agree before legislation is passed regulating any aspect of policing or internal security.'[48] Such a rule, however, has consequences for the voting power of 'the others' (neither As nor Bs) who may not be pivotal—that is, capable of being decisive in the outcome of a vote.[49] A qualified majority requirement may, however, also be accomplished another way—one that protects both A and B through a difference-blind majority decision-making rule: for example, 'No legislation regarding policing or internal security may pass without the consent of two-thirds of all elected representatives'. This rule would seem to make it difficult to pass legislation against the preferences of a majority in group A or B. Moreover, it treats the non-As and non-Bs equally with the As and Bs. Note, however, that this difference-blind rule does not provide the same measure of reassurance to the larger peoples as did the previous corporate naming rule. Consider people B: in a 100-seat assembly with forty-seven members being in the A party, forty-three in the B party, and ten among the others, it is possible for a two-thirds majority (sixty-seven) to be formed (forty-seven As *plus* ten Bs *plus* ten others) against the wishes of a large majority of the B group (thirty-three out of forty-three). Such a possibility may lead large minorities to prefer designated or corporate forms of concurrent decision-making to difference-blind rules, especially because

---

46. Northern Ireland currently approximates this picture (although two major parties exist among the nationalists and unionists, respectively).

47. In Northern Ireland, the single transferable vote (STV) system of PR is used to elect the Assembly and the proportional 'd'Hondt rule' is used as a sequential allocation rule for forming the Executive: see Brendan O'Leary, Bernard Grofman, and Jørgen Elklit, 'Divisor Methods for Sequential Portfolio Allocation in Multi-Party Executive Bodies: Evidence from Northern Ireland and Denmark' (2005) 49 American Journal of Political Science 198.

48. In Northern Ireland, 'In this Act ... "cross-community support", in relation to a vote on any matter, means—(a) the support of a majority of the members voting, a majority of the designated Nationalists voting and a majority of the designated Unionists voting; ...': Northern Ireland Act 1998, s. 4(5).

49. For discussion, see John McGarry and Brendan O'Leary, 'Stabilising Northern Ireland's Agreement' (2004) 75 Political Quarterly 213; for a rigorous treatment, see Alex Schwartz, 'How Unfair is Cross-Community Consent? Voting Power in the Northern Ireland Assembly' (2010) 61 Northern Ireland Legal Quarterly 349.

they seem more likely to immunize them against demographic shifts that are adverse to their group. This example illustrates why advocates of power-sharing in deeply divided places may favour laws made by concurrent majorities among the key (constituent) peoples who make up the relevant polity, provided that they are working within a viable and just settlement. When that standard cannot be met, advocates of power-sharing may settle for the use of concurrent majorities ('co-decision-making') for key matters, such as constitutional change, provided that the initial constitution is judged fair.

These arguments become more controversial when one people is significantly larger than another. Imagine, for example, that people C comprises 75 per cent of the electorate, people D comprises 20 per cent, and the others (neither Cs nor Ds) comprise 5 per cent. Imagine again that all voters in each category vote for one party of their category under pure PR. In this scenario, it is far more difficult to combine parity and proportionality principles without sharp tension. In a 100-seat assembly, with seventy-five members being in party C, twenty being in party D, and five among the others, then, under a concurrent majority rule, giving parity to C and D would mean that a blocking veto among D would comprise just eleven members. When a people's position resembles that of D and it is sufficiently powerful in its resources (such as threat power, wealth, or external support), its representatives will insist on parity in the executive and a full veto right over all executive and legislative decision-making. Otherwise, they face the prospect of being constantly outvoted by representatives of people C. This could easily happen in this scenario, even under PR, and even under a difference-blind qualified-majority rule for the passage of legislation set at 75 per cent of the legislature or executive.

For the representatives and negotiators of a people with a large or significant majority, ceding parity to any other group for any decisions is the most difficult power-sharing principle to accept. This example should not, however, be considered abstract. Where the ratios of people C to people D are roughly four to one, people C's position resembles that of Greek Cypriots confronting Turkish Cypriots, the Hutus in Rwanda and Burundi confronting Tutsis, the Sinhalese confronting Tamils in Sri Lanka, and Anglophone Canada confronting the Québécois, to name some obvious examples of largely dualistic antagonisms.

Bosnia, however, has not been a case of largely *dualistic* antagonisms; rather, its recent conflicts have largely been three-cornered in nature—triangular—although there have been occasional polarizations when an unstable coalition of two groups formed against one. Almost all external observers agree that three significantly sized peoples and their representatives have been in major conflict. Analysts and partisans have differed in whether they emphasize ethno-national or religious differences. Table 1.1 provides recent demographic estimates of ethno-national distributions in Bosnia in 1991 and 2000. The data suggest that, in 1991, if all Bosniaks had allied with all of the people from one of the other two groups, they would, in principle, have jointly commanded a majority of the population as a whole: either of 60.9 per cent (a Bosniak–Croat alliance) or 74.6 per cent (a Bosniak–Serb alliance). The Bosniaks would also have dominated if they had managed to incorporate small factions of both Croats or Serbs. By contrast, a Serb–Croat alliance would have fallen just short of a potential majority (48.6 per cent) in 1991. Defined ethno-nationally, no single group commanded a majority on its own, but on paper the Bosniaks had the greatest capability of leading a winning electoral alliance.

Bosnia's demography is not only triangular in its ethno-national configuration, but is also primarily triangular in its religious configuration. Table 1.2 compares ethno-national identifications with religious identifications in

Table 1.1 Ethno-national identifications in Bosnia 1991 and 2000 (%)★

	Bosniaks	Serbs	Croats
1991	43.5	31.2	17.4
2000	48.0	37.1	14.3

★ In 1991, 5.5 per cent identified as 'Yugoslavs', 0.2 per cent as 'Montenegrins', 0.2 per cent as Roma, and 2.0 per cent either did not declare or chose 'Other'. In 2000, 'Other' comprised just 0.6 per cent. Killings and flight account for some of the changes in the ethno-national distribution over this decade, as do differences in birth rates. Of those who had identified as 'Yugoslavs', 'Other', or 'Montenegrins' in 1991, we must assume that some were subsequently killed or fled, and others were now likely to identify as 'Bosniaks' or 'Serbs'.
Sources: 1991 Yugoslavia Census; US Central Intelligence Agency (CIA), *The World Factbook* (2000), available online at <https://www.cia.gov/library/publications/the-world-factbook/index.html>

Table 1.2 Ethno-national identifications in Bosnia compared with religious identifications in 2000

National identity	%	Religious identity	%
Bosniaks	48.0	Muslims	40
Serbs	37.1	Orthodox	31
Croats	14.3	Roman Catholics	15

Sources: 1991 Yugoslavia Census; US Central Intelligence Agency (CIA), *The World Factbook* (2000), available online at <https://www.cia.gov/library/publications/the-world-factbook/index.html>

Bosnia in 2000. These crude data, which naturally simplify the scale, intensity, and singularity of these identifications, nevertheless suggest what is confirmed by historians and ethnographers. There is a very strong congruence between ethno-national and religious identifications, even though significant numbers of Bosniaks and significant numbers of Serbs are respectively neither Muslim nor Orthodox in belief, and overall 14 per cent of the population does not identify with any of the three major religions.

These two triangular configurations, which frequently correspond, provide the elementary political sociology for understanding recent (and past) group politics in Bosnia. The 'others', by contrast, do not comprise a significant ethno-national pole. According to the 1991 census, Roma comprised 0.2 per cent of the population, but unofficial estimates identify higher numbers of the total population as Roma; the lower end of the range (that is, around 2 per cent) is more plausible than some of the higher estimates in circulation. There are currently about 500 Jews in Bosnia (mostly in Sarajevo). The non-religious also do not form a strongly unified secular pole—although hopes have been vested in such a project.

These simple data suggest that it should not have been surprising that significant numbers among all three major groups, in either the ethno-national or the religious configuration, would feel politically insecure in 1991, especially given strong memories of communal conflict in the Second World War. If future politics in an independent Bosnia were to divide ethnically or religiously (or in ways in which these two divisions reinforced one another), then each group would face a credible risk of being dominated, or threatened, by the other two under standard majority-rule, 'one person, one vote', arrangements. The democratization and breakup of Yugoslavia posed these risks in excruciating form. Many among the second and third largest groups thought that their lives might be better in a 'Greater Serbia' or a 'Greater Croatia' than in a multinational Bosnia. The governments of Croatia and Serbia (still nominally Yugoslavia) directly sponsored and supplied parties and emerging militias who shared these beliefs.

This sketch of recent conflict in and over Bosnia should not be misunderstood. Our summary does not imply any commitment to 'ontological groupism'—namely, the belief that there are only groups not individuals. This summary entails no 'methodological holism'—namely, the belief that analysis should proceed as if groups, rather than individuals, are the sole active explanatory agents in politics. War happened in Bosnia because individuals, and organizations of individuals, engaged in mortal combat. The motivations for conflict among those individuals who fought, killed, and expelled were highly varied. The evidence suggests, we believe, that leaders and the combative organizations that they mobilized acted because of fears among their group—fears that they sometimes manipulated, but which they often held sincerely. Leaders and organizations in Bosnia, before and after 1992, frequently acted as if groups mattered more than individuals—but to emphasize the importance of their beliefs requires no commitment to accepting their veracity.

In the 1990s, Bosnia and the wider Balkans taught the world the menacing joke: 'Why should I be a minority in your country when you can be a minority in mine?' When the leaders of Serbia and Croatia, and representatives of Bosnian Serbs and Bosnian Croats, insisted on corporate consociational assurances in the redesign of Bosnia that culminated in the Dayton Peace Agreement, they were not making jokes.

2

Bosnia as a consociation

The Bosnian constitutional text suggests a classic corporate consociation. In 1995 the consociational components were combined with the recognition of two entities, namely the Serb Republic and the Federation of Bosnia and Herzegovina. But whether the relationship between the two entities was confederal or federal was deliberately left ambiguous. No one doubted that the political system was the result of an internationally negotiated end to the most violent war on European soil since 1945—a civil war that was anything but civil, and an international war, in which Serbia and Croatia backed their co-ethnics in Bosnia, while a curious undeclared alliance of the United States, Turkey, Iran, and Saudi Arabia eventually helped to arm the Bosniak-dominated government in Sarajevo.

A. The war in Bosnia and the peace of Dayton

The war developed after Bosnia declared itself independent of the former Yugoslavia on 6 March 1992. Its independence was most contested by the Bosnian Serbs who had boycotted the referendum held in support of independence. They argued that the Bosniaks and Croats who had legislated for the referendum had broken the existing constitution to do so.[1] The radical leaders of the Bosnian Serbs pursued a mixed strategy, carving out a secessionist Serb Republic by force and seeking to keep all, or most,

---

1. For an account that is sympathetic to Serb preferences, see Robert M. Hayden, *Blueprints for a House Divided: The Constitutional Logic of the Yugoslav Conflict* (Ann Arbor, MI: University of Michigan Press 1999).

of Bosnia within the Serb-dominated rump Yugoslavia. Brutal war continued until 1995. It has been estimated that more than 100,000 people were killed.

The Research and Documentation Centre (*Istraživačko Dokumentacioni Centar*, or IDC) published *The Bosnian Book of the Dead* in Sarajevo in June 2007, providing the names of 97,207 victims of the war.[2] Of the total victims named, 59 per cent were soldiers and 41 per cent were civilians, although the former may have been overreported and the latter underreported, because welfare support for soldiers' families was higher than it was for families of civilian victims. A majority of the total victims were young adults, but 3.5 per cent were children; 90 per cent were men and 10 per cent were women. The ethnic breakdown of victims was 66 per cent Bosniak, 26 per cent Serb, and 8 per cent Croat. (Rounding to whole numbers removes the 0.49 per cent of victims who are classed as 'Other'.) Compared to their share of the 1991 population, the proportion of Bosniak/Muslim deaths was twice that of Serbs and three times that of Croats. It has separately been estimated that more than 2.2 million people left their homes because of organized programmes of ethnic expulsions ('ethnic cleansing') and generalized violence, mostly fleeing to areas controlled by their own ethnic group.[3] Almost 30,000 people went missing and one third of them were still missing a decade later. The war radically altered the territorial distribution of Bosnia's ethnic groups. Before the war, the pattern of ethnic residential location was frequently described as a 'patchwork quilt'; by the time the war ended, the groups had predominantly chosen, or had been forced, to live apart in distinct enclaves. What became the Serb Republic had very few Muslims or Croats.

Multiple European-led mediation efforts to end the war failed for three years. An audacious Croatian and Serbian plan to partition Bosnia was defeated,[4] but the Bosniak-led government in Sarajevo did not hold even all territory predominantly settled by Bosniaks. In 1994, the United States

---

2. Three international experts favourably assessed the database behind the book, while observing some difficulties: Patrick Ball, Ewa Tabeau, and Philip Verwimp, *The Bosnian Book of the Dead: Assessment of the Database (Full Report)*, Households in Conflict Network Research Design Note 5. They emphasized that the total should be seen as an approximation of a minimum.

3. Gerard Toal and Carl T. Dahlman, *Bosnia Remade: Ethnic Cleansing and its Reversal* (Oxford: Oxford University Press 2011) e-book loc. 2105.

4. Attila Hoare, 'The Croatian Project to Partition Bosnia-Hercegovina, 1990–94' (1997) 31 East European Quarterly 121.

encouraged Bosniak and Bosnian Croat leaders to form a federation. Later, also under US diplomatic leadership and after intensive negotiations, a comprehensive peace agreement was initialed at Dayton, Ohio, in November 1995.

One of the appendixes to the 1995 Dayton Peace Agreement (DPA) contains Bosnia's constitution. It was the culmination of some forty-four months of intermittent negotiations under the auspices of the International Conference on the former Yugoslavia, and the Contact Group. The conflict formally ended on 14 December 1995, when the General Framework Agreement for Peace (that is, the DPA), signed in Paris, entered into force.[5]

There are two features of the negotiations leading to the DPA that are important for understanding the resulting political settlement. The first is that the negotiations were, in practice, effectively limited to a small group of participants. Effectively, the Contact Group of western powers (particularly the United States and, to a much lesser extent, the European Union) led attempts to secure agreement between the Bosniak leadership and the leaders of Croatia and Serbia. This was a calculated move by US diplomats. James O'Brien, one of the lead negotiators, has described how 'late in 1993, if not before, it was evident that there were three centers of power among the warring parties': Zagreb, for all of the Croat groups; Belgrade, for all of the Serbs; and Sarajevo among the Bosniaks.

> As a simple matter of power politics, then, talks could be reduced to a few parties ... Once the United States took a more active role in the diplomacy, one of its major objectives ... was to reduce the number of voices at the table.[6]

5. A bibliographical guide to materials on Bosnia is provided at the end of the book. We are highly indebted to the meta-review of the literature in Sabrina P. Ramet, *Thinking about Yugoslavia: Scholarly Debates about the Yugoslav Breakup and the Wars in Bosnia and Kosovo* (Cambridge: Cambridge University Press 2005).

6. James C. O'Brien, 'The Dayton Agreement in Bosnia: Durable Ceasefire, Permanent Negotiation' in I. William Zartman and Viktor Aleksandrovich Kremenyuk (eds) *Peace versus Justice: Negotiating Forward- and Backward-Looking Outcomes* (Lanham, MD: Rowman and Littlefield 2005) 96. In his memoir, the US chief negotiator recounts his meeting with President Slobodan Milosevic in Belgrade on 17 August 1995:

   The United States, we said, would never again deal directly with the Bosnian Serbs who rained artillery and racist rhetoric down upon the Muslims and the Croats from their mountain capital of Pale. 'You must speak for Pale,' I said. 'We won't deal with them ever again.'

                              (Richard Holbrooke, *To End a War*, London: Random House 1998,
                                                                    e-book loc. 297)

The result was that the 'mediators dealt only with those leaders or individuals authorized by them. Bosnian Croats played little role in negotiations, and Bosnian Serbs were ignored'.[7] Other groups were excluded entirely.

The composition of the negotiators suggests, as Florian Bieber has observed, that the 'conflicts were not over dominance within the state, but whether the state should exist at all. [The] Dayton Peace Accords secured a weak commitment of the Bosnian Serb and Croat elite to the joint state'.[8] Ruti Teitel suggests that if the dispute were perceived as an inter-state dispute, it 'could explain, without necessarily justifying, the absence of representatives of the other communities (such as local Roma and Jewish communities) at the peace negotiations'.[9] Shortly after the Agreement was concluded, Fionnuala Ní Aoláin argued that, for the short term, 'Dayton has provided a home to group identity and has created spaces in which some (though not all) people may feel secure to rebuild'.[10]

The second important feature of the negotiations is that the consociational arrangements challenged in *Sejdić and Finci* were 'deal-breakers'. They were seen by some of the participants as not only desirable, but also necessary if a comprehensive peace agreement were to be secured. Florian Bieber is correct that it was critical to the US-led negotiation that a commitment to recognize Bosnia's existence was given from the leaders of Serbia and Croatia. Yet that commitment was tied to institutional arrangements within Bosnia that would prevent any one group achieving dominance. Without this bargain, neither Slobodan Milosevic nor Franjo Tudjman could have shepherded their respective co-ethnics into accepting the agreement. Consociational arrangements were part of the price for the recognition of Bosnia. In an interview with one of the authors, Peter W. Galbraith, former US ambassador to Croatia when the Dayton Agreement was made, emphasized that 'absent explicitly ethnic power-sharing assurances to the three main groups the negotiations would neither have begun nor concluded'.[11]

---

7. O'Brien (n. 6) 101.
8. Florian Bieber, 'The Balkans: The Promotion of Power-Sharing by Outsiders' in Joanne McEvoy and Brendan O'Leary (eds) *Power-Sharing in Deeply Divided Places* (Philadelphia, PA: University of Pennsylvania Press, in press).
9. Ruti Teitel, 'Transitional Justice and the Transformation of Constitutionalism' in Tom Ginsburg and Rosalind Dixon (eds) *Comparative Constitutional Law* (Cheltenham: Edward Elgar 2011) 71.
10. Fionnuala Ní Aoláin, 'The Fractured Soul of the Dayton Peace Agreement: A Legal Analysis' (1998) 19 Michigan Journal of International Law 957, 1003.
11. Interview of Vermont State Senator Peter W. Galbraith by Brendan O'Leary, in Townshend, VT, 17 August 2012.

James O'Brien writes:

> Croat and Serb negotiators ... [insisted] on a second house (the 'House of
> Peoples'), which would embody Bosnia's divisions among three groups and,
> more practically, would be selected by means susceptible to control by the
> nationalist parties. ... Fueled by this success, Croat representatives argued in
> the closing days of the talks that ethnic caucuses controlled by the nationalist
> parties should select members of the presidency. The international medi-
> ators—backed by some in the Bosniak delegation—refused and insisted on
> direct elections, admittedly among candidates identified by ethnicity.[12]

Differently put, not only were these institutional aspects of the Agreement
necessary to the making of the Dayton settlement, but they were also
already a compromise for Bosnian Croats and Serbs. For Nystuen, 'the
very rules that have been alleged as being incompatible with human rights
standards ... were also the rules that had made an agreement possible'.[13]
Ambassador Galbraith concurs.[14]

B. Key consociational aspects of Bosnia's constitution

The content of the Constitution of Bosnia and Herzegovina, defined at
Dayton, is complex, but obviously combines federal and consociational
principles.[15] The state of Bosnia and Herzegovina ('Bosnia') consists of
two 'entities': the Federation of Bosnia and Herzegovina (predominantly
Bosniak and Croat); and the Republika Srpska (predominantly Serb).[16] We
have previously called, and shall continue to call, the latter the 'Serb
Republic'.[17] To avoid deciding whether to describe the state officially as

---

12. O'Brien (n. 6) 105.
13. Gro Nystuen, *Achieving Peace or Protecting Human Rights? Conflicts between Norms Regarding
    Ethnic Discrimination in the Dayton Peace Agreement* (The Hague: Martinus Nijhoff 2005) 192.
14. Like many of the US negotiators, including the late Richard Holbrooke, Galbraith regrets that
    the negotiations partially rewarded reprehensible behaviour by Bosnian Serb leaders, but
    observes that 'realism required mutual concessions': Interview (n. 11).
15. For a detailed discussion of the ethnic differentiation rules in the Bosnian constitution, see
    Nystuen (n. 13) ch. 6.
16. In addition, because of an arbitral award of 5 March 1999, the Brčko District has been created
    under the exclusive sovereignty of the state.
17. The recognition of this name was most troublesome for the Bosniak negotiators, who were
    not impressed by US arguments that US states such as Texas and Massachusetts were called
    'republics' and 'commonwealths': Holbrooke (n. 6) e-book loc. 2944–74. The Bosniaks knew

'confederal' (the Serb preference), 'federal', or 'unitary' (the Bosniak preference), the negotiators agreed that its name would simply be 'Bosnia and
Herzegovina'. Likewise, to avoid deciding whether the status of the Federation and the Serb Republic was that of two sovereign republics (which
would have meant 'the state' being officially confederal) or that of provinces
within a two-unit federation, they were described as 'entities'.

New institutional arrangements were introduced at the state level,
including a forty-two-member House of Representatives and a fifteen-
member House of Peoples, the members of which are referred to as
'delegates'—language that many would associate with confederal arrangements. Two-thirds of the House of Representatives are elected from the
territory of the Federation and one third from the *territory* of the Serb
Republic. Therefore 'others' who live in these territories may be elected
to this House, although in practice the House 'has never had a member
drawn from the ranks of "Others"'.[18] By contrast, the House of Peoples,
insisted upon as the price of Croatia's and Serbia's signatures, is composed of
five Bosniaks and five Croats from the Federation of Bosnia and Herzegovina, and five Serbs from the Serb Republic. Croat and Bosniak delegates
from the Federation of Bosnia and Herzegovina are separately elected by the
Croat and Bosniak caucus in the Federation's House of Peoples. Serb
delegates and delegates of the 'Others' to the Federation's House of Peoples
are not permitted to participate in the process of electing Bosniak and Croat
delegates for the state's House of Peoples. However, Bosniak and Croat
delegates and delegates of the 'Others' to the National Assembly of the Serb
Republic are permitted to participate in the process of electing delegates
from the Serb Republic to the state House of Peoples.

The state House of Representatives and the House of Peoples were
therefore constructed to oblige power-sharing among the different 'constituent peoples', and to prevent the adoption of decisions against the will of
the representatives and delegates of any 'constituent people'. Legal scholar
Sheri P. Rosenberg argues that the understanding of 'constituent people'
amounts 'essentially to being a "state creating" people and not to being a

---

that it was linked to the Serb preference that Bosnia be remade officially as a confederation and
feared, following the immediate precedent of Yugoslavia, that republican status would be
interpreted to include the right of self-determination (and therefore of secession).

18. Edin Hodžić and Nenad Stojanović, *New/Old Constitutional Engineering? Challenges and
Implications of the European Court of Human Rights Decision in the Case of* Sejdić and Finci v
BiH (Sarajevo: Analitika 2011) 14.

national minority'.[19] In this case, in the language of political science, each of the three peoples has parity status as a nation in a multinational state. There are only three recognized nations in Bosnia. Sociologically, each of the three peoples is a national minority, since there is no national majority, but legally and politically the three named constituent peoples are constituent nations.[20]

All legislation in the state requires the approval of both chambers. Strong bicameralism is a typical feature of a 'consensus' democracy and of a federation,[21] but the rules governing the passage of legislation in Bosnia are also strongly consociational. Although decisions in both chambers are by a majority of those present and voting, delegates and members are required to 'make their best efforts' to see that the majority includes at least one third of the votes of delegates or members from the territory of each entity. If a majority vote does not achieve this target, the chair and deputy chairs (one Serb, one Bosniak, and one Croat) are required to meet as a commission and to attempt to obtain approval within three days of the vote. If those efforts fail, decisions are taken by a majority of those present and voting, provided that the dissenting votes do not include two-thirds or more of the delegates or members elected from either entity. A proposed decision of the Parliamentary Assembly may, however, be declared to be destructive of a 'vital interest' of the Bosniak, Croat, or Serb people by a majority of, as appropriate, the Bosniak, Croat, or Serb delegates of the House of Peoples. To pass, a decision that has been so designated requires the approval of a concurrent majority of the Bosniak, Croat, and Serb delegates present and voting in the House of Peoples. A majority of the Bosniak, Croat, or Serb delegates may object to the invocation of the 'vital interests' safeguard, in which case the chair of the House of Peoples is required immediately to convene a joint commission comprising three delegates—one selected by the Bosniak, Croat, and Serb delegates, respectively—to resolve the issue. If the commission fails to do so within five days, the matter is referred to the Constitutional Court, which is required, in an expedited process, to 'review it [only] for procedural regularity'.

19. Sheri P. Rosenberg, 'Promoting Equality after Genocide' (2007) 16 Tulane Journal of International and Comparative Law 329, fn. 62.
20. For the origins of the concept of the 'constituent peoples' as 'nations' in the Yugoslav constitutional structure, see Nystuen (n. 13) 139.
21. Arend Lijphart, *Patterns of Democracy: Government Forms and Performance in Thirty-Six Countries* (New Haven, CT: Yale University Press 1999) 200–15.

There is also, famously, provision for a collective presidency. Eligibility for election to the presidency of the state combines both a territorial and an ethno-national requirement. The presidency consists of three members: one Bosniak and one Croat, each directly elected from the territory of the Federation, and one Serb directly elected from the territory of the Serb Republic. The members of the presidency from the territory of the Federation are elected by voters registered to vote in the Federation. A voter registered to vote in the Federation may vote for either the Bosniak or Croat member of the presidency, but not for both. The Bosniak and Croat member who receives the highest number of votes among candidates from the same constituent people is elected. The member of the presidency who is directly elected from the territory of the Serb Republic is elected by voters registered to vote in the Serb Republic. The candidate who receives the highest number of votes is elected.[22]

A veto right also applies to decisions of the presidency. A member of the presidency may declare a presidency decision to be destructive of a vital interest of the entity from the territory from which the member is elected, provided that the member does so within three days of its adoption. Such a decision must then be referred immediately to: the National Assembly of the Serb Republic, if the declaration was made by the member from that territory; the Bosniak delegates of the House of Peoples of the Federation, if the declaration was made by the Bosniak member; or the Croat delegates of that body, if the declaration was made by the Croat member. If the declaration is confirmed by a two-thirds vote of those persons within ten days of the referral, the challenged presidency decision does not take effect.

---

22. These arrangements create separate electoral rolls for the presidency, unambiguously when we compare the Federation and the Serb Republic. This explains why a simple 'winner takes all' (plurality rule) electoral system may seem to fit comfortably in this consociational design. All accounts show that most Serbs are happy with the method through which the presidency is elected. But within the Federation, the voters choose to vote in the Bosniak or Croat contest. Since 2006, Croats have become deeply dissatisfied with this method. This is because significant numbers of Bosniak voters have chosen to cast their votes in 'the Croat contest', thereby selecting Croat nominees to the presidency who do not command the support of Croat voters. A Croat, Željko Komšić, was elected in 2006 and in 2010, mainly through Bosniak votes. For that reason, Croat politicians—and voters—are insistent that future winners of contests to the presidency must be the choice of their respective communities. See e.g. International Crisis Group, *Bosnia's Gordian Knot: Constitutional Reform*, Europe Briefing No. 68 (2012) 7 and 9.

The constitution contains no provisions regarding how a person's ethno-national status is to be determined. It appears that self-classification by the individual is sufficient.[23] No 'objective' criterion, such as belonging to a specific religion or proof of descent, is required. Nor, importantly, is there any requirement of acceptance by other members of the constituent people with which the person has self-identified. In practice, the 'Others' consist of members of other national minorities and of persons who do not declare affiliation with any particular group, perhaps because of intermarriage or mixed parenthood. The Election Act 2001 (as amended) provides that the list of candidates displayed for voters is required to contain the address of each candidate's permanent residence and each candidate's declared affili-ation with a particular 'constituent people' or the group of 'others'. A candidate is fully entitled not to declare his or her affiliation to a 'constitu-ent people' or the group of 'others', but a failure to declare such an affiliation is considered to be a waiver of the right to hold an elected or appointed position for which such declaration is required.

C. European commitments and the failure of proposed changes

Bosnia became a member of the Council of Europe in 2002. It committed itself to 'review within one year, with the assistance of the [Venice Com-mission], the electoral legislation in the light of Council of Europe stand-ards, and to revise it where necessary'.[24] In July 2002, Bosnia ratified the European Convention on Human Rights (ECHR), including Protocol No. 1, which entered into force immediately. Bosnia ratified Protocol No. 12 in July 2003 and it came into force in April 2005. In June 2008, Bosnia signed a stabilization and association agreement (SAA) with the European Union. A stated priority was to 'amend electoral legislation regarding members of the Bosnia and Herzegovina Presidency and House of Peoples delegates to

---

23. See Nystuen (n. 13) 143:

It was assumed [by negotiators] that the traditional Yugoslav 'self classification' would suffice, and as the Contact Group drafters wanted to weaken the ethnicity aspect as much as possible, there were no attempts to elaborate on procedures for establishing a person's ethnicity.

24. Parliamentary Assembly of the Council of Europe, *Opinion No. 234* (2002) para. 15(iv)(b).

ensure full compliance with the [ECHR] and the Council of Europe post accession requirements'.[25]

Céline Tran considers that these commitments were critical in affecting the approach of the European Court of Human Rights (ECtHR) in *Sejdić and Finci* because Bosnia 'had voluntarily agreed to abide by ECHR standards and to review its electoral legislation for compliance, when it joined the Council of Europe, and given the same promise when entering the Stabilization and Association Agreement with the EU'.[26] It was not obvious in advance, however, how the Court would react. On the one hand, since no relevant reservations or derogations to the ECHR were submitted by Bosnia on its ratification, or subsequently, the Court's reaction might well be that club membership entails accepting the consequences. On the other hand, it was perhaps unlikely that Bosnia would be able to live up to these commitments, at least in the short term, yet it was nevertheless admitted to the Council of Europe and permitted to enter into an SAA with the European Union. How far, and, should it be held to unrealistic commitments?

Subsequent attempts to honour these commitments have certainly demonstrated the difficulty of doing so with the requisite levels of support across the three constituent peoples. At the beginning of 2006, the Bosnian presidency proposed a series of constitutional amendments (the 'April package'). These were unsuccessful.[27] Mr Sejdić initiated the litigation before the ECtHR that is the subject of this book after the failure of these proposed amendments.[28] The 'Prud proposals' were subsequently agreed by the leaders of most of the parties in 2008 and these seemed to offer a way forward—yet these too were abandoned. The 'Butmir package', a remake of the previous proposals, was prepared by EU and US mediators in 2009. This intervention failed too. As Florian Bieber has argued, 'there has been a constant outbidding within each community as the [currently] dominant

---

25. Annex to Council Decision 2008/211/EC of 18 February 2008 on the principles, priorities and conditions contained in the European Partnership with Bosnia and Herzegovina and repealing Decision 2006/55/EC, OJ L 80/21 (2008).
26. Céline Tran, 'Striking a Balance between Human Rights and Peace and Stability: A Review of the European Court of Human Rights Decision *Sejdić and Finci v. Bosnia and Herzgovina*' (2011) 18 Human Rights Brief 3, 5.
27. Rudi Kocjančič, 'Bosnia and Herzgovina between Dayton and Brussels' (2011) 4 Journal of Comparative Politics 68.
28. Maja Šoštarić, 'Waiting for Godot: Efficiency of the BiH Judicial System in the Protection of Political Rights of Minorities' in Azra Šehić et al. (eds) *Access to Justice on Bosnia and Herzegovina: Collection of Public Policy Analyses in the Field of Judiciary* (Sarajevo: Justice Network in Bosnia and Herzegovina 2011).

party is pressured by international actors to compromise with other communities whereas the challenger can accuse the party of jeopardizing group interests'.[29] Outbidding, of course, can usually succeed only when fears about group interests have some credible foundation.

D. The role of international supervision

Bosnia's constitutional arrangements have had very extensive external involvement, both in their genesis and in their operation. Such roles for external agents were not anticipated when Lijphart and others first theorized what has been called 'classical consociationalism'.[30] These founding exponents focused on the endogenous, rather than the exogenous, sources of consociation.[31] In Bosnia, extensive external involvement has occurred not only in the negotiation of the DPA and in the mediation of subsequent difficulties among the signatories to the agreement, but is also evident in the direct role of non-Bosnians in Bosnia's institutions. The composition of its Constitutional Court, which has three international appointments from countries that are not contiguous to Bosnia, is a striking example. Yet even this extraordinarily prominent role for foreigners has been overshadowed by the subsequent appointment of a High Representative of the Contact Group to ensure that the governmental structures functioned, at a minimal level.[32] The role granted to the Office of the High Representative (OHR) under the DPA was subsequently radically expanded under 'the Bonn powers'.[33] These powers not only temper the self-governing consociational and federal features of Bosnia's constitution, but have also frequently been used to override the veto rights of one of the three constituent peoples. Even well-disposed analysts consider the High Representative's powers to limit Bosnia's sovereign independence.

29. Bieber (n. 8).
30. John McGarry and Brendan O'Leary, *The Northern Ireland Conflict: Consociational Engagements* (Oxford: Oxford University Press 2004) 4–9.
31. McGarry and O'Leary (n. 30).
32. For a discussion of the legal powers of the High Representative, see Nystuen (n. 13) 244–7.
33. See Marc Weller and Stefan Wolff, 'Bosnia and Herzegovina Ten Years after Dayton: Lessons for Internationalized State-Building' (2006) 5 Ethnopolitics 1.

Subsequently, we shall consider several decisions of the Bosnian Constitutional Court, one of which required significant modification of the constitutions of the two entities. The activities of the High Representative after what is known as the *Constituent Peoples* case illustrates the paradoxes of what some have called the 'European Raj'.[34] The decision of the Constitutional Court was not self-executing. Changes were necessary in the entities' constitutions that politicians in the two entities were responsible for introducing. After extensive negotiations between the parties and after an agreement had been secured, the last stage of implementation ended in failure. This deadlock was broken only by the intervention of the High Representative, who imposed the necessary changes.[35] The High Representative has no jurisdiction, however, to impose changes in *Bosnia*'s constitution—only in the constitutions of the entities.[36] Besides the normal democratic path of building the requisite legislative and executive support, there was therefore no available alternative, other than the judicial route, to those who sought faster constitutional change at the state level.

The effect of this pattern of external interventions in the operation of consociations is not fully diagnosed or understood.[37] Arguably, however, the availability of external mechanisms to overcome (and, in some cases, to override) local standoffs between the political agents serves to encourage irresponsibility by these agents. They are able to present an intransigent position to their supporters,[38] while knowing that the consequences of such intransigence will be resolved by the external power(s). It may indeed be easier for external officials to make 'necessary changes', but this in turn may

---

34. Gerald Knaus and Felix Martin, 'Lessons from Bosnia and Herzegovina: Travails of the European Raj' (2003) 14 Journal of Democracy 60 *passim*; see also Oisán Tansey, *Regime-Building, Democratization and International Administration* (Oxford: Oxford University Press 2009), ch. 6, 167, 172.

35. For a detailed account of the negotiations and the final imposition of the necessary reforms, see Peter Neussl, 'Implementation of the Constitutional Court Decision on the "Constituent Peoples" in Bosnia and Herzegovina' (2003) 24 Human Rights Law Journal 309; see also Tansey (n. 34) 175–82. See the full text of the case in (2001) 22 Human Rights Law Journal 127.

36. For the reasons justifying this conclusion, see Nystuen (n. 13) 247.

37. Anne Marie Wieman, 'Consociationalism with an External Actor in Bosnia: Blueprint for Success or Instability' (Unpublished MA dissertation, Rijksuniversiteit Groningen 2010) 23, citing Ulrich Schneckener, 'Making Power-Sharing Work: Lessons from Successes and Failures in Ethnic Conflict Regulation' (2002) 39 Journal of Peace Research 203.

38. The 'external imposition has undermined the compromise-seeking processes of local actors and created incentives for confrontational political posturing as imposition could break deadlock': Bieber (n. 8).

stunt rather than help the growth of more responsible and cooperative politics in the longer term. Differently put, the use of external supervision or arbitration means that the consociational partners do not bear the costs of stalemates that might otherwise encourage them to work more productively together.[39]

39. Brendan O'Leary, 'Power-Sharing in Deeply Divided Places: An Advocate's Conclusion' in Joanne McEvoy and Brendan O'Leary (eds) *Power-Sharing in Deeply Divided Places* (Philadelphia, PA: University of Pennsylvania Press, in press).

3

Human rights law and courts in consociations

There has, until recently, been little cross-fertilization between political science and academic legal considerations of consociation.[1] It is clear, however, that when the political science and political theory debates are translated into legal language, consociational principles are often regarded as possible violators of human rights norms, whether domestic, regional, or international. Two particular rights are seen to be the most often challenged: the right not to be treated on the basis of particular prohibited characteristics, such as race and ethnicity; and the dilution of a person's right to participate in the political process on equal terms with others.[2] The human rights critique is primarily coextensive, then, with the first two of the liberal political criticisms.[3]

A. Human rights law opposition to consociation

Henry Steiner's influential 1991 article pointed to the legal problems that consociational arrangements may face regarding equality and non-discrimination rights. Steiner wrote that a state 'must give all its citizens equal protection. Power-sharing schemes proceed on a contradictory premise.

---

1. Sujit Choudhry, 'Bridging Comparative Politics and Comparative Constitutional Law: Constitutional Design in Divided Societies' in Sujit Choudhry (ed.) *Constitutional Design for Divided Societies: Integration or Accommodation?* (Oxford: Oxford University Press 2008) 13 and *passim*.
2. Restrictions on freedom of movement and residence have been identified as another possible right that may be breached by some consociational arrangements: David Wippman, 'Practical and Legal Constraints on Internal Power-Sharing' in David Wippman (ed.) *International Law and Ethnic Conflict* (Ithaca, NY: Cornell University Press 1998) 231.
3. See Chapter 1, 'B. Opposition to consociationalism'.

They are cast in ethnic terms...and thus explicitly discriminate among groups on grounds like religion, language, race, or national origin'.[4] David Wippmann, in 1998, also pointed to the tension between consociations resting 'explicitly on the differential provision of tangible and intangible goods to individuals on the basis of their ethnicity', and human rights principles 'mandating equal rights of political participation for all and barring discrimination on the basis of race, religion, or ethnicity'.[5] Consociational arrangements, he wrote, 'explicitly differentiate among the members of groups on the basis of characteristics such as race, religion, and language',[6] instead of according all individuals equal rights. Power-sharing models 'have the effect of favoring [one section of the population] over another on the basis of their membership in an ethnic group'.[7] Closely connected to these fears are more polemical suggestions about possible violations of the prohibition of forced segregation of groups based on race or ethnicity.

There has, relatedly, long been a significant debate concerning the fundamental underpinnings of equality law. In the traditional debates, the identity group is often considered to be merely a collection of individuals and the group becomes the conduit through which the individual is seen as able to assert his or her interests—most particularly, his or her interests in equality. The group is seen as a means to an end, rather than an end in itself. Therefore, when group interests are seen as suppressing or limiting individual interests, the latter should trump the former in standard liberal interpretations, certainly in the long term and (arguably) even in the short term. The conflict between 'formal' and 'substantive' equality is played out in a similarly largely individualized discourse. In these legal debates, a common term of abuse of one's opponents is to suggest that they 'essentialize' the characteristics of groups.[8]

Wippmann's critique, quoted above points toward the second major set of human rights norms most often alleged to be infringed by consociations— namely, the right to political participation, including:

---

4. Henry J. Steiner, 'Ideals and Counter-Ideals in the Struggle over Autonomy Regimes for Minorities' (1991) 66 Notre Dame Law Review 1539, 1551.
5. Wippman (n. 2) 213.
6. Wippman (n. 2) 231.
7. Wippman (n. 2) 232.
8. In political debates over consociation, topical standard tropes in polemical accusation include 'essentialist', but also 'primordialist', 'methodological holist', and 'Balkanist'. 'Pre-constructivist' may be acquiring currency.

the right to take part in the conduct of public affairs, the right to vote and to be elected at genuine periodic elections, and the right to have access to, on general terms of equality, to public service in the country.[9]

Mohammad Shahabuddinas claims that:

> Consociational arrangements essentially violate these rights of the members of the majority community by providing minority ethnic groups political power disproportionate to their number through reserved seats and offices, minority veto rights, or similar devices.[10]

More generally, however, human rights law scholars identify conflicts between consociational principles and the underlying *foundations* of human rights thinking. For Wippmann, 'consociational structures . . . may conflict with the liberal individualist paradigm that underpins contemporary international human rights norms'. For Steiner, also, consociational arrangements threaten to submerge the individual within the community, whereas:

> all persons should be seen as empowered by human rights norms to decide whether to remain on one side of a cultural boundary, to shift to another side, or to seek a life not committed to one or the other community.

These, in some ways, deeper concerns are one way in which the anti-essentialism in liberal political theory echoes the older human rights law discourse. More recently, the liberal anti-essentialist stance has been translated into a claimed legal right not to be classified as a member of a racial or ethnic group, except voluntarily.

B. Human rights in consociational arrangements

For liberal human rights lawyers, the preferred approach to ethnic disputes is often to emphasize the potential for more and better constitutional

9. Mohammad Shahabuddinas, *A Normative Analysis of International Law Compatibility with Ethnic Conflicts* 8. Available online at <http://www.inter-disciplinary.net/ati/els/els2/Shahabuddin%20paper.pdf>
10. Shahabuddinas (n. 9). This argument presumes that consociation ubiquitously requires disproportionality, which is not so, *and* that it requires reserved seats and offices, which may not be so if standard proportional representation electoral formulae are applied: see Brendan O'Leary, Bernard Grofman, and Jørgen Elklit, 'Divisor Methods for Sequential Portfolio Allocation in Multi-Party Executive Bodies: Evidence from Northern Ireland and Denmark' (2005) 49 American Journal of Political Science 198. When parity among peoples is claimed, then its proponents insist that proportions should be one people per vote, and reject individualist proportionality ('one person, one vote') or a census headcount, as the basis for decision-making.

protections, such as the judicial protection of individual rights, instead of consociational or autonomy provisions. The trend, however, in many diverse places appears to have gone in the opposite direction. Sujit Choudhry has drawn attention to the popularity of consociations in managing ethnic disputes by contrast with the more individual rights-based approach, which would place greater importance on mechanisms such as bills of rights.[11] Drawing on the work of Christine Bell,[12] he argues that 'debates over the character and content of bills of rights are no longer at the center of more recent rounds of post-conflict constitutional politics'. His tentative conclusion is that 'constitutional actors have come to understand that rights-based constitutionalism cannot do all the work it has been expected to do'.

That said, however, peace settlements are now seldom *solely* consociational in the package of measures adopted to resolve national, ethnic, religious, or linguistic conflicts, and therefore are likely to contain elements infused with other ideological orientations.[13] In particular, bills of rights and equivalent mechanisms tend to be omnipresent in peace agreements that include consociational elements.[14] Some defenders of liberal consociationalism see strong human rights protections as an important safeguard for liberal values. Stefan Wolff notes that they consider that:

> ...the rights of communities—minorities and majorities alike—are best protected in a liberal consociational system if its key provisions are enshrined in the constitution and if the interpretation and upholding of the constitution is left to an independent constitutional court whose decisions are binding on executive and legislature.[15]

Andrew Finlay, a vigorous anti-consociationalist, maintains that:

---

11. Sujit Choudhry, 'After the Rights Revolution: Bills of Right in the Post-Conflict State' (2010) 6 Annual Review of Law and Social Science 301.
12. Christine Bell, *Peace Agreements and Human Rights* (Oxford: Oxford University Press 2000) and 'Peace Agreements: Their Nature and Legal Status' (2006) 100 American Journal of International Law 373.
13. Marc Weller, Barbara Metzger, and Niall Johnson (eds) *Settling Self-Determination Disputes: Complex Power-Sharing in Theory and Practice* (The Hague: Martinus Nijhoff 2008).
14. See e.g. Bell, *Peace Agreements* (n. 12) and Stefan Wolff, 'Complex Power Sharing as Conflict Resolution: South Tyrol in Comparative Perspective' in Jens Woelk, Francesco Palermo, and Joseph Marko (eds) *Tolerance through Law: Self-Governance and Group Rights in South Tyrol* (The Hague: Martinus Nijhoff 2008) 35–7.
15. Wolff (n. 14) 7, citing Brendan O'Leary, 'Power-Sharing, Pluralist Federation and Federacy' in Brendan O'Leary, John McGarry, and Khaled Salih (eds) *The Future of Kurdistan in Iraq* (Philadelphia, PA: University of Pennsylvania Press 2005) 55–8.

Because of their universalism, the notion that they offer protection to all, including 'others', it is hoped that human rights will act as a unifying mechanism in the aftermath of conflict. In other words, a significant part of the political rationale for human rights provisions in consociational peace agreements is that they can transcend ethnic divisions. For this reason human rights organizations tend to be the first place that people who do not fit the specified categories look for support.[16]

C. Courts as part of the consociational agreement

In consociations, however, courts are themselves the object of consociational design impulses. Courts that are likely to play a significant constitutional role will probably, for example, be composed to reflect the ethno-national or linguistic makeup of the state or region. This was certainly the case in Cyprus during its period of unambiguous consociation between 1960 and 1963.[17] In Northern Ireland, reforms in the administration of justice mandated by the 1998 Belfast Agreement (also known as the 'Good Friday Agreement') have led to a far more representative High Court. The composition of Belgium's Court of Arbitration squarely reflects consociational, and federal, arrangements.[18]

The Constitutional Court of Bosnia is also consociational in design. It consists of nine judges. Four are selected by the House of Representatives of the Federation of Bosnia and Herzegovina (FBiH), and two are selected by the National Assembly of the Serb Republic (RS). In practice, as David Feldman authoritatively describes, 'the House of Representatives of the FBiH has selected two Bosniacs and two Croats, and the RS Assembly has

16. Andrew Finlay, *Governing Ethnic Conflict: Consociation, Identity and the Price of Peace* (London: Routledge 2011) 76. Finlay is no methodological fanatic. Responding to the views attributed to Rogers Brubaker, he writes (at 110), 'it is not my view that identities and groups do not exist or that they should not be recognized'. We agree when he insists that 'ethnic identity does not exist for everyone, all the time, in the same way', but, unlike him, we regard the use of ethnic categorization—for policy intended to achieve equality or proportionality—as frequently unavoidable.
17. Christalla Yakinthou, *Political Settlements in Divided Societies: Consocialism and Cyprus* (Basingstoke: Palgrave Macmillan 2009) 55: 'The High Court and the Supreme Constitutional Courts were composed of Greek Cypriots, Turkish Cypriots, and "neutrals"'.
18. Patriek Peeters, 'Expanding Constitutional Review by the Belgian "Court of Arbitration"' (2005) 11 European Public Law 475, 478 (a balance is required between Dutch and French speakers on the Constitutional Court); Ivan Verougstraete, 'Judicial Politics in Belgium' in Mary L. Volcansek (ed.) *Judicial Politics and Policy-Making in Western Europe* (London: Frank Cass 1992) 93.

selected two Serbs'.[19] The remaining three members are selected by the President of the European Court of Human Rights (ECtHR), after consultation with the presidency of Bosnia unless and until the Parliamentary Assembly of Bosnia provides for a different method of selecting these judges. The judges selected by the ECtHR President may not be citizens of either Bosnia or of its neighbouring states. The Constitutional Court of Bosnia therefore exemplifies the consociational principles of parity and proportionality, but also includes external 'arbitrators'.

The composition of the courts is important, of course, because their role in consociational polities may be crucial. Political scientists' discussions have shown that consociations require satisfactory methods of dispute resolution when the political elites of the major communities clash on vital interests. Courts may fulfil the function of helping to resolve these tensions.[20] When the courts do not play this role, they may contribute to instability. The inability of the Cyprus Constitutional Court to operate effectively is thought to have contributed to the breakdown of the consociational arrangements in 1963.[21] The reactions of the courts in Fiji to its consociational arrangements, by contrast, have been seen more positively as contributing to their survival (if only briefly).[22] Work by Gordon Anthony and John Morison on litigation following Northern Ireland's consociational agreement demonstrates the same supportive phenomenon.[23]

The difficult role that courts have to play in consociations that have entrenched human rights protections should now be apparent. The likely constitutional arrangements are Janus-faced: one face looks to individualist

---

19. David Feldman, 'Renaming Cities in Bosnia and Herzegovina' (2005) 3 International Journal of Constitutional Law 649, 655.

20. Ulrich Schneckener, 'Making Power-Sharing Work: Lessons from Successes and Failures in Ethnic Conflict Regulation' (2002) 39 Journal of Peace Research 203, 205.

21. Thomas W. Adams, 'The First Republic of Cyprus: A Review of an Unworkable Constitution' (1966) 19 Western Political Quarterly 475.

22. Venkat Iyer notes, in 'Enforced Consociationalism and Deeply Divided Societies: Some Reflections on Recent Developments in Fiji' (2007) 3 International Journal of Law in Context 127, the 'constitution-reinforcing' judicial review and how, on one particular occasion, the judges 'decisively stopped the abrogation' of the power-sharing agreement. For the coup that ended Fiji's most recent experiment, see Jon Fraenkel and Stewart Firth, *The 2006 Military Takeover in Fiji: A Coup to End all Coups?* (Canberra: Australia National University, E Press 2009).

23. Gordon Anthony, 'Public Law Litigation and the Belfast Agreement' (2002) 8 European Public Law 401; Gordon Anthony and John Morison, 'The Judicial Role in the New Northern Ireland: Constitutional Litigation and Devolution Disputes' (2009) 21 European Review of Public Law 1219.

citizenship, as encapsulated in the bill of rights; the other, towards identity-based or group-regarding consociation. There is an inherent ambiguity presented to the courts for resolution in particular cases. Neither of the two, however, is likely to be entrenched to the complete exclusion of the other. In other constitutional contexts, Hannah Lerner has identified the value in retaining ambiguity and duality, when negotiators refrain from 'entrenching one or another normative perspective'.[24] She does, however, identify potential dangers in such an approach, such as 'the risk of compromising basic rights, potential over-rigidity of the material constitutional arrangement that evolved in the absence of a formal constitutional decision, and the risk of inter-institutional polarization between the legislature and the judiciary'.[25]

The possible role of the judiciary in consociations is not, however, necessarily restricted to domestic courts. Increasingly, it may involve international and regional human rights courts. In particular, the jurisdiction of the ECtHR has been extended to include an ever-widening set of rights—particularly the right to non-discrimination—and has been applied to an ever-widening group of states—particularly those countries with a history of bloody ethno-religious, or ethno-national, disputes. European judges are, therefore, likely to be faced with further disputes in consociational contexts that require judicious resolution.

The ECtHR is no stranger to such disputes. Consociational arrangements in Belgium have been before the Court in several high-profile cases from the earliest days of its existence. Indeed, as we shall discuss in the next chapter, the Court first cut its teeth on the meaning and extent of the non-discrimination principle and the principle of fair elections in cases arising from challenges to the Belgian arrangements.[26] So, too, the Court of Justice of the European Union is likely to play an increasingly important role in adjudicating such issues, given that its jurisdiction has been extended geographically and substantively, in ways that are likely to engage consociational arrangements, especially if and when the European Union incorporates the entire Balkans. James Sweeney has argued that:

---

24. Hanna Lerner, *Making Constitutions in Deeply Divided Societies* (Cambridge: Cambridge University Press 2011) 10.
25. Lerner (n. 24) 12.
26. See Chapter 4, Section B, '2. Meaning of "discrimination" under Article 14' and '1. Summary of the facts of the case [*Mathieu-Mohin and Clerfayt*]'.

... international human rights enforcement bodies, including the European Court, [should] engage far more robustly with the difficult question of when, and in what circumstances, national transitional policies that might secure peace or democratic consolidation are trumped by international human rights concerns.[27]

A key question is whether the involvement of international and regional courts is more or less legitimate than the similar involvement of state courts. On the one hand, state courts are closer to the ground, more familiar with the background, and better able to judge whether a particular legal interpretation will succeed in practice. On the other hand, a regional or international court may have greater legitimacy because it is seen as above the fray, reflecting opinion beyond the state itself, and able to draw on deeper reservoirs of international support in having its decision implemented. As we have seen, in Bosnia, those devising the arrangements sought to combine the benefits of the local and the supranational in the construction of the domestic constitutional court by requiring a degree of supranational representation. Three members of the Bosnian Constitutional Court, who jointly outnumber each of the pairs of judges nominated by the respective constituent peoples, are selected by the ECtHR President after consultation with the state presidency. The Constitutional Court is therefore one of only two important institutions (the other being the central bank) in which the representatives of each constituent people does not have a veto 'over all essential decision-making'.[28]

D. Courts as potential 'unwinders' of consociational arrangements?

Given the potential conflict between the consociational and the human rights aspects of the same peace agreement or political settlement, courts are likely to be called on to perform an even more delicate role than adjudicating disputes arising within long-established consociational arrangements. Since much of the liberal criticism insists that consociations are normatively

---

27. James Sweeney, 'Freedom of Religion and Democratic Transition' in Antoine Buyse and Hamilton Michael (eds) *Transitional Jurisprudence and the ECHR: Justice, Politics and Rights* (Cambridge: Cambridge University Press 2011) 126.
28. Zaid Al-Ali, 'Constitutional Drafting and External Influence' in Tom Ginsburg and Rosalind Dixon (eds) *Comparative Constitutional Law* (Cheltenham: Edward Elgar 2011) 82.

unacceptable as a permanent set of institutions, one important question is whether (and if so, how) to move from a consociational to a (more acceptable) non-consociational future. One of the obstacles to the dissolution of consociations, according to sceptics, is said to be that political elites that benefit from such an arrangement will be loath to give it up. Within this vein of thought, courts are sometimes considered to have a pivotal role in ensuring that such a transition nevertheless takes place. Richard Pildes, in particular, has identified the courts as potential 'unwinders of ethnic political bargains'.[29]

We have already suggested that the performance of the courts in consociations may be a significant determinant of the success or failure of consociational agreements. However, very little recent comparative empirical research appears to have been conducted on how courts react in practice to challenges to consociational agreements on human rights grounds. There has also, as far as we are aware, been no sustained legal theory devoted to how judges *should* treat consociations. Recent work by Samuel Issacharoff[30] and Richard Pildes,[31] however, provides useful opening hypotheses for such research.

Issacharoff, whose principal scholarly interests lie in American constitutional law, anti-discrimination law, and civil procedure, makes the important point that, in this area of controversy, courts are often considering a first-order challenge[32]—that is, they are called upon to determine the nature and the proper composition of the polity itself. These challenges may arise in several different ways, but these types of dispute are 'challenges to political compromises that condition political participation on defined membership in subordinate constituencies'.[33] Such 'first-order challenges' pose a set of problems for courts 'that may not be unique in nature, but the consequences of which are uniquely serious and can be highly destabilizing for otherwise menaced democratic regimes'—namely, the breakdown of civil peace and the onset (or recurrence) of widespread political violence.[34] Issacharoff stresses how frequently the challenges to the political bargains

---

29. Richard Pildes, 'Ethnic Identity and Democratic Institutions: A Dynamic Perspective' in Sujit Choudhry (ed.) *Constitutional Design for Divided Societies: Integration or Accommodation?* (Oxford: Oxford University Press 2008) 195.
30. Samuel Issacharoff, 'Democracy and Collective Decision-Making' (2008) 6 International Journal of Comparative Law 231.
31. Pildes (n. 29) 173.   32. Issacharoff (n. 30) 232.
33. Issacharoff (n. 30) 232.   34. Issacharoff (n. 30) 262.

in such cases are based on 'fundamental rights' arguments that 'are almost invariably addressed by reference to higher authority at either the national level or even at the international level'.[35] This possibility may pit not only the legal against the political spheres, but, more importantly, the universalist orientation of human rights against the intense particularity of consociational politics. Precisely 'because context-sensitive local accommodations tend to be idiosyncratic,' Issacharoff writes, 'the homogenizing effect of a rights template threatens the political accommodations...'.[36] He reasons that the potential difficulties posed by controversial decisions should lead us to expect that the courts may adopt 'exit strategies' 'by means of which the courts could restore a measure of deference to the institutional realities of politics'.[37] In short, for Issacharoff, courts are hypothesized to prioritize public order and stability rather than to engage in what some politicians will see as usurpationist universalist rights activism—'usurpationist' because the court may be radically modifying a democratically endorsed settlement, and drawing upon outside sources and resources to do so.

Pildes, drawing too on his American and comparative constitutional law background, also identifies the increasing tendency of domestic and international courts to use constitutional rights doctrines to revisit basic structural issues about the design of democratic institutions.[38] However, Pildes' reaction to these developments is mixed: on the one hand, 'there are serious normative and pragmatic concerns' when judges play 'the role of institutional agents for transitioning away, even modestly, from ethnic accommodation in the design of democratic institutions'. The normative concern arises from 'the legitimacy of courts in partially undoing political agreements reflected in legislation' or, we might add, with Bosnia in mind, in a constitution. Pildes' pragmatic concern is that, 'to the extent [that] judicial interventions of these sorts rest, in part, on the view that circumstances have changed enough to justify moves toward a more integrationist political sphere, they require exquisitely charged judgments'. If the court gets that judgment wrong, 'its decision could fuel ethnic conflicts'. On the other hand, as we have seen, he is prepared to envisage an active role for courts in changing constitutional design, in relatively confined circumstances. Like Issacharoff, however, Pildes' concern about particular courts' legitimacy is

35. Issacharoff (n. 30) 262.   36. Issacharoff (n. 30) 242.   37. Issacharoff (n. 30) 262.
38. Richard H. Pildes, 'Foreword: The Constitutionalization of Democratic Politics' (2004) 118 Harvard Law Review 25, 28.

lessened 'the longer the interval between the original agreement and the court's action'.[39]

Turning now from the theory to the practice, it would appear that state courts have been highly restrained in intervening to unwind ethnic political bargains, in most cases upholding consociational arrangements and in some cases even cautiously extending the logic of consociation beyond its original scope. This pattern appears to have been the case, for example, in Italian judgments on consociational arrangements in Alto Adige/South Tyrol,[40] and in judgments considering questions arising under Northern Ireland's constitutional arrangements established after the Belfast, or Good Friday, Agreement,[41] as well as in the decisions of the Belgian courts when consociational arrangements were in issue.[42] If state courts have prudently maintained or cautiously extended consociational arrangements, we may wonder when and why regional or international courts would consider it wise to find against such institutions on human rights grounds. As we shall show in the next chapter, the ECtHR initially conformed with Issacharoff and Pildes' hypotheses, which predict judicial restraint in finding consociational arrangements incompatible with human rights.

---

39. Pildes (n. 29) 197.
40. Emma Lantschner and Giovanni Poggeschi, 'Quota System, Census and Declaration of Affiliation to a Linguistic Group' in Jens Woelk, Francesco Palermo, and Joseph Marko (eds) *Tolerance through Law: Self-Governance and Group Rights in South Tyrol* (The Hague: Martinus Nijhoff 2008) 219, although the Italian Supreme Court in the *Beltramba* case in 1999, Judgment No. 11048 of 24 February 1999, held that a person's failure to declare an ethno-linguistic identity should not result in denial of the right to stand for election: see Lantschner and Poggeschi, 230.
41. See Anthony (n. 23); Brice Dickson, 'The House of Lords and the Northern Ireland Conflict: A Sequel' (2006) 69 The Modern Law Review 383; Marie Lynch, '*Robinson v Secretary of State for Northern Ireland*: Interpreting Constitutional Legislation' [2003] Public Law 640; John Morison, 'Ways of Seeing? Consociationalism and Constitutional Law Theory' in Rupert Taylor (ed.) *Consociational Theory: McGarry and O'Leary and the Northern Ireland Conflict* (London: Routledge 2009) 94. See also *Parsons, Re Application for Judicial Review* [2003] NICA 20 (6 June 2003).
42. For an early assessment, see Verougstraete (n. 18) 93. Over time, the role of the Constitutional Court has been somewhat expanded, with a concomitant increase in judicial activity: see Peeters (n. 18).

4

The Belgian consociational cases in the European Court of Human Rights

We have suggested that the practice of *domestic* courts has been broadly consistent with the hypotheses of Issacharoff and Pildes of what courts are likely to do in weighing consociations against human rights— namely, to maintain or extend consociational arrangements. We argue in this chapter that their hypotheses are also useful guides to how *international and regional* courts have reacted to similar challenges in the past. Indeed, their hypotheses partly derived from earlier decisions of the European Court of Human Rights (ECtHR), particularly those in the Belgian consociational cases, *Belgian Linguistics* and *Mathieu-Mohin*. These two judgments stood for many years as the only major cases of the ECtHR, or indeed of any other international human rights court, to consider the application of human rights norms to consociations.

There have been three major cases that have brought consociational designs before the ECtHR: the two from Belgium, and the *Sejdić and Finci* case from Bosnia. We believe that these constitute the complete set of cases in which the Court has dealt directly with human rights challenges to consociational arrangements.[1] Although limited in number, they enable us to test Issacharoff and Pildes' hypotheses. Let us begin with the Belgian cases.

---

1. The (now abolished) European Commission on Human Rights considered two cases of some relevance. One case was from Northern Ireland, in which somewhat similar challenges were made to voting arrangements, which pre-dated the fuller consociational arrangements introduced by the Belfast (or 'Good Friday') Agreement: *Lindsay v. United Kingdom*, Application no. 8364/78, 8 March 1979, [1979] 3 CMLR 166. The Commission found that a system of proportional representation was legitimate, particularly in areas in which voting behaviour was significantly influenced by ethnic and religious affiliation. The Commission also

A. Consociationalism and Belgium

Language policies were developed in Belgium to resolve intermittently violent conflicts between French-speaking Walloons and Dutch-speaking Flemings that had erupted in Belgium after the Second World War. These clashes, in turn, need to be understood in the context of the perceived (and actual) domination of Flemings by the Walloons during the nineteenth century and the growth of a Flemish secessionist movement in the first half of the twentieth. The complex constitutional developments at issue in the two cases that we consider here have been part of the project to keep Belgium as a single country, rather than to see it break up into a Flemish-speaking and a French-speaking state.

The Belgian constitutional system that has developed is complex and multilayered. Powers and responsibilities have been distributed between state-wide institutions, regions, and communities. The Belgian experience may be briefly described as having evolved in the last forty years from a consociation within a unitary state to a consociational federation, based on communities and territorial regions.[2] In all of the centres of influence within Belgium, complex internal arrangements have protected the interests of the different language groups. The Brussels region, situated geographically between the two main language regions, and inhabited and claimed by both linguistic communities (as well as newcomers), is both a site of contestation and arguably a magnet that has kept Belgium together, because neither Flemings nor Walloons wish to let it go.

Legislation in 1932 had placed the two languages on a more or less equal footing in state institutions. The approach designated territories as officially French- or Dutch-speaking. However, the legislation did not fix the language boundaries permanently and it was envisaged that changes to the language boundaries could change as a result of censuses held every ten years. In consequence, political instability accompanied the occasion of each

considered a case from Alto-Adige/South Tyrol in which a party representing the German-speaking and Ladin-speaking majority in the region alleged that they were prevented from qualifying for a seat in the national parliament under a system of proportional representation by a minimum threshold requirement. The Commission rejected the complaint as inadmissible: *Magnago and Südtiroler Volkspartei v. Italy*, Application no. 25035/94.

2. For the literature in English on consociation and federation in Belgium, see the bibliographical guide at the end of this book.

census.[3] Under legislation adopted in 1963, Belgium was divided into four linguistic regions: the Dutch, French, and German regions, and the Brussels conurbation. In the first three regions, the Acts required the exclusive use of Dutch, French, and German, respectively, by public sector institutions. As importantly, under the 1963 legislation, each linguistic region was given permanent boundaries, which would not be subject to subsequent change driven by demographic shifts.

At the time of the cases considered by the ECtHR,[4] the language regions defined the territorial scope of the use of languages in administrative and judicial matters, as well as in education. In addition to these language regions, the three 'political' regions have since become the territorial components of the federation: the Walloon Region; the Flemish Region; and the Brussels Region.

The issue at the heart of the first case, the famous *Belgian Linguistics* case, was what language could be used in teaching children in public schools in Belgium, and the relationship between this issue and the designation of territories within Belgium, in which particular languages were regarded as dominant. The litigation particularly challenged attempts to ensure that designated Dutch-speaking areas would remain Dutch-speaking, and not be slowly made to change through pressure from French-speaking residents to accommodate the French language. This challenge was almost entirely rejected by the ECtHR, for reasons that we shall examine.[5]

For critical political decision-making in the Belgian government, the elected members of each of the two houses of the legislature were divided into a French-language and a Dutch-language group. In the House of

---

3. In this respect, Belgium's consociation may be contrasted with Lebanon's, where no census has been held since 1932 because Christians know that Muslims now outnumber them and because the Christians insist that any census should count the Lebanese diaspora (which is assumed to contain more Christians than Muslims). 'So long as a census is not held, each of the confessional blocs can maintain that it is in the majority and make corresponding demands with respect to the distribution of power': Theodor Hanf, *Coexistence in Wartime Lebanon: Decline of a State and Rise of a Nation* (tr. John Richardson, London: I.B. Tauris & Co 1993) 96.

4. In this outline, we detail only the (often-changing) elements of Belgium's institutions necessary to follow the cases to be discussed. We do not consider the changes that have occurred since the cases. For these, see the useful analysis in Kris Deschouwer, *Ethnic Structure, Inequality and Governance of the Public Sector in Belgium* (Geneva: United Nations Research Institute for Social Development 2004), and see the Re-Bel initiative, including the Re-Bel e-book series, run by Paul de Grauwe and Philippe van Parijs, online at <http://www.rethinkingbelgium.eu/>

5. *Case 'Relating to Certain Aspects of the Laws on the Use of Languages in Education in Belgium' v. Belgium* *(Merits)*, Application nos 1474/62, 1677/62, 1691/62, 1769/63, 1994/63, and 2126/64, Judgment 23 July 1968, (1979–80) 1 EHRR 252.

Representatives, the French-language group included, as of right, the members elected by the constituencies of the French-speaking region and by the constituency of the district of Verviers, while the Dutch-language group comprised the members elected by the constituencies of the Dutch-speaking region. The members elected in the Brussels electoral district belonged to one or the other group, depending on whether they chose to take the parliamentary oath in French or in Dutch. Similar criteria applied to the language groups in the Senate.

When the parliamentary language groups had a role to play, the constitution required a concurrent majority of votes in each language group of each house, but that concurrent majority was further qualified. The total of the affirmative votes cast in the two language groups was required to amount to at least two-thirds of the votes cast. In addition, there was an 'alarm bell' procedure, which, to be triggered, required a motion signed by at least three-quarters of the members of one of the language groups, stating that the provisions of a specified Bill were likely to be seriously detrimental to relations between the two language communities. Upon the alarm bell being rung, parliamentary proceedings were suspended and the motion was referred to the Cabinet, which was required to give a reasoned opinion on it within thirty days and to request the parliamentary chamber concerned to vote either on this opinion or on the Bill. These provisions were designed primarily to protect the speakers of the country's minority language—that is, French. The Cabinet was required to comprise as many French-speaking ministers as Dutch-speaking.

The French and Flemish communities each had a council and executive, which were able to exercise the powers of the Walloon or Flemish regions, respectively, but only if prescribed by law. The law provided for this only in the Flemish region, where the council and executive of the Flemish community therefore additionally exercised the powers invested at the regional level. The councils consisted of elected delegates. The Flemish Council consisted of the members of the Dutch-language group in the House of Representatives and, if directly elected by the electorate, in the Senate.

In *Mathieu-Mohin and Clerfayt*, the applicants complained to the ECtHR about the legislation that determined the membership of the Flemish Council.[6] They claimed that it did not, in practice, enable French-speaking

---

6. *Mathieu-Mohin and Clerfayt v. Belgium*, Application no. 9267/8, Judgment of 2 March 1987, (1988) 10 EHRR 1.

electors in a Dutch-speaking administrative district to appoint French-speaking representatives to the Council, while Dutch-speaking electors could appoint Dutch-speaking representatives. They also claimed that it prevented any parliamentarian elected in that electoral district and resident in one of the municipalities of that district from sitting on the Flemish Council if he or she belonged to the French-language group in the House of Representatives or the Senate; they argued that this was an obstacle not faced by the elected representatives who belonged to a Dutch-language group and were resident in one of the same municipalities. Even more comprehensively than in the *Belgian Linguistics* case, these challenges failed before the ECtHR. Let us consider the reasoning in these two cases in some detail.

B. The *Belgian Linguistics* case

The *Belgian Linguistics*[7] case is such an iconic case in European human rights jurisprudence that it is sometimes forgotten that the plaintiffs' challenge was to a central pillar of Belgium's consociational arrangements—namely, the way in which the substantial autonomy granted to each language region operated to ensure that its school system perpetuated the survival of the language of that region.

1. Summary of the facts of the case

Policies had been adopted to strengthen the protection of the languages in each community. In the unilingual regions, no state schools were to be established, nor was any subsidy provided to private schools in which instruction was given in a language other than the official language of the region. All public subsidies were withdrawn from any provincial, commune, or private schools providing full or partial instruction in a language other than the 'majority' language of the region, even where this took place in non-subsidized classes and along with the instruction given in the

---

7. We will not discuss the issue of whether Flemish is Dutch. The official language spoken in Flanders is standard Dutch: see Kenneth D. McRae, *Conflict and Compromise in Multilingual Society, Vol. 2: Belgium* (Waterloo, ON: Wilfrid Laurier University Press 1986) 56–9. In this chapter, we follow the Belgian government and the ECtHR judgment, which speaks of 'Dutch'.

'majority' language. In the Dutch-speaking region, a 'Dutch-language' school that opened classes either completely or partially in French at the nursery, primary, or secondary level lost its public subsidies. 'Bilingual' schools that, in the same region, formerly maintained such classes were obliged to close, or to split into two, if they wished to preserve access to state subsidies. As the Court said, in analysing these provisions, the two policies were closely related: 'What is in issue, therefore, is a whole series of provisions with a common aim, namely, the protection of the linguistic homogeneity of the region.'[8]

Several other measures were adopted to strengthen this policy. Classes were abolished that enabled children to make a gradual transition from the 'minority' language of the language region to the 'majority' language of the region ('transmutation classes'), while being taught initially in the 'minority' language. Leaving certificates issued by private schools that did not conform to the language legislation were not fully recognized ('homologated'), disadvantaging students from these schools in achieving entry to certain professions. It was generally accepted that the purpose of these policies was to ensure that, as far as possible, the language regions' schools (public and private) would teach only in the language of the region.

Special provisions were made for the Brussels region, however, which was permitted to remain substantially pluri-linguistic. Parents from outside Brussels were permitted to send their children to the Brussels schools, but even here there were restrictions. They were permitted to send their children only to schools that taught in the language in which the children had been raised. In addition, six Dutch-speaking communes on the periphery of Brussels were accorded a special status, in which limited 'minority' languages could be taught in defined circumstances: education in French in these Dutch communes was subject to the deposit of a request by sixteen heads of family living in the commune; and such French education had to be accompanied by an in-depth study of Dutch. A further relaxation of the prohibition on French-language teaching in the Dutch-speaking region was provided regarding the higher education institutions of Louvain and Heverlee. Although situated in the Dutch-speaking region, these institutions were authorized to maintain French-language education—and indeed these continued to be subsidized by the state—in consideration of the needs arising from the (then) bilingual University of Louvain. Admission to these schools, however, was granted only to four types of child: children

8. *Belgian Linguistics* (n. 5) [13].

who attended the classes during the school year 1962–63; children of employees, students, and teaching staff of the university, as well as members of their family living with them; children of foreign nationality, when the head of the family belonged to an international law organization, embassy, legation, or consulate; and finally, children of French-speaking Belgians if the head of the family lived outside the Dutch-speaking region.

The development of Brussels as an employment and residential magnet soon meant that there were significant numbers of French-speaking children in the other Dutch-speaking communes around Brussels, which were not specially designated for exemptions and not permitted the same relaxation of the rules as those who lived in the specially designated communes. Nor were their parents able to send their children to the schools in those 'special' areas in which French-language teaching was permitted. Resident children were not permitted to attend French-language schools in Louvain and Heverlee, for example; nor were parents resident in unilingual regions permitted to send their children to French-language classes in the six designated communes enjoying 'special status' on the periphery of Brussels if the head of the family resided elsewhere than in one of the six communes, such as in the Dutch-speaking region.

The applicants in the *Belgian Linguistics* case were French-speaking and lived in predominantly Dutch-speaking areas. The cumulative effect of these policies, they complained, required them to enrol their children in a local school, where they would be taught through Dutch, which was contrary to their language preferences, or to send their children to school in Brussels, where instruction was given in Dutch or French depending on the child's mother tongue or usual language, or to send them to school in the French-speaking region. Such 'scholastic emigration', as the parents termed it, was alleged to entail dangers and hardships for the children and their parents. They alleged that the provisions of which they complained were in breach of their right to education under Article 2 of Protocol No. 1 of the European Convention on Human Rights (ECHR), their right to a protected home and family life under Article 8 ECHR, and their right not to be discriminated against under Article 14 ECHR. For our purposes, the issue of discrimination is the central focus of attention. The Court rejected all of the applicants' complaints except one. By a majority, the Court upheld only the complaint that the restrictions on parents in the Dutch-speaking region being able to send their children to French-speaking schools in one of the six 'special' communes were discriminatory.

2. Meaning of 'discrimination' under Article 14

Belgian Linguistics was not only the first case in which the ECtHR considered consociational arrangements, but it was also the first decision of the Court in which it interpreted Article 14 ECHR.[9] The Court therefore considered it important to set out its interpretation more generally, before turning to apply that interpretation to this particular case.

The Court decided that Article 14 was not a free-standing non-discrimination provision and was parasitic on other substantive rights protected under the Convention. This did not mean, however, that another right had to be found to have been breached before Article 14 had any purchase. If the area of activity in which there was alleged to be discrimination was 'within the ambit' of another right, such as the right to education, then Article 14 was engaged. The Court also decided that 'discrimination' under Article 14 was a concept that incorporated a significant possibility of justification. Unlike some other systems that developed subsequently in the European context, such as under European Union anti-discrimination law, where direct discrimination could not be 'justified' unless there was a specific exception provided, discrimination arose under Article 14 only:

> ... if the distinction has no objective and reasonable justification. The existence of such a justification must be assessed in relation to the aim and effects of the measure under consideration, regard being had to the principles which normally prevail in democratic societies. A difference of treatment in the exercise of a right laid down in the Convention must not only pursue a legitimate aim: Article 14 ... is likewise violated when it is clearly established that there is no reasonable relationship of proportionality between the means employed and the aim sought to be realised.[10]

Article 14 ECHR, the Court held:

> ... does not prohibit distinctions in treatment which are founded on an objective assessment of essentially different factual circumstances and which, being based on the public interest strike a fair balance between the protection of the interests of the community and respect for the rights and freedoms safeguarded by the Convention.[11]

The assessment of whether the distinction was 'arbitrary' required a contextual understanding of the 'legal and factual features which characterize

---

9. For the text of Article 14 ECHR, see the Preface, n. 11.
10. *Belgian Linguistics* (n. 5) [10].   11. *Belgian Linguistics* (n. 5) [6].

the life of the society in the state which, as a Contracting Party, has to answer for the measure in dispute'.

> In so doing it cannot assume the role of the competent national authorities, for it would thereby lose sight of the subsidiary nature of the international machinery of collective enforcement established by the Convention. The national authorities remain free to choose the measures which they consider appropriate in those matters which are governed by the Convention.[12]

This judgment became one of the classic articulations by the Court of the doctrine of 'margin of appreciation', under which states are accorded a significant degree of discretion in how they comply with the Convention. In *Belgian Linguistics*, the Court emphasized from the beginning of its judgment that 'the Court will take into account the factual and legal features that characterise the situation in Belgium, which is a plurilingual state comprising several linguistic areas'.

3. Treatment of specific allegations

In so far as the complaints challenged the prohibition on the establishment or the subsidy by the state of schools not in conformity with the general linguistic requirements, the applicants accepted that the legislation under attack did not prohibit children from pursuing their studies in French. But they argued that the possibilities of doing so were more theoretical than real. It was unrealistic to expect the applicants to home-school their children. There were 'material and moral obstacles' to sending their children to Brussels, Wallonia, or abroad. The establishment of private French-language schools in Flanders involved prohibitive expense, because they would operate without state subsidies. French-speaking children in Flanders were denied a public or subsidized education in their mother tongue, while Dutch-speaking children were able to benefit from education in their mother tongue. The fact that the same situation would occur in Wallonia, but in reverse (so-called 'parallelism'), did not lessen the discrimination against the French-speaking children; nor did the history of the Belgian language disputes provide a justification. Their advocates maintained that, 'The incontrovertible "abuses" of "the last century" were remedied a "long

---

12. *Belgian Linguistics* (n. 5) [10].

time ago" and in no way justify "the opposite abuse" introduced "by the 1932 legislation and markedly aggravated by that of 1963".'[13]

The Belgian government argued, however, that the legislation ensured 'a strict parallelism between the regulations for the Dutch-speaking and French-speaking areas'. It had been passed by 'very large majorities of chambers elected by universal suffrage' and, therefore, had democratic legitimacy. In spite of some 'inevitable imperfections', it represented a democratic compromise between 'values of liberty and social values'. The purpose of the legislation was to deal with 'grave national crises' by rehabilitating the 'Flemish language and Flemish culture' through developing an 'intelligentsia with a good knowledge of Dutch', able to play a formative role in public leadership and, in a more general sense, to give to the country a stable structure based mainly on two large homogeneous regions with a bilingual capital.[14]

The Court held that the challenged legislation did not amount to discrimination under Article 14 ECHR. The purpose of the legislation 'is to achieve linguistic unity within the two large regions of Belgium in which a large majority of the population speaks only one of the two national languages'. The Court accepted that:

> This legislation makes scarcely viable schools in which teaching is conducted solely in the national language that is not that of the majority of the inhabitants of the region. In other words, it tends to prevent, in the Dutch-unilingual region, the establishment or maintenance of schools which teach only in French.

Yet in the Court's view:

> Such a measure cannot be considered arbitrary. To begin with, it is based on the objective element which the region constitutes. Furthermore it is based on a public interest, namely, to ensure that all schools dependent on the State and existing in a unilingual region conduct their teaching in the language which is essentially that of the region.

The challenged legislation did not prevent 'in the Dutch-unilingual region, the organisation of independent French-language education, which in any case still exists there to a certain extent'. The Court concluded that it did not consider 'the measures adopted in this matter by the Belgian legislature [to

---

13. *Belgian Linguistics* (n. 5) [4].   14. *Belgian Linguistics* (n. 5) [5]ff.

be] so disproportionate to the requirements of the public interest which is being pursued' as to constitute discrimination.[15]

The Court's response to the withdrawal of subsidies from provincial, communal, or private schools providing instruction in the minority language was the same, even where this instruction took place in non-subsidized classes and along with the instruction given in the 'majority' language. The Court had already held that requiring that the teaching language of official or subsidized schools in the unilingual regions should be exclusively that of the region was not arbitrary and, therefore, not discriminatory. The withdrawal of subsidies went somewhat further, how-ever, making it impossible for teaching in French to be conducted as a secondary activity by a subsidized Dutch-language school in a Dutch-speaking region, and the Court accepted that 'this is a harsh measure'. Nevertheless, the Court held that the purpose of the measure was to avoid the possibility, for legitimate reasons, of education that the state did not wish to subsidize benefiting from such subsidies. 'This purpose', held the Court, 'is plausible in itself and it is not for the Court to determine whether it is possible to realise it in another way.' The measures were therefore not discriminatory.[16]

A challenge was also mounted to the legislation providing for the special status of the six traditionally Dutch-speaking communes on the periphery of Brussels. The applicants' complaint was based in part on the requirement that a certain number of heads of family were required to request French-language teaching and that, where permission was given to have teaching of the 'minority' language in a public school in one of these communes, it was a requirement that French-language tuition should be accompanied by inten-sive study of Dutch as well. The Court, again, upheld the requirements. The provision did not:

> . . . go outside limits drawn according to objective criteria and is based on a
> public interest. Furthermore, the establishment and maintenance of education
> conducted in French is possible in the communes concerned. Finally, the fact
> that this education is tied to a study in depth of Dutch, whereas the study of
> French remains optional in Dutch schools in the same communes, does not
> constitute a discrimination as the latter belong to a region which is, by
> tradition, Dutch-speaking.[17]

15. *Belgian Linguistics* (n. 5) [7].   16. *Belgian Linguistics* (n. 5) [13].
17. *Belgian Linguistics* (n. 5) [19].

The refusal to 'homologate' (that is, to confirm officially) certificates relating to secondary schooling not in conformity with the language requirements in education was also upheld. Again, the Court considered that the objective of this measure was legitimate, 'to favour linguistic unity within the unilingual regions and, in particular, to promote among pupils a knowledge in depth of the usual language of the region'. The Court had greater difficulties in upholding the 'relationship of proportionality between the means employed and the objective aimed at'. The Court found, for example, that, although in general the measure was proportionate, it was:

> ... not, however, impossible that the application of the legal provisions in issue might lead, in individual cases, to results which put in question the existence of a reasonable relationship of proportionality between the means employed and the objective aimed at, to such an extent as to constitute discrimination.[18]

In the case before the Court, this was not the case, however, and the Court upheld the measure.

The Court only found a violation of Article 14 ECHR regarding the measure that prevented certain children, on the single premise of their parents' place of residence, from attending French-language schools in the six communes on the outskirts of Brussels that enjoyed a special status. The Court carefully distinguished conditions of access to the French-language schools in the city of Louvain and the adjacent commune of Heverlee, which were upheld, from the conditions of access to the French-language schools in the six communes. Regarding access to French-language education at Louvain and Heverlee, the Court accepted that French-language education had been maintained there, despite the schools being in Dutch-speaking communes, 'in consideration of the needs arising from the bilingual nature of the University of Louvain'. 'Consequently,' the Court held:

> ... the exclusion of French-speaking children living in the Dutch unilingual region whose parents are not members of the teaching staff, students or employees of the University, does not amount to a discriminatory measure in view of the legitimacy of the specific objective of the legislature.[19]

The situation was 'completely different' in the case of the six communes. The residence condition affected only one of the two linguistic groups. The

---

18. *Belgian Linguistics* (n. 5) [42].   19. *Belgian Linguistics* (n. 5) [32].

Court held that this amounted to discrimination under the Convention. The measure was 'not applied uniformly to families speaking one or the other national language'. The Dutch-speaking children resident in the French unilingual region had access to Dutch-language schools in the six communes, whereas French-speaking children living in the Dutch unilingual region were refused access to French-language schools in those same communes. Likewise, the Dutch classes in the six communes were open to Dutch-speaking children of the Dutch unilingual region, whereas the French classes in those communes were closed to the French-speaking children of that region. The Court therefore considered that:

> ...the residence condition is not imposed in the interest of schools, for administrative or financial reasons: it proceeds solely, in the case of the Applicants, from considerations relating to language. Furthermore the measure in issue does not fully respect, in the case of the majority of the Applicants and their children, the relationship of proportionality between the means employed and the aim sought.[20]

It was the decision to uphold a complaint of discrimination in this one respect that elicited a collective dissenting opinion from Judges Holmbäck, Rodenbourg, Ross, Wiarda, and Mast. In particular, they objected to the failure of the majority, as they saw it, to take sufficiently into account the margin of appreciation:

> ...the rule according to which the national authorities, who are in the first place those who must appreciate the requirements implied by the factual and legal features in issue, remain free to choose the measures which they consider appropriate in those matters which are governed by the Convention.

The dissent sought to give considerably more weight than the majority to the state's goal of ensuring 'the linguistic homogeneity of the two communities which would...be threatened by an extension of an exceptional system beyond the territory of the six communes'. All that the measure intended to do was 'to limit the effects of the exception...to the principle of territoriality only to the children of families whose head lives in the communes "with special facilities" '.[21] The difference between the majority and the minority on this point appeared to lie in differing judgments as to whether the six communes were 'Dutch-speaking' or not. For the

---

20. *Belgian Linguistics* (n. 5) [32].
21. *Belgian Linguistics* (n. 5), Dissenting opinion I.

dissenting minority, they were, and the provisions for French-language schools were exceptions that were legitimately narrowly applied. For the majority, the six communes 'no longer form part of the Dutch unilingual region, but constituted a "distinct administrative district" invested with its own "special status"', more akin to Brussels, and the Court saw no clear reason why the Brussels solution could not be adopted.

C. *Mathieu-Mohin and Clerfayt*

In *Mathieu-Mohin and Clerfayt v. Belgium*,[22] another central feature of Belgian consociationalism was challenged, and again the Court showed itself sympathetic to consociational methods of dealing with fundamental ethnic (in this case, ethno-linguistic) disputes. Like *Belgian Linguistics* regarding the scope and meaning of Article 14 ECHR, *Mathieu-Mohin and Clerfayt* distinguishes itself as the first case in which the Court considered the meaning of Article 3 of Protocol No. 1.[23] The consociational arrangements that are at the heart of both cases have, therefore, indirectly influenced the approach that the Court has adopted to the interpretation of two key Articles of the Convention.

1. Summary of the facts of the case

The case before the Court concerned the administrative district of Halle-Vilvoorde, which came within the Dutch-language region and the Flemish Region and was under the authority of the Flemish Council and Executive. It was, accordingly, not subject to the authority of the French community institutions or those of the Walloon Region. It nevertheless contained a sizeable French-speaking minority. Nothing prevented those who were French-speaking, whether resident in Halle-Vilvoorde or not, from standing for election in that district, or the voters, whether French-speaking or not, from voting for them. If they were elected, they would be able to take the parliamentary oath in French or Dutch as they wished, irrespective of the language that they personally spoke. If they were to take the oath in French, however, although their consequent membership of the French-language

---

22. See (n. 6).
23. For the text of Article 3 of Protocol No. 1, see the Preface, n. 12.

group in the House of Representatives or the Senate would entitle them to sit on the French Community Council, this body had no responsibility for the district of Halle-Vilvoorde. They would not be permitted to sit on the Flemish Council, nor on the Walloon Regional Council, which did have responsibility for the district. Conversely, if they were to take the oath in Dutch, they would be members of the Dutch-language group and would accordingly sit on the Flemish Council, but not on the French Community Council nor on the Walloon Regional Council. They would therefore lose the right to vote in the French-language group on those matters concerning which the constitution required qualified concurrent majorities. The consequence was that French-speaking voters in Halle-Vilvoorde could be represented on the Flemish Council only by parliamentarians who had taken the oath in Dutch.

2. Treatment of specific allegations

The majority of the Court, sitting in plenary, held that this system did not breach Article 3 of Protocol No. 1 and that, since the arguments regarding Article 14 were the same as those regarding Article 3 of Protocol No. 1, there was also no breach of Article 14. To begin with, the Court was willing to accord a significant 'margin of appreciation' to the states in the context of electoral systems:

> For the purposes of Article 3 of Protocol No. 1, any electoral system must be assessed in the light of the political evolution of the country concerned; features that would be unacceptable in the context of one system may accordingly be justified in the context of another, at least so long as the chosen system provides for conditions which will ensure the 'free expression of the opinion of the people in the choice of the legislature'.[24]

The scope of application of the Article was also flexible. The Court observed that:

> Article 3 applies only to the election of the 'legislature', *or at least of one of its chambers if it has two or more* . . . The word 'legislature' does not necessarily mean only the national parliament, however; it has to be interpreted in the light of the constitutional structure of the state in question.[25]

---

24. *Mathieu-Mohin and Clerfayt* (n. 6) [54].
25. *Mathieu-Mohin and Clerfayt* (n. 6) [53] (emphasis added).

For the purposes of this case, the Court held that, applying this approach, the Flemish Council had been given competence and powers wide enough to make it, alongside the French Community Council and the Walloon Regional Council, a constituent part of the Belgian 'legislature' in addition to the House of Representatives and the Senate.

The Court's explanation implied that only one of the chambers of a bicameral legislature may need to be elected to satisfy the requirements of the Protocol; what was significant was 'the constitutional structure' of the state. In his concurrence, however, Judge Pinheiro Farinha made clear his unease with the Court's phrase 'or at least of one of its chambers if it has two or more', which he regarded as 'inadequate and dangerous'. He continued: 'As it stands, it would allow of a system at variance with "the opinion of the people in the choice of the legislature" and might even lead to a corporative, elitist or class system which did not respect democracy.' The fact that the issue of whether second chambers were included within the scope of Article 3 of Protocol No. 1 was not before the Court in this case merely served to demonstrate how broad the discretion was for states to organize their own systems free of judicial constraints.

The same breadth of discretion was demonstrated by the Court in assessing the issue of justification. The Court considered that the purpose of the system that had been devised was legitimate. The legitimate aim, it considered, was 'to defuse the language disputes in the country by establishing more stable and decentralized organizational structures'.[26] Given the context:

> The system does not appear unreasonable if regard is had to the intentions it reflects and to the respondent State's margin of appreciation within the Belgian parliamentary system—a margin that is all the greater as the system is incomplete and provisional.

The system would not thwart 'the free expression of the opinion of the people in the choice of the legislature', which is what the Court considered the relevant test to be under Article 3 of Protocol No. 1. The French-speaking electors in the district of Halle-Vilvoorde enjoyed:

> ...the right to vote and the right to stand for election on the same legal footing as the Dutch-speaking electors. They are in no way deprived of these rights by the mere fact that they must vote either for candidates who will take

---

26. *Mathieu-Mohin and Clerfayt* (n. 6) [57].

the parliamentary oath in French and will accordingly join the French-language group in the House of Representatives or the Senate and sit on the French Community Council, or else for candidates who will take the oath in Dutch and so belong to the Dutch-language group in the House of Representatives or the Senate and sit on the Flemish Council.

The Court did not consider this to constitute 'a disproportionate limitation'.

D. Features of the two Belgian consociational cases

Four features of these two precedent-establishing cases are important here. First, the Court took a highly deferential approach to state decision-making, not only regarding electoral systems, but also, more generally, through the 'margin of appreciation' doctrine. In particular, the Court was, in most respects, unwilling to second-guess the Belgian state in deciding whether alternative policies were available that would satisfy the same objectives as the impugned measures with less adverse effect on the rights claimed.

Second, a low-intensity standard of review was adopted in the interpretation of the non-discrimination norm, which essentially amounted to little more than a test of arbitrariness. Passing a relatively low-threshold justification test nullified a determination of discrimination.

Third, the Court accorded considerable weight to the legitimacy of the purposes sought by the impugned measures, as defined by the state itself.

Fourth, considerable support for the legitimacy of the measures was gleaned from the democratic and inclusive nature of the support received across the different communities affected by the arrangements.

E. Influence of the cases

Although these cases under the ECHR were not explicit interpretations of *international* (as opposed to European) human rights norms, they were often seen subsequently as stating clearly the approach that would, and should, be adopted in international human rights law more generally.[27] The *Belgian*

27. In general, for the position in international law before the *Sejdić and Finci* case, see Marc Weller and Katharine Nobbs (eds) *Political Participation of Minorities: A Commentary on International Standards and Practice* (Oxford: Oxford University Press 2010).

Linguistics case, in particular, has been extensively drawn on by other courts interpreting human rights law in other jurisdictions.[28] Those scholars who assessed the compatibility of consociational arrangements with international human rights norms also drew significantly on these cases. Wippmann, writing in 1998, based his arguments on *Mathieu-Mohin and Clerfayt v. Belgium*. He argued that the flexibility embedded in the legal definition of 'discrimination', in which it is not discrimination if the contested measures are 'based on criteria that are "reasonable and objective", if their aim "is to achieve a purpose which is legitimate" under the applicable covenant, and if the measures employed are "proportionate" to the ends sought',[29] meant that consociations are 'not inherently incompatible'[30] with international human rights provisions prohibiting discrimination. He argued similarly that rights of political participation also allowed a significant degree of discretion to states on how to organize their electoral systems, provided that they are 'reasonable and proportionate to the ends sought',[31] and that even ensuring proportionality in civil service and other government posts would 'probably pass muster'.[32]

For Issacharoff, the 'key holding' in *Mathieu-Mohin and Clerfayt* was 'to endorse as a legitimate objective an institutional structure that tries to find a mediating equilibrium between popular sovereignty and the risk that a narrow majority could claim too much power'. He was complimentary about features of the Court's management of the issues. He stressed the importance attached by the ECtHR to the fact that the entire consociational structure derived from 'recent public, negotiations' and was subject to approval by the Belgian Parliament, in which the claimants 'were able to participate on a free and equal basis'. Indeed, overwhelming majorities passed the contested measures. These factors indicated that there was no 'oppression resulting from the operation of the unique voting arrangements'.[33] For Issacharoff, this approach suggested important implications

---

28. See e.g. *Proposed Modification to the Political Constitution of Costa Rica Relating to Naturalization*, Advisory Opinion OC-4, 19 January 1984, Inter-Am Ct HR (Ser A), No. 4, [56]–[57].
29. David Wippman 'Practical and Legal Constraints on Internal Power-Sharing' in David Wippman (ed.) *International Law and Ethnic Conflict* (Ithaca, NY: Cornell University Press 1998) 233, citing, inter alia, *Mathieu-Mohin and Clerfayt v. Belgium* (n. 6).
30. Wippman (n. 29) 240.
31. Wippman (n. 29) 236, again citing *Mathieu-Mohin and Clerfayt v. Belgium* (n. 6).
32. Wippman (n. 29) 237.
33. Samuel Issacharoff, 'Democracy and Collective Decision-Making' (2008) 6 International Journal of Comparative Law 231, 242–3.

that might guide future courts in similar situations: courts should be more willing to intervene where such arrangements continue in existence because of 'a lock up of power by self-interested incumbents or the calcification of institutional arrangements when there is insufficient political will for change',[34] but 'where political arrangements are more recent and reflect a genuine compromise, there should be a much greater presumption of legal tolerance of experimentation'.[35]

In short, until recently, academic legal commentators who evaluated the compatibility of consociational arrangements with human rights norms, based on these Belgian cases, generally accepted that they would survive a human rights challenge in domestic and international courts. Granted, this judgement was sometimes tinged with a significant set of caveats, which may be summarized as suggesting that consociation should be permitted primarily because it was often the least worst option. Steiner's basic argument illustrates the dilemma in which several legal writers have found themselves. Autonomy regimes—within which he included consociation— 'find indirect but significant support in several prominent norms of the human rights movement', such as self-determination and minority protection. On the other hand, 'these regimes can undermine other powerful human rights ideals, and to that extent embody a morally problematic counter-ideal'. In such circumstances, 'autonomy regimes may be justified as "least worst" solutions to almost intractable problems, perhaps frustrating the full realization of important ideas but ending or forestalling unjust rule'.[36] So, too, despite his argument that such regimes were probably compatible with international human rights law, Wippmann concluded that 'consociational settlements clearly do not fit comfortably within the dominant individual rights paradigm of contemporary international law', in that they tend to 'favor collective over individual rights', and 'may seem inherently regressive and atavistic in their emphasis on the importance of

---

34. Issacharoff (n. 33) 265.
35. Issacharoff (n. 33) 265. Partly based on conversations with Isaacharoff, we believe that his reading of the ECHR jurisprudence in these cases is results-oriented. We think that he wishes to enable courts to be agents for the dissolution of consociational bargains when the courts judge them to have outlived their usefulness and legitimacy—a reading consistent with his explicit preference, derived from the South African experience, to time-limit consociational bargains. By contrast, we think that consociational bargains are best unwound by the parties to the bargain, under the provisions of that bargain: see Conclusions and policy implications.
36. Henry J. Steiner, 'Ideals and Counter-Ideals in the Struggle over Autonomy Regimes for Minorities' (1991) 66 Notre Dame Law Review 1539, 1540.

ethnicity'; 'Compared to [the] ... alternatives, [however], consociational solutions are likely to represent the least worst alternative, in at least some cases.'[37]

This pragmatic assessment plainly depended on whether the consociational arrangement in question was likely to be 'successful'—that is, to create and maintain the conditions for a peaceful modus vivendi between the parties.[38] It is not our goal here to assess the facts of this issue scientifically. We note, however, that, unlike the human rights scholars and legal writers whom we have discussed, some political scientists have tried to assess the relevant facts. Caroline Hartzell and Matthew Hoddie, for example, examined thirty-eight civil wars that ended through negotiated settlements between the years 1945 and 1998. They found that the creation of an array of power-sharing institutions is 'positively associated with a durable peace'.[39] More recently, Michaela Mattes and Burcu Savan have examined all peace agreements made to end civil wars between 1945 and 2005. Their statistical tests report that the presence of ('parity-' or 'proportionally-' based) power-sharing provisions in such agreements, in conjunction with appropriate security arrangements, significantly reduces the likelihood of conflict recurrence.[40]

---

37. Wippman (n. 29) 240–1.
38. Caroline Hartzell and Matthew Hoddie, 'Institutionalizing Peace: Power Sharing and Post-Civil War Conflict Management' (2003) 47 American Journal of Political Science 318; see also Caroline Hartzell and Matthew Hoddie, *Crafting Peace: Power-Sharing Institutions and the Negotiated Settlement of Civil Wars* (University Park, PA: Penn State University Press 2007).
39. Hartzell and Hoddie, 'Institutionalizing Peace' (n. 38); see also Hartzell and Hoddie, *Crafting Peace* (n. 38).
40. Michaela Mattes and Burcu Savun, 'Fostering Peace after Civil War: Commitment Problems and Agreement Design' (2009) 53 International Studies Quarterly 737.

5

Departing from precedent

What explains the decision of the European Court of Human Rights (ECtHR) in the *Sejdić and Finci* case, especially its departure from the precedents of the Belgian cases? Our explanation highlights four significant developments that occurred between the Belgian cases and the Bosnian case: the growth of a considerably more robust approach to discrimination and minorities by the Council of Europe and the ECtHR; changes to the approach to interpreting rights to political participation by the ECtHR; the increasing adoption of the liberal criticisms of consociations by other human rights organizations, in particular by the Venice Commission; and particular understandings of the conflict in Bosnia, taken together with Bosnia's subsequent commitments to the Council of Europe and the European Union. We consider each in turn.

A. The European Court of Human Rights develops a more robust anti-discrimination jurisprudence

Following the Belgian cases, but before the *Sejdić and Finci* case, there were significant developments in the Council of Europe's and the Court's approach to non-discrimination issues. We can begin with developments in the Council of Europe, before considering the evolving approach of the ECtHR.

1. Council of Europe developments

Article 14 of the European Convention on Human Rights (ECHR) provides that '*the enjoyment of the rights and freedoms set forth in [the] Convention shall be secured without discrimination*'.[1] In 2000—that is, well after the

---

1. Emphasis added.

Belgian cases—the Council of Europe adopted a new equality provision (Protocol No. 12) that was seen as going some way toward remedying some of the limits of Article 14 ECHR arising from the words emphasized.[2] This Protocol, in effect, adds an additional provision to Article 14 that prohibits discrimination on any grounds such as those set out in Article 14 by a public authority even in circumstances in which other Convention rights are not engaged. It was also important in reaffirming that 'the principle of non-discrimination does not prevent States Parties from taking measures in order to promote full and effective equality, provided that there is an objective and reasonable justification for those measures'.[3] This Protocol entered into force on 1 April 2005 for those states that had ratified the provision, including Bosnia. As reported by Edin Hodžić and Nenad Stojanović, this ratification stimulated both the applicants in *Sejdić and Finci* to take their case to Strasbourg, since before that ratification 'neither applicant believed he had a legal basis for an application'.[4] The extension by Protocol No. 12 of protection from discrimination in the 'enjoyment of any right set forth by law' meant that protection against discrimination applied to the enjoyment of any right specifically granted to an individual under member-state law, 'not just in the enjoyment of Convention rights'.[5] In *Sejdić and Finci*, the right to stand for elections to the presidency was covered by Protocol No. 12 because the right to stand for election was provided by Bosnia's law.

Along with Protocol No. 12, the Council of Europe has adopted further conventions relevant to ethnic equality: on national minorities, the Framework Convention for the Protection of National Minorities 1995; and on minority languages, the European Charter for Regional or Minority Languages 1992. Of these two instruments, the most significant for the purposes of this book is the Framework Convention—in particular, Article 3(1), which provides:

> Every person belonging to a national minority shall have the right freely to choose to be treated or not to be treated as such and no disadvantage shall result from this choice or from the exercise of the rights which are connected to that choice.

---

2. Council of Europe, Protocol No. 12 to the Convention for the Protection of Human Rights and Fundamental Freedoms, 4 November 2000.
3. Protocol No. 12, Preamble.
4. Edin Hodžić and Nenad Stojanović, *New/Old Constitutional Engineering? Challenges and Implications of the European Court of Human Rights Decision in the Case of* Sejdić and Finci v. BiH (Sarajevo: Analitika 2011) 27.
5. Sandra Fredman, *Discrimination Law* (2nd edn, Oxford: Oxford University Press 2011) 147.

This provision has come to have considerable significance for the issue of whether consociational arrangements impermissibly inhibit the right of 'exit'.[6]

2. Suspect classifications and heightened scrutiny

In explaining the approach taken by the ECtHR in *Sejdić and Finci*, a particularly important development was the extent to which the Court adopted a US Supreme Court-style 'suspect classifications' approach to the interpretation of Article 14 ECHR, under which a two-tier standard of review is applied. A less intensive standard of review is applied to most of the prohibited grounds of discrimination. A more intensive standard of review is applied to a select group of prohibited grounds, and the ECtHR requires the state to present particularly convincing reasons justifying the difference in treatment. Some grounds of discrimination, therefore, are considered to be particularly serious, requiring a higher degree of justification than others. Differentiations based on gender and race appear to be given such heightened scrutiny. Other grounds of discrimination, such as religion,[7] nationality,[8] illegitimacy,[9] and sexual orientation,[10] may attract a similar high degree of justification to survive scrutiny, but this is more uncertain.

Heightened scrutiny has been of importance in cases concerning Roma and other vulnerable national minorities, relevant to the *Sejdić and Finci* case. In *DH*, for example, the Court considered that 'the vulnerable position of Roma/Gypsies means that special consideration should be given to their needs and their different lifestyle both in the relevant regulatory framework and in reaching decisions in particular cases'.[11] This approach was reiterated in *Chapman v. United Kingdom*,[12] in which the Court stated that:

---

6. See Chapter 1, 'B. Opposition to consociationalism'.
7. *Hoffmann v. Austria* (1994) 17 EHRR 293.
8. *Gaygusuz v. Austria* (1997) 23 EHRR 364.
9. *Marckx v. Belgium* (1979) 2 EHRR 330; cf. *McMichael v. United Kingdom* (1995) 20 EHRR 205.
10. *Smith and Grady v. United Kingdom* (2000) 29 EHRR 493, [90]; *Lustig-Prean and Beckett v. United Kingdom* (2000) 29 EHRR 548, [82]; cf. *Fretté v. France* (2004) 38 EHRR 21.
11. *DH v. Czech Republic* (2008) 47 EHRR 3.
12. (2001) 33 EHRR 18, [96]. See also *Connors v. United Kingdom* (2005) 40 EHRR 9, [84].

... there could be said to be an emerging international consensus amongst the Contracting States of the Council of Europe recognizing the special needs of minorities and an obligation to protect their security, identity and lifestyle, not only for the purpose of safeguarding the interests of the minorities themselves but to preserve a cultural diversity of value to the whole community.[13]

3. Discrimination as 'degrading treatment'

Since the Belgian cases, the ECtHR has also developed Article 3 of the ECHR prohibiting 'torture or inhuman or degrading treatment or punishment' into a more far-reaching anti-discrimination standard. The Court had stated that discrimination may breach Article 3 under certain conditions, even before *Mathieu-Mohin and Clerfayt*.[14] In *Abdulaziz v. United Kingdom*, although the Court held that racial discrimination could amount to a breach of Article 3, there was no violation here because the differences in treatment complained of (allegedly based on race) 'did not denote any contempt or lack of respect for the personality of the applicants and . . . it was not designed to, and did not, humiliate or debase'.[15] Since then, the Court has gone somewhat further. In *Smith and Grady v. United Kingdom*, the Court was willing to extend the coverage of Article 3 to prohibit sexual orientation discrimination,[16] although it held that the discrimination must attain a minimum level of severity that will be assessed taking into account all of the circumstances of the case, such as the duration of the treatment and its physical or mental effects. The Court stated that:

> Treatment may be considered degrading if it is such as to arouse in its victims feelings of fear, anguish and inferiority capable of humiliating and debasing them and possibly breaking their physical or moral resistance. Moreover, it is sufficient if the victim is humiliated in his or her own eyes.[17]

---

13. *DH* (n. 11) [181].
14. *Abdulaziz v. United Kingdom* 7 (1985) EHRR 471, [90]–[91]; *Smith and Grady* (n. 10) [120]–[121].
15. *Abdulaziz* (n. 14) [90]–[91]. See also *Moldovan and others v. Romania (No. 2)* (2005) 44 EHRR 16.
16. *Smith and Grady* (n. 10) [121].
17. *Smith and Grady* (n. 10) [120]. See also *Cyprus v. Turkey* (2002) 35 EHRR 30, [302]–[311] (in which Greek Cypriots in Northern Cyprus were subjected to discrimination amounting to degrading treatment).

B. Voting rights developments

There has also been significant evolution of the rights to vote and to stand for elections protected by Article 3 of Protocol No. 1 since *Mathieu-Mohin*.[18] We saw earlier[19] that the approach taken by the Court in that case had been to accord significant discretion to states to devise their own legislative arrangements and, in the main, that continued to be the case. Thus, in *Zdanoka v. Latvia*,[20] the Grand Chamber reaffirmed that:

> ...the margin [of appreciation] in this area is wide...There are numerous ways of organising and running electoral systems and a wealth of differences, inter alia, in historical development, cultural diversity and political thought within Europe, which it is for each Contracting State to mould into its own democratic vision...[21]

The Court continued to hold that Article 3 of Protocol No. 1 did not impose an absolute obligation to hold democratic elections for both chambers in each and every bicameral system. However, subsequent cases made clear that the Court was prepared to apply Article 3 of Protocol No. 1 more broadly, when it considered this necessary. In *Matthews v. United Kingdom*,[22] in particular, the Court applied the provision to the European Parliament, holding that it was sufficiently involved in the specific legislative processes leading to the passage of legislation, and was sufficiently involved in the general democratic supervision of the activities of the European Community, to constitute part of the 'legislature' of Gibraltar for the purposes of Article 3 of Protocol No. 1:

> The Court must ensure that 'effective political democracy' is properly served in the territories to which the Convention applies, and in this context, it must have regard not solely to the strictly legislative powers which a body has, but also to that body's role in the overall legislative process.[23]

---

18. For an authoritative discussion of the Court's development of Article 3 of Protocol No. 1, see Michael O'Boyle, 'Electoral Disputes and the ECHR: An Overview' (2009–10) 30 Human Rights Law Journal 1.
19. See Chapter 4, Section C, '2. Treatment of specific allegations'.
20. *Zdanoka v. Latvia* (2007) 45 EHRR 17.
21. *Zdanoka* (n. 20) [103].
22. *Matthews v. United Kingdom* (1998) 28 EHRR 361, [40].
23. *Matthews* (n. 22) [49].

In a second significant development, some cases subsequent to *Mathieu-Mohin* appeared to accord a significantly reduced margin of appreciation to states where the right to vote was effective denied on ethnic grounds. In *Aziz v. Cyprus*,[24] under the Cypriot consociational agreement that operated briefly in the early 1960s, two separate voters' rolls were established: one for the Greek community, and one for the Turkish community. Voters on these rolls could vote only for candidates from that community, so Greek Cypriot voters could only vote for Greek Cypriot candidates, and Turkish Cypriots voters for Turkish Cypriot candidates. When the agreement collapsed and Turkish Cypriots established their own unrecognized 'state' in northern Cyprus, the Turkish Cypriot representatives withdrew from the Cypriot legislature. However, the system of separate rolls was kept in operation. For the Turkish Cypriots who remained within that portion of the island controlled by the official Republic of Cyprus, the rule meant that they had no one for whom they were able to vote. In *Aziz*, the ECtHR held that the applicant, who was Turkish Cypriot, was deprived of his right to vote because of his ethnic origin. One key dispute in *Sejdić and Finci* was how far the decision in *Aziz* applied. In contrast to the situation in *Aziz*, the Bosnian government argued in *Sejdić and Finci* that the situation of 'Others' in Bosnia did not amount to a complete inability to exercise a vote or stand as a candidate: 'Others' could be elected to serve in the House of Representatives, and a person in the category of 'Others' is not in any way restricted 'in exercising his guaranteed right to vote for the candidates nominated in the election lists'.[25]

C. Adoption of liberal individualist criticisms of Bosnia by international human rights institutions

The ECtHR is not the only body that has considered the compatibility of consociational arrangements with human rights law. During the 2000s, consociational arrangements were greeted less than sympathetically in other

---

24. (2005) 41 EHRR 11. See further Lindsey E. Wakeley, 'From Constituent Peoples to Constituents: Europe Solidifies Fundamental Political Rights for Minority Groups in *Sejdić v. Bosnia*' (2010) 36 North Carolina Journal of International Law and Commercial Regulation 245, 246.
25. *Sejdić and Finci v. Bosnia (Submissions)* Application nos 27996/06 and 34836/06, 22 December 2009, [12].

European forums, particularly those that are concerned with the protection of human rights and equality, such as the Advisory Committee that oversees the implementation of the Council of Europe Framework Convention for the Protection of National Minorities and the European Commission for Democracy through Law (known as the 'Venice Commission'). We consider these criticisms in this section. In many instances, these critical assessments were made in the specific context of Bosnia's arrangements, and this somewhat paradoxical situation has not gone unnoticed. One writer frames matters as follows: this 'clearly discriminatory regime was endorsed by all the external actors that participated in the [Dayton] drafting process, including the United States and the European Union'.[26] Yet, almost as soon as the ink was dry on the Agreement, 'the international community began to push for reforms' that sought to move the Bosnian arrangements from being consociational to integrationist in nature.[27]

1. Advisory Committee of the Framework Convention for the Protection of National Minorities

Aspects of consociational arrangements in Cyprus, Belgium, South Tyrol, and Northern Ireland have been subject to scrutiny by the Advisory Committee of the Framework Convention for the Protection of National Minorities. Several of these criticisms raise issues that also arise in the *Sejdić and Finci* case. The Advisory Committee has criticized arrangements in which communities other than the main competing communities appear to have been 'squeezed' between the two main communities. A recurring example is from Cyprus: the Committee regards a requirement that Armenians, Latins, and Maronites are required to affiliate to either the Greek Cypriot or the Turkish Cypriot communities as contrary to Article 3 of the Framework Convention.[28] Criticisms have been forthcoming from the Advisory Committee where individuals are required to declare linguistic

---

26. Zaid Al-Ali, 'Constitutional Drafting and External Influence' in Tom Ginsburg and Rosalind Dixon (eds) *Comparative Constitutional Law* (Cheltenham: Edward Elgar 2011) 82.
27. Allison McCulloch, 'The Track Record of Centrieptalism in Deeply Divided Places' in Joanne McEvoy and Brendan O'Leary (eds) *Power-Sharing in Deeply Divided Places* (Philadelphia, PA: University of Pennsylvania Press, in press). See also Sumantra Bose, *Bosnia after Dayton: Nationalist Partition and International Intervention* (Oxford: Oxford University Press 2002) 204–52.
28. Advisory Committee on the Framework Convention for the Protection of National Minorities, *Third Opinion on Cyprus*, ACFC/OP/III(2010)002, 19 March 2010, [28] and [35].

affiliation, or to suffer disadvantages, such as in the South Tyrol.[29] It has also been consistently critical of provisions in Bosnia's election law that prevent minorities not affiliated with the Croat, Serb, or Bosniak communities from being able to stand for the state presidency, or for the House of Peoples, raising issues of compatibility with Article 4 of the Framework Convention. 'The legitimate objective of ensuring fair and balanced representation of the constituent peoples', the Committee said in 2008, 'should not result in excluding from political representation those who do not belong to the constituent peoples, and in particular, persons belonging to national minorities.'[30]

2. Venice Commission

Another body that has been centrally involved in assessing the compatibility of consociational arrangements with human rights–particularly equality–standards is the Venice Commission. The Venice Commission's criticism of the method of election to the presidency and the House of Peoples echoes that expressed by the Advisory Committee.

The Venice Commission initially became involved following a request in 2001 by the Legal Affairs Committee of the Parliamentary Assembly of the Council of Europe, which asked for an opinion on the draft Election Law then under discussion in Bosnia and subsequently adopted. The purpose of the request was to assist the Committee in preparing the decision of the Assembly on commitments to be entered into by Bosnia upon accession to the Council of Europe. The subsequent opinion was that 'the provisions of the Election Law governing elections to the Presidency and the House of Peoples of Bosnia raise questions as to their compatibility with international standards'.[31] The Commission noted, however, that:

> [Alt]hough both . . . the provisions use ethnic references, . . . the terms Bosniak, Croat and Serb, used throughout . . . may be more flexible than they appear, as

---

29. Advisory Committee on the Framework Convention for the Protection of National Minorities, *Opinion on Italy*, ACFC/OP/I(2002)007, 14 September 2001, [19]–[20]; Advisory Committee on the Framework Convention for the Protection of National Minorities, *Second Opinion on Italy*, ACFC/OP/II(2005)003, adopted 24 February 2005, [46].
30. Advisory Committee on the Framework Convention for the Protection of National Minorities, *Second Opinion on Bosnia and Herzegovina*, ACFC/OP/II(2008)005, 9 October 2008, [68].
31. Venice Commission, *Opinion on the Electoral Law of Bosnia and Herzegovina*, CDL-INF(2001) 21, 24 October 2001, [30].

there is no constitutional or legal definition of who is a Bosniak, Croat or Serb. Current electoral rules simply require electoral candidates to make a declaration as to their ethnicity.

Since these provisions were required by the constitution, the Commission recognized that 'its recommendations cannot be implemented overnight', but emphasized that the necessary revisions 'could be carried out in a manner which would safeguard the position and equality of the constituent peoples by maintaining the multi-ethnic character of both institutions'.[32]

When the Commission returned to consider the question in 2005, its position had hardened.[33] It concluded that 'the time seems ripe to start a process of reconsideration of the present constitutional arrangements',[34] the first stage of which should include reform of the provisions on the composition and election of the presidency and the House of Peoples, 'which seem either now or following the entry into force of Protocol No. 12 . . . incompatible with the ECHR'. It made clear, however, that its longer-term goal was much more far-reaching: 'Further constitutional reforms, changing the emphasis from a state based on the equality of three constituent peoples to a state based on the equality of citizens, remain desirable in the medium and long term.'[35]

The Venice Commission here intimated nothing less than the eventual overturning of the multinational federal and consociational agreement for three peoples negotiated at Dayton in 1995, and its replacement with an integrated state of equal citizens (as long sought by the Bosniaks)—although perhaps the drafters of the opinion would suggest that they were merely commending a change of emphasis.

The specific options for change identified by the Venice Commission were complex and wide-ranging and a full discussion is beyond the bounds of this book.[36] In essence, regarding the House of Peoples, the Commission identified three options: to abolish it and move the vital interests veto to the

---

32. Venice Commission (n. 31) [14], [30], and [31].
33. Venice Commission, *Opinion on the Constitutional Situation in Bosnia and Herzegovina and the Powers of the High Representative*, CDL-AD(2005)004, 11–12 March 2005, [101].
34. '"The Principle of Unripe Time" is that people should not do at the present moment what they think right at the moment, because the moment at which they think it right has not yet arrived': Francis Macdonald Cornford, *Microcosmographia Academica: Being a Guide for the Young Academic Politician* (Cambridge: MainSale Press 1993 [1908]) 29. 'Ripe time' for the Venice Commission, likewise, is when it is now right to do what it had previously thought to be right, but had judged inopportune.
35. Venice Commission (n. 33) [102], [104].
36. For a fuller discussion, see Hodžić and Stojanović (n. 4) 88*ff*.

House of Representatives; to include representatives of the 'Others' in the House of Peoples; or to retain the present composition, but restrict its powers solely to the exercise of the vital interests veto. Regarding the presidency, three options again were identified: to abolish the three-headed presidency and have one president only; to remove the ethnic qualification for standing as president; or to transfer most powers of the president to the House of Representatives and have an individual president elected by the Parliamentary Assembly.[37]

The Commission sought leave in October 2008 to intervene as a third party in proceedings before the ECtHR in the *Sejdić and Finci* case, a submission that was successful and which, as we shall see, was also highly influential.[38] The Venice Commission's position, which the Court referenced extensively, was that the provisions of the constitution and the Electoral Code preventing the election of 'Others' to the House of Peoples 'cannot be considered proportionate', and are therefore contrary to Article 14 ECHR read with Article 3 of Protocol No. 1. The Commission argued, however, that there was no violation of Article 14 ECHR, read with Article 3 of Protocol No. 1, because Article 3 was not applicable to elections to the presidency, since it had no legislative functions.

Although it considered that the *original* inclusion of these restrictions '[did] not deserve criticism', they could not be justified on a permanent basis. The Commission advanced four reasons why they should be removed. First, the approach adopted 'does not really help to overcome the problems' in Bosnia: 'It is not proportionate to nullify rights guaranteed in the Convention in order to preserve a constitutional structure that has not helped to acquire the desired results within a period of about 13 years.'

Second, penalizing those who have 'opted out' of the existing ethnic categories was likely to produce the most counter-productive result:

> It is precisely this change [opting out] which, if made by the majority of citizens, can lead Bosnia and Herzegovina to overcome the current political *impasse*. This attitude should therefore be encouraged, inter alia through the enhancement of the position of the 'Others' at the constitutional level.

37. See Venice Commission (n. 33), *Opinion on Different Proposals for the Election of the Presidency of Bosnia and Herzegovina*, CDL-AD(2006)004, 20 March 2006, and *Opinion on the Draft Amendments to the Constitution of Bosnia and Herzegovina*, CDL-AD(2006)019, 12 June 2006.
38. Venice Commission, *Amicus Curiae Brief in the Cases of* Sejdić and Finci v. Bosnia and Herzegovina *(Applications no. 27996/06 and 34836/06) Pending before the European Court of Human Rights*, CDL-AD(2008)027, 17–18 October 2008.

Third, there were mechanisms of power-sharing available elsewhere in Bosnia that demonstrated that the 'Others' did not need to be excluded for the mechanisms to operate.

Lastly, there was a 'significant change of mentality' occurring in Bosnia, evidenced by constitutional reform negotiations that showed 'a real readiness to change the basic functioning of the institutions', even though these had been unsuccessful.[39]

3. Other international and European official bodies

These criticisms of the Bosnian arrangements and of other consociations were not restricted to the Advisory Committee and the Venice Commission. In 2004, the European Commission against Racism and Intolerance (ECRI), another body established by the Council of Europe, reported on its assessment of Bosnia. Among a wide-ranging set of recommendations, it was particularly critical of the extensive use of ethnic affiliation and 'of institutional arrangements essentially designed to cater for the needs and interests of the three main constituent peoples'. It accepted that these may have been necessary 'in a post-conflict situation', but it identified 'growing support among the general population' for a change in this approach.[40] It found that:

> . . . persons who do not identify with one of the three constituent peoples, either because they have other ethnic affiliations or because [they] are unable or willing to choose an ethnic affiliation, are in a position of serious disadvantage and, in many cases, victims of ethnic discrimination.[41]

In its report on Lebanon, the Human Rights Committee, the body responsible for overseeing the implementation of the United Nations International Covenant on Civil and Political Rights (ICCPR), noted:

39. Venice Commission (n. 38) [26], [33], and [36]. The Opinion provides no survey or public opinion research demonstrating a change in mentality among citizens. The evidence consisted of the failed attempt to change the constitution in response to the terms of the EU accession agreement.
40. European Commission against Racism and Intolerance, *Report on Bosnia and Herzegovina*, CRI (2005)2, 15 February 2005, [70] and [71].
41. ECRI (n. 40) [70]. The report also expressed concern at 'the extensive use made by political parties of a nationalist discourse that fosters division, including geographical separation, between constituent peoples and, more generally among the different ethnic groups': [56]. As ECRI reports say of themselves, however, they are 'not the result of inquiries or testimonial evidences': ECRI (n. 40) Foreword. The Bosnia report commissioned, and cites, no social science surveys of public opinion. It was produced after confidential dialogue with 'national authorities'.

...with concern that every Lebanese citizen must belong to one of the religious denominations officially recognized by the Government, and that this is a requirement in order to be eligible to run for public office. This practice does not comply with the requirements of Article 25 of the Covenant.[42]

In 2006, the Human Rights Committee, in its concluding observations on Bosnia's periodic report, urged the adoption of 'constitutional reform... with a view to adopting an electoral system that guarantees equal enjoyment of... rights... to all citizens irrespective of ethnicity'.[43]

4. Dependence of the Court on such bodies

The ECtHR has, it must be emphasized, become highly dependent in practice on these organizations for information. Institutionally, one of the most important developments since the Belgian cases has been the abolition of the European Commission on Human Rights. The Commission had become the major mechanism by which the Court was relieved of quite a lot of the burden of fact-finding. In the new structure, there is a tiered Court, in which the lower tier finds the facts and reaches a judgment, which is then subject to an appeal to the Grand Chamber. In exceptional cases, however, a case can be referred by the lower tier directly to the Grand Chamber, which is what occurred in the *Sejdić and Finci* case. Formally, the Court may itself engage in extensive original fact-finding, but in practice this seldom happens, not least because of the pressure on the Court to reduce its backlog of cases (at the time of writing, numbering some 150,000). The abolition of the Commission has obliged the Court to rely in practice on alternative methods of fact-finding, and one of these methods has been to place considerably greater reliance in some cases on fact-finding by other human rights bodies associated with the Council of Europe, such as the Advisory Committee and the Venice Commission, as occurred in the *Sejdić and Finci* case. Of the three factors that Céline Tran considers particularly affected the Court's judgment in *Sejdić and Finci*, the Venice Commission was centrally involved in two—namely, the identification of 'positive developments' in Bosnia suggesting significant political progress, and the

---

42. Human Rights Committee, *Concluding Observations on Lebanon*, UN Doc. CCPR/C/79/ Add.78, 1 April 1997, [23]; Steven Wheatley, *Democracy, Minorities, and International Law* (Cambridge: Cambridge University Press 2005) 164, fn. 235.
43. Human Rights Committee, *Concluding Observations on Bosnia and Herzegovina*, CCPR/C/ BIH/CO/1, 22 November 2006, [8].

identification of alternative means to maintain power-sharing without discriminating.[44]

In this case, the opinions of these bodies also appear to have been accorded considerably greater weight than they might otherwise have had because of the weakness of the case presented by the government of Bosnia. It is not clear why the government's case was so weakly presented, but it seems reasonable to surmise that the government was itself made up of parties with radically different views on the acceptability of the arrangements, which likely contributed to the lack of a robust defence. Given also the absence of any interventions from other bodies supporting the arrangements under challenge, the Court was left in a particularly difficult position; not surprisingly, then, it relied heavily on whatever 'independent' assessments it could find—particularly those that it considered reflected a European consensus. In contrast to the usual method of identifying a consensus, which is to engage in a comparative assessment of the laws and practices of other European states,[45] there is a notable absence of comparative reasoning in the Court's opinion in *Sejdić and Finci*, and a correspondingly heavier reliance on the findings of the Venice Commission.

5. The 'international community' and representation before the Court

It is noticeable, too, that the legal representation of the applicants, and the interveners, had common links with the network of international critics. The legal representation of the applicants before the Court all had extensive experience in Bosnia, both in non-governmental organizations (NGOs) and in several different governmental institutions.

Mr Finci was represented by Clive Baldwin, an English solicitor, on behalf of Minority Rights Group International (MRG).[46] Mr Baldwin had

---

44. Céline Tran, 'Striking a Balance between Human Rights and Peace and Stability: A Review of the European Court of Human Rights Decision *Sejdić and Finci v. Bosnia and Herzgovina*' (2011) 18 Human Rights Brief at 5. The third was that Bosnia had voluntarily agreed to abide by ECHR standards and to review its electoral legislation for compliance when it joined the Council of Europe, and had given the same promise when entering the stabilization and association agreement (SAA) with the EU: see Chapter 2, 'C. European commitments and the failure of proposed changes'.

45. Kanstantsin Dzehtsiarou, 'Does Consensus Matter? Legitimacy of European Consensus in the Case Law of the European Court of Human Rights' [2011] Public Law 534.

46. See <http://www.hrw.org/bios/clive-baldwin-0>

been senior legal adviser at Human Rights Watch since 2007, had previously worked for the Organization for Security and Co-operation in Europe (OSCE) Mission in Kosovo, and was head of advocacy for MRG. Before joining Human Rights Watch, Baldwin had been a practising lawyer in London for human rights law firm Bindman and Partners, and had worked on European human rights litigation at the AIRE (Advice on Individual Rights in Europe) Centre. While at MRG, he implemented the organization's first global litigation programme. Professor Sheri Rosenberg, a New York attorney who was then director of the Human Rights and Genocide Clinic at the Cardozo Law School of Yeshiva University in New York, also represented Mr Finci.[47] Previously a practising lawyer, Professor Rosenberg was selected in 2000 by the US Department of State to be one of two US lawyers to work for the Bosnia Human Rights Chamber, established under the Dayton Peace Agreement.[48] She was subsequently awarded a Human Rights Fellowship at Columbia University, where she worked for the United Nations, Office for the Coordination of Humanitarian Affairs, Policy Branch, before joining Cardozo Law School.

Javier Leon Diaz, of the Madrid Bar, represented Mr Sejdić.[49] Diaz had worked with the European Union Police Mission (EUPM) to Bosnia and Herzegovina as a legal adviser, as an international lawyer with the Human Rights Chamber for Bosnia and Herzegovina, and with the OSCE Mission to Bosnia and Herzegovina as a senior legal adviser. He was also an independent expert consultant for the Venice Commission of the Council of Europe and an expert consultant for the Council of Europe Directorate-General (DG) Human Rights and Rule of Law.

The strong interconnections that operated were equally apparent as regards the intervenors who were permitted to make submissions to the Court. There were several third-party intervenors, all supporting the position of the applicants—notably including the Open Society Justice Initiative (funded by George Soros and involved in an earlier case before the Court on issues of Roma discrimination),[50] the AIRE Centre (also with

---

47. See <http://www.cardozo.yu.edu/MemberContentDisplay.aspx?ccmd=ContentDisplay&ucmd=UserDisplay&userid=10690>
48. An article flowed partly from this experience and reviews the Bosnia's Constitutional Court's equality jurisprudence: Sheri P. Rosenberg, 'Promoting Equality after Genocide' (2007) 16 Tulane Journal of International and Comparative Law 329.
49. See <http://www.javier-leon-diaz.com/docs/Curriculum_Vitae.htm>
50. *Sejdić and Finci v. Bosnia (Third Party Observations)*, 15 August 2008. The earlier case was *Nachova and others v. Bulgaria* (2006) 42 EHRR 43.

an impressive track record of cases taken to the Court),[51] and the Venice Commission itself.

D. Bosnia in European eyes, and Bosnia's commitments to the Council of Europe and the European Union

While they are courts of *law*, human rights courts are also influenced by the climate of opinion on particular issues. Assessing the climate of educated opinion that may affect judicial decisions, and which may shape the way in which information is framed and digested, is necessarily a difficult and inexact enterprise. In the *Sejdić and Finci* case, however, it is not particularly difficult to identify the currents and contours of the dominant trends in international educated opinion. Two of these trends were, in our view, of particular importance.

The first trend is the notable absence of any organized international or European movement that actively supports consociations. In contrast to the international human rights and minority rights movements, there is no 'Consociations International' to which the governments of consociational polities subscribe. This absence is not hard to explain. No advocate of power-sharing commends the global implementation of consociation. Consociations are not invented or reinvented because of the global diffusion of an ideology, or because of the spread of the expertise of political scientists and constitutional lawyers; rather, they emerge from negotiations, as practical resolutions to prevent or to resolve conflicts. They generally flow from a balance of power—military or political, or both. They arise from practical wisdom, rather than the application of high-minded doctrine. Today, as we suggested in Chapter 1, there is much greater self-conscious diffusion of consociational theory and practice. Its exponents, however, rarely make their case in universalist language—and are rarely heard when they do. When they are effective in their advice, their arguments and proposals are richly context-specific. Consociations historically have been composed with proper names, with particular peoples in mind; they have been supremely difference-conscious; they have been negotiated under the

51. *Sejdić and Finci v. Bosnia (Third Party Intervention)*, 15 August 2008.

shadow of past or future armed conflict; and, as Lijphart suggests, have exhibited significant variety.[52] These are among the reasons why there is no 'Consociations International'. There is another: consociations are not easy to love, partly because they are rarely anyone's first design preference. Consociation was no one's first-preference resolution in Bosnia, or among Bosnia's immediate neighbours. Consociation—as opposed to celebrating 'diversity' and 'inclusivity'—is not a cause championed by human rights activists.

The second trend that played a role in influencing the ECtHR in *Sejdić and Finci* arose from the perceived role among educated public opinion of consociational arrangements in Bosnia specifically. Bosnia in the 1990s was an international human rights cause par excellence—and for good reason. Genocide, ethnic expulsion, war crimes, crimes against humanity, mass rapes, and coercive assimilation occurred and recurred on European soil. Zealous mono-ethnic nationalists, especially among Serbs and Croats, were reviled and treated as the principal culprits in the ruin of Bosnia. 'Slobodan Milosevic, Butcher of the Balkans' became a staple of commentary (as a Google search will establish in any language). The palpable xenophobia, anti-Semitism, and contempt for Roma among ultra-nationalist Serbs and Croats added to their deserved poor press. There was, by contrast, considerable general sympathy for the Bosniaks (especially secular Muslims) among western human rights activists. Such activists thought that the Bosniaks shared a common vision of an integrated Bosnia in which all human rights would be respected, the crimes of the mono-ethnic nationalists punished, and the consequences of their crimes—especially expulsions and

---

52. In 1990, Arend Lijphart wrote:

> The necessity of power-sharing was recognized and consociational rules and institutions were developed by Dutch politicians in 1917, by Lebanese politicians in 1943, by Austrian politicians in 1945, by Malaysian politicians in 1955, by Colombian politicians in 1958, and, of course, by British politicians for the Northern Ireland problem in 1972. The pattern is one of reinvention instead of learning from prior foreign examples. The logic of power-sharing is so compelling that it is readily recognized even when established political traditions, such as the strong British majority-rule tradition militate against it ... A factor that complicates the adoption of power-sharing in practice to some extent is that power-sharing can come in very many forms.
>
> (Arend Lijphart, 'Foreword: One Basic Problem, Many Theoretical Options—and a Practical Solution?' in John McGarry and Brendan O'Leary, eds, *The Future of Northern Ireland*, Oxford: Clarendon Press 1990, viii).

displacements—reversed. For many in this high-minded constituency, the Dayton Peace Agreement (DPA) was a betrayal. They thought of it as a pact among war criminals. They regarded the recognition of the Serb Republic as a victory for the ethnic cleansers. They thought that Dayton had legitim-ized the partition of Bosnia.[53]

The international diplomats who mediated and arbitrated the DPA did not regard its contents as ideal. They thought, however, that it had pre-vented the secession of the Serb Republic, and its partition between Croatia and Serbia. Its power-sharing institutions were, in their view, a regrettable necessity, but a necessity nonetheless.[54] They believed that they had put in place commitments to reverse 'ethnic cleansing'[55] and to establish high human rights standards, so that Bosnia's future remained open, as they saw it, to voluntary reintegration. They thought that international assistance would productively help this goal. The international organizations that settled in Bosnia after Dayton, however, were dominated by western or western-educated personnel with cosmopolitan, international, and integra-tionist values. They manned the security forces—NATO's Implementation Force (IFOR) and its later Stabilization Force (SFOR), the OSCE, the European Union, and the World Bank; their efforts were coordinated by the Office of the High Representative (OHR), which reported to the Peace Implementation Council. With exceptions, they shared the outlook of the human rights advocates abundantly present in NGOs and international NGOs (INGOs) engaged in post-conflict reconstruction.[56]

---

53. See Bose (n. 27) *passim*, esp. chs 4 and 5. Few, except Albanians, noticed that the Dayton Agreement had done nothing to address the position of the Albanians of Kosovo: see Alexandra D.R. Channer, 'Defeat and Resurrection: A Political History of the Pan-Albanian Revolutionary Movement, 1912–2010' (Unpublished PhD thesis, University of Pennsylvania 2012).

54. James C. O'Brien, 'The Dayton Agreement in Bosnia: Durable Ceasefire, Permanent Nego-tiation' in I. William Zartman and Victor A. Kremenyuk (eds) *Peace versus Justice: Negotiating Forward- and Backward-Looking Outcomes* (Lanham, MD: Rowman and Littlefield 2005); Richard Holbrooke, *To End a War* (London: Random House 1998) *passim*. See also Interview of Vermont State Senator Peter W. Galbraith by Brendan O'Leary, in Townshend, VT, 17 August 2012.

55. Office of the High Representative, General Framework Agreement for Peace in Bosnia and Herzegovina, Annex 7: Agreement on Refugees and Displaced Persons (1995). In 2004, the Bosnian Ministry of Human Rights and Refugees announced that 'one million of a total wartime displacement population of over two million had returned home': Gerard Toal and Carl Dahlman, *Bosnia Remade: Ethnic Cleansing and its Reversal* (Oxford: Oxford University Press 2011) ebook loc. 223.

56. Very different analysts of Bosnia's post-conflict development share this assessment: see e.g. Bose (n. 27); David Chandler, *Bosnia: Faking Democracy after Dayton* (2nd edn, London:

Pro-consociational voices for Bosnia, by contrast, have not been internationally prominent in western democracies. If heard at all, they were treated as akin to those of realpolitik realists—although exponents of the latter worldview generally favoured the partition of Bosnia[57]—or, worse, pro-consociational voices were seen as appeasers of hardline Serbs and Croats, at the expense of the Bosniaks and democracy. After all, within Bosnia, the keenest exponents of veto rights appeared to be hardline nationalists, especially Bosnian Serbs and Croats. It was their leaders who had insisted on and championed the collective presidency and a powerful second chamber based on constituent peoples.

This climate of opinion, we suggest, reinforced all of the foregoing intellectual and jurisprudential trends: the shift toward a more robust approach to discrimination and defence of minorities by the Council of Europe and the ECtHR; changes to interpreting the right to political participation by the ECtHR; and the adoption of the liberal criticisms of consociations by other human rights organizations—in particular, by the Venice Commission.

Lastly, Bosnia's formal commitments when it joined the Council of Europe, given also to the European Union when it accepted the latter's terms for association, made it appear, as suggested by many of the NGO and INGO reports cited in this chapter, that Bosnia's leadership and its communities had come to share this opinion.

Pluto Press 2000); Andrew Finlay, *Governing Ethnic Conflict: Consociation, Identity and the Price of Peace* (London: Routledge 2011); Sabrina P. Ramet, *Thinking about Yugoslavia: Scholarly Debates about the Yugoslav Breakup and the Wars in Bosnia and Kosovo* (Cambridge: Cambridge University Press 2005); Toal and Dahlman (n. 55).

57. See e.g. John J. Mearsheimer and Robert A. Pape, 'The Answer: A Three-Way Partition Plan for Bosnia and How the US Can Enforce It' *The New Republic*, 14 June 1993.

6

The Bosnian Constitutional Court and consociation

We should be wary, however, of adopting an overly deterministic approach to judicial adjudication, assuming that the decision of the European Court of Human Rights (ECtHR) in *Sejdić and Finci* was in some sense inevitable or preordained. The decisions of the Constitutional Court of Bosnia, itself composed as a consociational institution, are of crucial significance in showing that different courts could address the same issues differently, with entirely different results. Despite the developments discussed in the previous chapter and despite predictions from well-informed observers before the cases were decided,[1] the Bosnian Constitutional Court has so far rejected all of the challenges to the ethnic differentiation requirements of the consociational arrangements that it has adjudicated. The decisions of this Court are therefore fascinating in their own right, but they are also of critical importance for another reason: applicants must exhaust domestic remedies before they proceed to the ECtHR, and the exhaustion of this domestic process was a necessary prelude to the case of *Sejdić and Finci* going before that Court.

A. The role of the Constitutional Court

The Constitutional Court's decisions conform to the hypotheses of Pildes and Issacharoff that predict judicial restraint when consociational institutions and human rights appear to clash. They also contrast sharply with the

1. Gro Nystuen, *Achieving Peace or Protecting Human Rights? Conflicts between Norms Regarding Ethnic Discrimination in the Dayton Peace Agreement* (The Hague: Martinus Nijhoff 2005) 157.

eventual approach of the ECtHR. This is particularly significant given that the European Convention on Human Rights (ECHR) features prominently in the history and context of Bosnia's Constitutional Court. Not only is the external appointment of its judges in the hands of the President of the ECtHR, but the Constitution of Bosnia and Herzegovina also provides that the rights and freedoms contained in the ECHR 'shall apply directly in Bosnia and Herzegovina. These shall have priority over all other law'.[2] This provision now includes priority over the constitution itself.[3] Sheri Rosenberg has therefore correctly observed that, on paper, Bosnia 'has one of the highest standards of human rights protection in the world'.[4]

B. The *Constituent Peoples* case

In a series of cases, the Bosnian Constitutional Court has trodden a delicate line between intervention and non-intervention.[5] On the one hand, the Court showed itself ready to overturn aspects of the entities' constitutions in its *Constituent Peoples* decision.[6] The constitution vested the entities with the power to determine and regulate their own citizenship, and they had taken advantage of that freedom to create priorities within the entities for particular groups. Alija Izetbegovic, 'the then-Chairman of the Presidency' and

2. In an interview given on 22 September 2011, Daniel Serwer, who served as State Department Special Envoy for the Bosnian Federation from 1994 to 1996 (that is, over the period of the negotiation of the Dayton Agreement), described this provision as having been 'snuck ... in' past the Bosnian negotiators. He is quoted as saying: 'If [the Bosnians] had noticed it, they probably would have insisted that it was taken out.' He also suggested that his team 'was well aware that [we were] planting [in] the constitution the seeds of its own destruction': quoted in Katie Engelhart, 'Bosnia's Three-Headed Beast: *Sejdić and Finci v. Bosnia and Herzegovina* and the case for 'reasonable' discrimination'. Available online at <http://www.sant.ox.ac.uk/esc/docs/Dahrendorf_k.engelhart.doc>
3. The Constitutional Court of Bosnia and Herzegovina, in Decisions U-5/04 of 31 March 2006 and U-13/05 of 26 May 2006, held that the ECHR did not have priority over the constitution, but it came to a different conclusion a few months later in decision AP-2678/06 of 29 September 2006.
4. Sheri P. Rosenberg, 'Promoting Equality after Genocide' (2007) 16 Tulane Journal of International and Comparative Law 329, 343.
5. For discussions of the role of the Constitutional Court of Bosnia, see David Feldman 'Constitutionalism, Deliberative Democracy, and Human Rights' in John Morison and Kieran McEvoy (eds) *Judges, Transition, and Human Rights* (Oxford: Oxford University Press 2007) 453ff; Anna Morawiec Mansfield, 'Ethnic but Equal: The Quest for a New Democratic Order in Bosnia and Herzegovina' (2003) 103 Columbia Law Review 2052; David Feldman, 'Renaming Cities in Bosnia and Herzegovina' (2005) 3 International Journal of Constitutional Law 649.
6. For a detailed discussion of this decision, see Nystuen (n. 1) 139–42.

'himself a Bosniak',[7] brought the constitutional challenge to the Serb Republic's approach. According to Issacharoff, Izetbegovic had 'objected strenuously to the final form of the Dayton Accords', but was 'forced under pressure from the U.S. to accede to the ethnic assignment of power through the territories'.[8] The *Constituent Peoples* decision by the Constitutional Court declared unconstitutional those provisions of the entity constitutions that identified only particular ethnic groups as constituent peoples of each entity and, therefore, used ethnicity as the sole criterion for citizenship of the entity.[9] The Court declared that all ethnic groups (including 'Others') were 'constituent peoples' and thus equal, irrespective of where they lived. 'Essentially,' wrote Sheri Rosenberg, 'the Constitutional Court held that the Constitution requires that all ethnic groups—Bosniaks, Croats, Serbs, and "Others" are "constituent peoples" and equal across the entire territory of Bosnia, regardless of where they reside.'[10]

Although apparently radical, the decision entrenched the ethnic aspect of the constitution, at the same time as it challenged the use of ethnicity by the entities. Under the Court's decision, it is the groups—namely, the peoples—that enjoy equality.[11] As Rosenberg wrote:

> The Court established that the Bosnia Constitution requires 'collective equality' among the constituent groups of Bosnia. In doing so, it wisely balanced the strong group identities found among citizens in Bosnia with notions of equality, interpreting the Bosnia Constitution as one that respects collective identity provided it does not morph into collective domination by any one group in any part of Bosnia.[12]

Even then, as Issacharoff points out, the 'opinion striking down the claims of ethnic hegemony in the entities was a five-to-four vote, with the majority comprising the two Bosniak judges and the three international judges, while the Serb and Croat judges dissented'.[13] There was, therefore, no concurrent majority among the judges from Bosnia. The Court's majority consisted of the outsiders and the judges from the largest group, the Bosniaks.

7. Samuel Issacharoff, 'Constitutionalizing Democracy in Fractured Societies' (2004) 82 Texas Law Review 1888.
8. Issacharoff (n. 7) fn. 149.
9. *Constituent Peoples* Decision, U 5/98, Partial decision Pt III, July 2000.
10. Rosenberg (n. 4) 383–91.
11. See Mansfield (n.5). See also Sujit Choudhry and Richard Stacey, 'Independent or Dependent? Constitutional Courts in Divided Societies' in Colin Harvey and Alexander Schwartz (eds) *Rights in Divided Societies* (Oxford: Hart 2012).
12. Rosenberg (n. 4) 385.   13. Issacharoff (n. 7) 1891.

C. Challenges to the presidency
election arrangements

While willing to strike down attempted constitutional innovations by the
entities, the Constitutional Court decided that the arrangements regarding
the presidency[14] were not in conflict with the non-discrimination requirements of the state's constitution.[15] Two cases were taken by Sulejman
Tihić, a Bosniak politician, one of the founding members of the Party of
Democratic Action (*Stranka Demokratske Akcije*, or SDA). In 2001, Tihić
was chosen to succeed Alija Izetbegovic as head of the SDA. He was
subsequently elected to the presidency in October 2002. In April 2004
and September 2005, while chair of the presidency, he submitted applications to the Constitutional Court seeking review of the compatibility with
the ECHR of constitutional provisions regarding elections to the presidency
and to the House of Peoples.[16] His arguments were substantially the same as
those later made by Mr Finci before the ECtHR.

The Constitutional Court rejected both applications as inadmissible
because the Court was not empowered to take a decision. In Case U-5/04,
it accepted that the ECHR was directly applicable in Bosnia and that therefore
domestic law must conform to the ECHR. However, the Constitutional
Court's jurisdiction did not extend to considering possible conflicts between
the Convention and the constitution itself. It held that 'the rights under the
European Convention cannot have a superior status in relation to the Constitution' of Bosnia, because 'the European Convention, as an international
document, entered into force on the basis of the Constitution of Bosnia and
thereby the constitutional authorities derive from the Constitution of Bosnia
and not from the European Convention'.[17] In Case U-13/05, the Court
reiterated this position.[18]

A third case was taken by Ilijaz Pilav, who had attempted to be registered
as a candidate for the Bosnian presidency as a member from the Serb
Republic. His registration was requested by the Party for Bosnia and

---

14. Described in Chapter 2, 'B. Key consociational aspects of Bosnia's constitution'.
15. Case AP-2678/06, 29 September 2006. A detailed consideration of the Constitutional Court's
    equality jurisprudence may be found in Rosenberg (n. 4) *passim*.
16. In Decisions U-5/04 and U-13/05.
17. Decision on Admissibility, U-5/04, 31 March 2006.
18. Decision on Admissibility, U-13/05, 26 May 2006.

Herzegovia, but rejected by the Central Election Commission, because he declared himself to be Bosniak. To be elected from the Serb Republic, candidates had to declare themselves to be Serb. The Central Election Commission's refusal to register him was challenged in the Constitutional Court as contrary to the ECHR, the United Nations International Covenant on Civil and Political Rights (ICCPR), and the Framework Convention for the Protection of National Minorities, and therefore in violation of the Bosnian constitution. Again, the majority of the Court decided against the applicant, but this time on the merits of the case. In particular, the majority considered whether the differential treatment lacked an objective or reasonable justification. Drawing specifically on the ECtHR case law on elections (including *Mathieu-Mohin*), the Court concluded that there was a margin of appreciation given to states:

> The ... restrictions are justified by the specific nature of internal order of Bosnia and Herzegovina that was agreed upon by Dayton Agreement and whose ultimate goal was the establishment of peace and dialogue between the opposing parties given that the said provision was intentionally incorporated into the Constitution so that the members of the Presidency come from amongst Bosniaks, Croats and Serbs.

The purpose of the provisions:

> ... is strengthening of constituent peoples in order to secure that the Presidency is composed of the representatives from amongst these three constituent peoples. Taking into account the current situation in Bosnia and Herzegovina, the restriction imposed ... is justified at this moment since there is a reasonable justification for such reasoning.

The restrictions imposed 'are proportional to the objectives of general community in terms of preservation of the established peace, continuation of dialogue, and consequently creation of conditions for amending' the challenged provisions. These were precisely the justifications that the Bosnian government subsequently used to defend itself before the ECtHR.[19]

The argument had two components. The first was that there was a legitimate justification for the arrangements originally and that the situation that justified these arrangements had not changed sufficiently to warrant any amendment. Second, it was accepted that the arrangements were temporary. Any changes, however, must be introduced gradually, 'in accordance with

19. Written Observations of Bosnia Herzegovina on Admissibility and Merits, 23 June 2008, [29].

the development of social relations'.[20] Indeed, if changes are desired, the current arrangements are most likely to lead to this change, because they provide a 'platform for amendments'.

D. The views of the international judges

In two cases, however, there were dissenting opinions from Judge Constance Grewe of France,[21] who was one of the two judges appointed by the President of the ECtHR (joined by Judge Palavric, one of the Bosniak members of the Court), and from Judge David Feldman of the United Kingdom, who was the second appointee of the ECtHR President at the time. The dissent conformed to sociological expectations (or stereotypes): the French judge displayed a principled, integrationist temperament; the British judge adopted a more pragmatic, pluralist, and territorially accommodationist outlook.

In Case U-13/05, Judge Grewe not only found the application admissible, but she also went on to uphold the challenge in part. Regarding admissibility, she held that the ECHR was part of the Constitution of Bosnia and Herzegovina; therefore the Court had jurisdiction. Regarding the merits of the application, she upheld all of the complaints, except that relating to the claimed right under Article 3 of Protocol No. 1, because she held that the presidency was not a legislative body. The presidency provisions were, however, in breach of Protocol No. 12. In Case AP-2678/06, Judge Grewe made more explicit her view that the time for change had come. Although she acknowledged that Bosnia 'has not yet completed its transition' and is 'still in a special situation requiring specific measures', she considered that 'the Dayton Agreement architecture is evolving and has to adapt to the different stages of evolution' in Bosnia. Drawing on the earlier *Constituent Peoples* decision, she argued that the goal of the Dayton Peace Agreement (DPA) was to establish a multiethnic state. She maintained that this goal was inconsistent with the existing arrangements, which combined a territorial and an ethnic restriction, because they excluded all Serbs living in the Federation and all Croats and Bosniaks living in the Serb Republic from standing for the presidency.[22]

---

20. At [31].   21. Decisions U-13/05 and AP-2678/06.

22. See further Constance Grewe, 'Making Minorities More Influential in Public Life: Opportunities Provided by Existing Constitutional Arrangements and Their Limitations' in Venice Commission, *The Participation of Minorities in Public Life, Science and Technique of Democracy* (Strasbourg: Council of Europe 2011) 48, where she describes Bosnia's arrangements as based

Judge Feldman, while concurring in the result in Case U-13/05, would have preferred to hold the applications admissible, but to reject them on their merits. His primary reasoning involved the application of the test of proportionality. He specifically argued that the Bosnian arrangements 'can be seen as a special form of representative democracy (sometimes called "consociation") modified to suit the special needs of the country'. The adoption of this system fulfilled a legitimate aim. In addition, the 'deviation from the normal system of elections' applied only to the presidency and not to a lawmaking body.[23] In Case AP-2678/06, Judge Feldman agreed with Judge Grewe that the justification was 'temporary rather than permanent', but disagreed over when and how the change should be made. He considered 'that the time has not yet arrived when the State will have completed its transition away from the special needs which dictated the unusual architecture' of the state. In addition, he considered that the distinctions were required by the constitution as currently drafted: 'The Constitutional Court has an express constitutional obligation to uphold the Constitution, and in my opinion has no power to set aside parts of it, or make them ineffective, by relying on rights arising in an international instrument...'[24] He pointed out, however, that an 'international tribunal such as the European Court of Human Rights might perhaps decide that the constitutional arrangements for electing members of the presidency violate rights under the European Convention,' although he stressed that 'nothing I write here should be taken to lend support to that suggestion under present conditions.'[25]

E. Overview

The general picture is, therefore, clear. The Constitutional Court of Bosnia, including some of its distinguished non-Bosnian members appointed by the ECtHR, has usually acted in line with the hypotheses of Issacharoff and Pildes. Its majorities have generally upheld consociational principles at the state level, respecting the constitution made at Dayton, even when ECHR rights have arguably been limited. The Constitutional Court has

on 'a principle of collective or ethnic equality that does not seem conducive either to optimum protection for minorities or to the development of democracy, or indeed to the integration of all the communities in society'.

23. Separate opinion, [8].   24. Separate opinion, [5].   25. Separate opinion, [5].

consistently observed that there are constitutional processes through which amendments can be made. It has displayed a patient disposition.

The track record of this Court, at least in key cases, also suggests a distinct pattern of judgment among the judges appointed from Bosnia. It is the Bosniak judges who have been more likely to favour integrationist constructions of the constitution and to express such commitments in their opinions. By contrast, the Serb and Croat judges have been more likely to uphold provisions emphasizing the multinational, federal, and consociational character of the constitution negotiated at Dayton. The internationally appointed judges to the Constitutional Court have not been as predictable as the Bosnian appointments, but they have generally displayed interpretive restraint and their judgments have also shown a deep immersion in, and appropriately professional knowledge of, local conditions. The Court's rejection of challenges to consociational arrangements at the state level meant that any further legal challenges had to take place outside Bosnia; applying to the ECtHR was the predictable next move.[26]

---

26. Another possibility would have been to lodge an individual complaint to the Human Rights Committee under the Optional Protocol to the UN International Covenant on Civil and Political Rights, to which Bosnia has acceded, which provides that individuals have the right to submit complaints, but states are 'not legally obliged to follow decisions of the Committee': Nystuen (n. 1) 249.

7

Analysing the Grand
Chamber judgment

We may now consider the judgment of the European Court of Human Rights (ECtHR) in *Sejdić and Finci v. Bosnia* in greater detail. The Court first dismissed two preliminary issues regarding admissibility. It held that the applicants had sufficient standing to be validly before the Court and that, leaving aside the question of whether Bosnia could be held responsible for putting in place the contested constitutional provisions, 'it could nevertheless be held responsible for maintaining them'.[1] The Court then turned to the merits of the applicant's claims. The operative part of the decision of the Grand Chamber on the discrimination issues is remarkably brief for such an important case, consisting of a mere eighteen paragraphs.[2] There were three dissents.

A. Majority opinion

1. Application of Article 3 of Protocol No. 1

We have seen that Article 14 of the European Convention on Human Rights (ECHR) prohibits discrimination, but it is not a free-standing equality provision: for there to be a breach of the right, the Court must find discrimination 'within the ambit' of one or more of the other protected rights in the Convention. The Court had to decide whether elections to the

---

1. *Sejdić and Finci v. Bosnia*, Application nos 27996/06 and 34836/06, 22 December 2009, [27]–[31].
2. *Sejdić and Finci* (n. 1) [38]–[56].

House of Peoples of Bosnia and Herzegovina fell within the 'ambit' of Article 3 of Protocol No. 1, which had previously been interpreted by the Court as applying to elections to a 'legislature'.

In previous cases, the ECtHR had noted that, in drafting Article 3, the contracting parties recognized that certain parliaments included non-elective chambers (such as the House of Lords in the United Kingdom). The Court had avoided this potential problem by holding that, although Article 3 of Protocol No. 1 did not impose an absolute obligation to hold elections for both chambers in each and every bicameral system,[3] it did apply to any of a parliament's chambers to be filled through *direct* elections.

Applying this distinction to Bosnia's legislature was not easy, however, because it was unclear whether the House of Peoples was 'directly' elected, at least as previously interpreted by the Court. The Court noted that the House of Peoples was composed through *indirect* elections, 'its members being appointed by the Entities' legislatures'.[4] The Court decided, however, that the method of election was not the crucial issue; rather, 'the extent of the legislative powers enjoyed by it' now constituted the 'decisive factor'.[5] Since the House of Peoples enjoyed 'wide powers to control the passage of legislation', 'decides upon the sources and amounts of revenues for the operations of the state institutions and international obligations', and 'its consent is necessary before a treaty can be ratified', elections to the House of Peoples fell within the scope of Article 3 of Protocol No. 1. Article 14 ECHR was therefore engaged.[6]

2. Ethnic discrimination

The key issue then became whether the distinctions complained of amounted to 'discrimination' under Article 14 ECHR. The Court had held in previous cases that 'discrimination' meant treating persons in similar situations differently, without an objective and reasonable justification. The Court viewed the discrimination at issue in the applicants' case as discrimination on ethnic grounds. The Court interpreted 'ethnicity' as originating 'in the idea of societal groups marked in particular by common nationality,

---

3. See *Mathieu-Mohin and Clerfayt v. Belgium* (1988) 10 EHRR 1, [53].
4. *Sejdić and Finci* (n. 1) [41].   5. *Sejdić and Finci* (n. 1) [41].
6. *Sejdić and Finci* (n. 1) [41].

religious faith, shared language, or cultural and traditional origins and backgrounds'.[7]

Drawing on the definition adopted by the United Nations International Convention on the Elimination of All Forms of Racial Discrimination (ICERD), the Court declared that discrimination on ethnic grounds is 'a form of racial discrimination'.[8] Following its recent jurisprudence, racial discrimination, in the Court's view, 'is a particularly egregious kind of discrimination and, in view of its perilous consequences, requires from the authorities special vigilance and a vigorous reaction'.[9] Because of its 'egregious' nature, the Court emphasized that 'the authorities must use all available means to combat racism, thereby reinforcing democracy's vision of a society in which diversity is not perceived as a threat but as a source of enrichment',[10] again echoing the approach that it had taken in recent cases.[11]

3. Margin of appreciation

For a distinction to be regarded as having an objective and reasonable justification, it must pursue a 'legitimate aim' and there must be a 'reasonable relationship of proportionality between the means employed and the aim sought to be realised'.[12] The Court, in this case, accorded the state a very narrow 'margin of appreciation' precisely because it involved ethnic discrimination. The Bosnian government had argued that it should be given the benefit of a wide margin of appreciation, because its current constitutional structure was established by a peace agreement after one of the most destructive conflicts in recent European history. The government claimed that 'the time was still not ripe for a political system which would be a simple reflection of majority rule, given, in particular, the prominence of mono-ethnic political parties and the continued international administration of Bosnia and Herzegovina'.[13] The Court did not agree. Relying on the *DH* case,[14] the Court held that where 'a difference in treatment is based on

---

7. *Sejdić and Finci* (n. 1) [43].   8. *Sejdić and Finci* (n. 1) [43].
9. *Sejdić and Finci* (n. 1) [43].   10. *Sejdić and Finci* (n. 1) [43].
11. See *Nachova and others v. Bulgaria* (2006) 42 EHRR 43, [145]; *Timishev v. Russia* (2007) 44 EHRR 37, [56].
12. See e.g. *Andrejeva v. Latvia*, Application no. 55707/00, 18 February 2009, (2010) 51 EHRR 28, [81].
13. *Sejdić and Finci* (n. 1) [34].
14. See *DH v. Czech Republic* (2008) 47 EHRR 3, [196].

race or ethnicity, the notion of objective and reasonable justification must be interpreted *as strictly as possible*.[15]

4. Not 'affirmative action'

The Court reiterated what it had held in *DH*—namely, that:

> no difference in treatment which is based exclusively or to a decisive extent on a person's ethnic origin is capable of being objectively justified in a contemporary democratic society built on the principles of pluralism and respect for different cultures.[16]

The Court did not, however, interpret Article 14 ECHR as 'prohibit[ing] Contracting Parties from treating groups differently in order to correct "factual inequalities" between them',[17] echoing the language of Protocol No. 12.

This qualification preserves the Court's freedom to allow affirmative action as a remedy in the future. Indeed, the Court recognized that, in several earlier cases,[18] 'a failure to attempt to correct inequality through different treatment may, without an objective and reasonable justification, give rise to a breach' of Article 14.[19] States therefore have to negotiate a narrow path between doing too much and not doing enough. The issue in *Sejdić and Finci* was whether Bosnia had negotiated that path successfully. The Court concluded that it had failed to do so. No argument was advanced by any of the parties that there was an affirmative action-type justification for the contested measures.

5. Legitimate purpose

The Court also considered whether the challenged exclusionary rule regarding election to the House of Peoples pursued a legitimate aim. The Bosnian government had argued that the history of the origins of the contested provisions should be given determinative weight in the assessment of whether

---

15. *Sejdić and Finci* (n. 1) [44], emphasis added.
16. *Sejdić and Finci* (n. 1) [44], relying on *DH* (n. 14) [176]. See also *Timishev v. Russia* (n. 11), [58].
17. *Sejdić and Finci* (n. 1) [44].
18. *Case 'Relating to Certain Aspects of the Laws on the Use of Languages in Education in Belgium' v. Belgium*, Application nos 1474/62, 1677/62, 1691/62, 1769/63, 1994/63, and 2126/64, Judgment 23 July 1968 (1979–80) IEHRR 252, [10]; *Thlimmenos v. Greece* (2001) 31 EHRR 15, [44]; *DH* (n. 14), [175].
19. *Sejdić and Finci* (n. 1) [44].

there was an 'objective and reasonable justification'. The government defended the central function of the constitution as follows:

> ... the constitutional provisions that differently treat the election rights of individual ethnical [*sic*] groups are not aimed to discriminate [against] individuals or groups but the introduction of corrective standards in the rule of simple majority thus preventing the majority to bring decisions to the detriment of other groups.[20]

In his originating application, Mr Finci argued that even in 1995 when the constitution was originally adopted 'and notwithstanding the need to secure a peace agreement, there could have been no legitimate aim which justified excluding completely the Jewish community (and other minorities) from representation and its consequent creation of their second-class status'.[21] In his 'Reply' to the government's 'Observations', Mr Finci repeated that 'The mere fact that discriminatory arrangements are established by a peace agreement cannot ... be a legitimate aim to justify such discrimination'.[22] The response continued:

> ... direct racial discrimination cannot be justified even for a temporary period, and certainly not for over thirteen years. The fundamental principle of non-discrimination constitutes a *jus cogens* norm of international law that should be implemented immediately, not a mere aspiration or subject only to gradual acceptance.[23]

On the other hand, Mr Finci appeared to accept that not all ethnic distinctions must be eradicated; he was 'simply saying that the current situation of complete exclusion of the Jewish and other minority groups from participation is not necessary and cannot be justified'.[24]

---

20. Additional written observations of Bosnia and Herzegovina, 20 April 2009, [19]. A more eloquent version of this argument is that 'the critical frailty of majoritarian democracy in any fractured society is the risk that elections turn into a referendum on which group will wield the instrumentalities of state power against the other': Samuel Issacharoff, 'Courts, Constitutions, and the Limits of Majoritarianism' in Joanne McEvoy and Brendan O'Leary (eds), *Power-Sharing in Deeply Divided Places* (Philadelphia, PA: University of Pennsylvania Press, in press).
21. At [60].
22. Reply of Mr Jakob Finci to the Government's Observations on Admissibility and Merits of 4 July 2008, 2 October 2008, [62].
23. Reply of Mr Jakob Finci (n. 22) [69].
24. Reply of Mr Jakob Finci (n. 22) [87].

The Court accepted that the exclusionary rule 'pursued at least one aim which is broadly compatible with the general objectives of the Convention ..., namely the restoration of peace'.[25] It accepted that:

> When the impugned constitutional provisions were put in place a very fragile cease-fire was in effect on the ground. The provisions were designed to end a brutal conflict marked by genocide and 'ethnic cleansing'. The nature of the conflict was such that the approval of the 'constituent peoples' (namely, the Bosniaks, Croats and Serbs) was necessary to ensure peace. This could explain, without necessarily justifying, the absence of representatives of the other communities (such as local Roma and Jewish communities) at the peace negotiations and the participants' preoccupation with effective equality between the 'constituent peoples' in the post-conflict society.[26]

The Court nevertheless sidelined the salience of this purpose, relying on the somewhat technical argument that 'the Court is only competent *ratione temporis*[27] to examine the period after the ratification of the Convention and Protocol No. 1 thereto by Bosnia and Herzegovina'.[28] The Court held, on this premise, that it:

> ... does not need to decide whether the upholding of the contested constitutional provisions after ratification of the Convention could be said to serve a 'legitimate aim' since ... the maintenance of the system in any event does not satisfy the requirement of proportionality.[29]

6. Proportionality

The exclusionary rule did not satisfy the requirement of proportionality for several reasons. While 'progress might not always have been consistent and challenges remain', the Court identified 'significant positive developments in Bosnia and Herzegovina since the Dayton Peace Agreement', which appeared to indicate progress towards normalization of security.[30] While the Court agreed with the government that there is 'no requirement under the Convention to abandon totally the power-sharing mechanisms peculiar to Bosnia and Herzegovina and that the time may still not be ripe for a political system which would be a simple reflection of majority rule', it relied on the

---

25. *Sejdić and Finci* (n. 1) [45].   26. *Sejdić and Finci* (n. 1) [45].
27. The ECtHR is generally restricted to addressing issues that have arisen after the state in question has ratified the ECHR.
28. *Sejdić and Finci* (n. 1) [46].   29. *Sejdić and Finci* (n. 1) [46].
30. *Sejdić and Finci* (n. 1) [47].

opinion of the Venice Commission to support its conclusion that 'there exist mechanisms of power-sharing which do not automatically lead to the total exclusion of representatives of the other communities'.[31] Therefore the state had failed to demonstrate that there were no alternative means of achieving the same end.[32]

The Bosnian government had indicated by several of its actions that it was agreeable to a review of the electoral system: it had ratified the ECHR and its Protocols without reservations; it had undertaken to the Council of Europe that it would review the electoral legislation under Council of Europe standards; and it had committed itself to the European Union to amend electoral legislation 'to ensure full compliance with the European Convention on Human Rights and the Council of Europe post-accession commitments'.[33] For these reasons, the Court concluded that 'the applicants' continued ineligibility to stand for election to the House of Peoples of Bosnia and Herzegovina lacks an objective and reasonable justification',[34] and therefore breached Article 14 ECHR, taken in conjunction with Article 3 of Protocol No. 1.[35]

7. Protocol No. 12

Regarding the presidency of Bosnia and Herzegovina, the applicants relied only on Article 1 of the new Protocol No. 12—no doubt because it was thought that the presidency would not be covered by the provisions of Article 3 of Protocol No. 1.

This was the first case in which the ECtHR considered the meaning of the new Protocol. Just as Article 14 ECHR and Article 3 of Protocol No. 1 were first interpreted in cases concerning consociation, the first judgment on Protocol No. 12 has arisen in a similar context. The Court held that whether elections to the presidency fell within the scope of Article 3 of Protocol No. 1 or not, this complaint concerned a 'right set forth by law', which made Article 1 of Protocol No. 12 applicable. Indeed, this was not contested before the Court.

31. *Sejdić and Finci* (n. 1) [48].
32. See *Glor v. Switzerland*, Application no. 13444/04, 30 April 2009, [94].
33. *Sejdić and Finci* (n. 1) [49].
34. *Sejdić and Finci* (n. 1) [50].
35. The Court did not consider it necessary to examine separately whether there had also been a violation of Article 3 of Protocol No. 1 taken alone, or under Article 1 of Protocol No. 12.

The main issue, rather, was how the Court would interpret the meaning of 'discrimination' under the new Protocol. Notwithstanding the difference in scope between the Protocol and Article 14 ECHR, the Court concluded that 'the meaning of [discrimination] in Article 1 of Protocol No. 12 was intended to be identical to that in Article 14'.[36] The Court therefore did not 'see any reason to depart from the settled interpretation of "discrimination" … in applying the same term under Article 1 of Protocol No. 12'.[37] Applying this definition to the exclusionary presidency election rules resulted in the same conclusion as that at which the Court had arrived regarding the House of Peoples rule—namely, that it constituted a violation of the Convention (in this case, Protocol No. 12), because the Court did not consider 'that there is any pertinent distinction to be drawn in this regard between the House of Peoples and the Presidency of Bosnia and Herzegovina'.[38]

B. Concurring and dissenting opinions

There was a significant partly concurring and partly dissenting opinion by Judge Mijović, the judge from Bosnia (nominated by the Serb Republic), and she was joined by Judge Hajiyev, from Azerbaïjan. Like the majority, Judge Mijović found there to be a violation regarding both sets of exclusionary rules. She disagreed with the reasoning adopted by the majority, however, in two important ways. There was also a separate dissent from Judge Bonello, the Maltese judge.

1. Proportionality

Judge Mijović's assessment of the potential for the majority's decision to bring catastrophic results stands in marked contrast to the majority's rosier assessment. The case, she argued, 'tackles the essence of the internal State structure of Bosnia and Herzegovina', raising issues that were 'the very heart of the post-war organisational structure of the State'.[39] Changing these structures 'might result in serious constitutional turmoil and rearrangements

---

36. *Sejdić and Finci* (n. 1) [55].   37. *Sejdić and Finci* (n. 1) [55].
38. *Sejdić and Finci* (n. 1) [56].
39. *Sejdić and Finci* (n. 1), partly concurring and partly dissenting opinion of Mijović J, at II.

in one of the Council of Europe member States'.[40] To deny 'legitimacy to norms that may be problematic from the point of view of non-discrimination but were necessary to achieve peace and stability and to avoid further loss of human lives would be very difficult'.[41] Making 'changes in the composition of specific political institutions requested by the applicants would actually require changes in the existing balance of power' and this could 'rekindle the serious tensions that are still present in Bosnia and Herzegovina'.[42] Her argument would appear to allow to Bosnia the defence of both proportionality and legitimate purpose.

2. Distinguishing the presidency from the House of Peoples

Judge Mijović also considered that there were important distinctions to be drawn between the exclusionary rules regarding the presidency and those relating to the House of Peoples. In particular, the House of Peoples 'has an important and sensitive role' in the protection of 'vital national interests', and in that context has a more central place than the presidency in the system of mutual veto rights characteristic of full consociational arrangements.[43] While Judge Mijović was prepared to take the risk of adverse reaction to requiring fundamental changes in the composition of the presidency, she was not prepared to do so in the context of similar changes in the composition of the House of Peoples. Although she was prepared to join with the majority in finding a violation of Protocol No. 12 regarding the rules governing eligibility for the presidency, she dissented from the finding of a violation of Article 14 ECHR taken in conjunction with Article 3 of Protocol No. 1 regarding the rules governing eligibility for the House of Peoples.

There were two different legal bases on which this dissent was based. First, Article 3 of Protocol No. 1 was not applicable, according to Judge Mijović. In her view, this was because of several features of the House of Peoples: there was no right in domestic law for any individual to stand for election to the House of Peoples; the House of Peoples was a non-elective organ, having neither the typical characteristics nor the powers of a second

---

40. *Sejdić and Finci* (n. 1), partly concurring and partly dissenting opinion of Mijović J, at I.
41. *Sejdić and Finci* (n. 1), partly concurring and partly dissenting opinion of Mijović J, at II.
42. *Sejdić and Finci* (n. 1), partly concurring and partly dissenting opinion of Mijović J, at II.
43. *Sejdić and Finci* (n. 1), partly concurring and partly dissenting opinion of Mijović J, at IV.

chamber; and its structure placed it outside the ambit of Article 3 of Protocol No. 1. Judge Mijović also raised serious questions concerning the majority's conclusions that security was becoming normalized. Following a detailed (and depressing) litany of continuing problems, she asked rhetorically: '[C]an one be absolutely certain of the lack of justification for these constitutional arrangements today?'[44] She dissented on the Court's conclusion that methods were available other than the use of ethnic affiliation. She asked: 'What other method would maintain the ethnic balance and build the confidence that is so needed in Bosnia and Herzegovina?'[45] The majority's judgment, in her view, was 'a missed opportunity to provide more decisive and convincing arguments'.[46]

3. Proportionality and legitimacy

Judge Bonello, like Judge Mijović, considered that the majority's judgment 'divorced Bosnia and Herzegovina from the realities of its own recent past'.[47] After sketching out the history of the negotiations that led to the Dayton Accords and the 'precarious equilibrium... laboriously reached, resulting in a fragile tripartite symmetry born from mistrust and nourished on suspicion', he expressed his unease that 'this Court has taken it upon itself to disrupt all that. Strasbourg has told both the former belligerents and the peace-devising do-gooders that they got it all wrong. They had better start all over again'.[48] For Judge Bonello, then, there were major issues over the legitimacy and competence of the ECtHR to decide a case involving an international peace agreement, underpinned by an international treaty, especially where instability was still the order of the day.

Like the majority, Judge Bonello accepted the necessity of balancing of rights with other rights and with other values:

> The whole structure of the Convention is based on a primordial sovereignty of human rights, but, saving the very core rights (to which that of standing for election certainly does not belong), [these are] always subject to their exercise in conformity with the rights of others and with the over-riding social good.[49]

---

44. *Sejdić and Finci* (n. 1), partly concurring and partly dissenting opinion of Mijović J, at V.
45. *Sejdić and Finci* (n. 1), partly concurring and partly dissenting opinion of Mijović J, at V.
46. *Sejdić and Finci* (n. 1), dissenting opinion of Bonello J.
47. *Sejdić and Finci* (n. 1), dissenting opinion of Bonello J.
48. *Sejdić and Finci* (n. 1), dissenting opinion of Bonello J.
49. *Sejdić and Finci* (n. 1), dissenting opinion of Bonello J.

In that context, he questioned the weight of the right of the applicants to stand for election when compared with the threat to the 'peace, security and public order [of] the entire population—including themselves'.[50] He accepted that the values of equality and non-discrimination are 'invaluable', but insisted that 'national peace and reconciliation are at least equally so'.[51] He questioned 'the Court's finding that the situation in Bosnia and Herzegovina has now changed and that the previous delicate tri-partite equilibrium need no longer prevail'.[52] He also asked whether 'a judicial institution so remote from the focus of dissension' was the 'best judge' of local realities:

> I doubt that the Court is better placed than the national authorities to assess the point in time when previous fractures consolidate, when historical resentments quell and when generational discords harmonise. I find that claims such as these, arguably based on self-delusory wishful thinking, show little or no respect for the inexhaustible resources of rancor. The Court does ill to shut its mind to histories in which hate validates culture.[53]

Given that the Court in previous cases had 'repeatedly accepted that the enjoyment of the majority of basic human rights—not least, the right to stand for election—is subject to intrinsic restrictions and extrinsic curtailment', he found it hard to understand how 'a clear and present danger of destabilising the national equilibrium' could not be found to be justified.[54] In a dramatic peroration, he concluded: 'I cannot endorse a Court that sows ideals and harvests massacre.'[55]

---

50. *Sejdić and Finci* (n. 1), dissenting opinion of Bonello J.
51. *Sejdić and Finci* (n. 1), dissenting opinion of Bonello J.
52. *Sejdić and Finci* (n. 1), dissenting opinion of Bonello J.
53. *Sejdić and Finci* (n. 1), dissenting opinion of Bonello J.
54. *Sejdić and Finci* (n. 1), dissenting opinion of Bonello J.
55. *Sejdić and Finci* (n. 1), dissenting opinion of Bonello J.

8

Sejdić and Finci and consociational futures

Several of the hypotheses derived from Issacharoff and Pildes on which we elaborated in Chapter 3[1] are supported by an examination of the *Sejdić and Finci* judgment. In particular, the European Court of Human Rights (ECtHR) was offered the opportunity to speed a transition from corporate consociational arrangements to other arrangements. That suggests the correctness of Pildes' hypothesis that courts might be expected to become the 'unwinders of ethnic political bargains'. In other key respects, however, Issacharoff's and Pildes' hypotheses have proven less accurate predictions of what a court is likely to do when asked to 'unwind' an ethnic political bargain. We can identify several respects in which the hypotheses developed by Issacharoff and Pildes have to be modified after *Sejdić and Finci*.

A. Cosmopolitan values versus local deals

The case supports Issacharoff's hypothesis that challenges to local political bargains are likely to be based on 'fundamental rights' arguments and are likely to be claimed through reference to higher authority at the international level. The distinction between local deals and international (more accurately, 'cosmopolitan') values is not, however, as clear as it might seem, and is open to a degree of manipulation.

In *Sejdić and Finci*, the international dimension was present on both sides of the argument. The Court majority was anxious, however, to put to one

---

1. See 'D. Courts as potential "unwinders" of consociational arrangements?'.

side the international origins of the consociational arrangements, suggesting that these origins had been largely superseded. The Court also put to one side whether Bosnia could be held responsible for *adopting* the contested constitutional provisions. It insisted that Bosnia 'could nevertheless be held responsible for *maintaining* them'. This argument allowed the Court to maintain that it was imposing *European* human rights standards on *local* political arrangements, rather than unwinding an internationally negotiated (and imposed) settlement. The Court considered that it was supporting the emerging consensus that things had to change, articulated at the European level by the Venice Commission, among others. This reasoning fits with the Court's view of its function as policing the boundaries of the European consensus and bringing to heel those states that act outside that consensus.

No doubt because their focus was primarily on the reaction of *domestic* courts to such bargains, neither did Issacharoff and Pildes appear to anticipate the extent to which what counted as the international or European consensus could be so selective. We have already seen the extent to which the ECtHR in *Sejdić and Finci*, intentionally or unintentionally, portrayed the Bosnian arrangements as unique, through the simple expedient of not referring to how the arrangements in Bosnia were similar to other consociational arrangements. This is particularly apparent in the Court's failure to distinguish Bosnia from Belgium, but the Court's approach failed more generally to consider Bosnia as one of a group of countries that are consociations; it therefore failed to consider whether consociational arrangements may be seen as *within* the European consensus rather than outside it. Because the Court essentially ignored the idea of Bosnia as a consociation, it did not consider how its judgment may impact on other consociational arrangements in Europe. Nor, despite the fact that the Court's judgments are closely followed in other international human rights dispute settlement bodies, was any consideration given to the implications of the Court's approach for consociational arrangements beyond Europe.

In the remainder of our discussion of the implications of *Sejdić and Finci*, we suggest how a knowledge of other consociational arrangements both tests the meaning of the judgment and problematizes it. We shall draw on the Belgian example, but also on two further examples: Northern Ireland and Burundi. The first has not come before the ECtHR, but one can imagine aspects of it doing so. The second, of course, can never come before the European Court, but one can imagine Burundi's provisions being considered by other international human rights bodies that do have jurisdiction. We first sketch out some particularly relevant aspects of these arrangements, before returning to consider the *Sejdić and Finci* judgment.

1. Northern Ireland

An essential element of the Northern Ireland arrangements, primarily to be found in the Northern Ireland Act 1998, giving statutory effect to the 1998 Belfast Agreement (also known as the 'Good Friday Agreement'), is the attempt to ensure power-sharing in government and this is achieved by the use of the 'd'Hondt rule'. This system of proportional and sequential allocation of ministerial portfolios in the government of Northern Ireland does not, on its face, allocate on the basis of religion or ethnicity; it is, to that extent, difference-blind.[2] Parties win the right to nominate government ministers in proportion to their shares of the popular vote. The rule would not have been accepted locally, however, had it not ensured that Ulster unionists and loyalists (primarily Protestant) and Irish nationalists and

2. For discussion of the d'Hondt rule in Northern Ireland and the ways in which it can be used for liberal consociational purposes, see Brendan O'Leary, Bernard Grofman, and Jørgen Elklit, 'Divisor Methods for Sequential Portfolio Allocation in Multi-Party Executive Bodies: Evidence from Northern Ireland and Denmark' (2005) 49 American Journal of Political Science 198. The d'Hondt rule of proportionality uses simple divisors, 1, 2, 3, 4, ... n in a highest averages procedure for allocation of seats (or ministries). The relevant average, a, is defined as a party's votes, v, in a given district, divided by the number of seats, s, already allocated to it in the district, plus one—that is, $a = v/(s + 1)$. Following Rein Taagepera and Matthew Soberg Shugart, *Seats and Votes: The Effects and Determinants of Electoral Systems* (New Haven, CT: Yale University Press 1989) 32, the procedure may be demonstrated through a simple example.

Imagine that there are seven seats to be allocated. Imagine that party A gets 48.5 per cent of the vote; party B, 29 per cent; party C, 14 per cent; party D, 7.5 per cent; and party E, 1 per cent. In the table below, each party's votes are listed in per cent at the top and the divisors ($s + 1$) down the left-hand side. The numbers in parenthesis, e.g. (1), indicate the order in which seats (or ministries) are allocated. The largest party, party A, gets the first seat, and its vote share is then divided by two (one seat plus one). Now the second largest party, party B, has the highest remaining average and it therefore obtains a seat. In this example, with seven seats (or ministries) to be allocated, party A obtains four, B, two, and C, one. The other parties win no seats.

s	s + 1	Party A	Party B	Party C	Party D	Party E
0	1	48.5 (1)	29.0 (2)	14.0 (6)	7.5	1.0
1	2	24.3 (3)	14.5 (5)	7.0		
2	3	16.2 (4)	9.7			
3	4	12.1 (7)				

The d'Hondt rule is but one of a number of ways of trying to achieve proportionality. For further discussions, see, inter alia, Michael Gallagher, 'Comparing Proportional Representation Electoral Systems: Quotas, Thresholds, Paradoxes and Majorities' (1992) 22 British Journal of Political Science 469; Steven J. Brams, *Mathematics and Democracy: Designing Better Voting and Fair-Division Procedures* (Princeton, NJ: Princeton University Press 2008).

republicans (primarily Catholic) would be proportionally represented in the Northern Ireland executive.[3] This electoral formula is, of course, widely used in Europe, including in the allocation of committee seats in the European Parliament.

The 1998 Agreement also explicitly required, however, that the two most important executive posts, the First Minister and Deputy First Minister (who are equal in their powers and status), would be held by a designated unionist and a designated nationalist, who had to affirm the relevant identity in the Northern Ireland Assembly. The initial rule to accomplish this end required that the two postholders be elected by a concurrent majority of designated nationalists and unionists (and a majority in the Assembly as a whole). The subsequent rule, agreed at St Andrews in 2006 after a further fraught set of negotiations, awards the first ministership to the largest designation in the Assembly (whether nationalist or unionist or other), and the deputy first ministership to the second largest designation in the Assembly.

The rules regarding the (single-chamber) Assembly are also designed to ensure that both designated communities agree to any important decision, by providing for qualified majority rules. These rules are of two types: one requires a concurrent majority of the Assembly, including a majority of designated nationalists and unionists respectively; the other, 'the parallel consent' procedure, requires that the majority include 60 per cent of the Assembly, and a minimum level of support of 40 per cent of designated nationalists and designated unionists respectively.

2. Burundi

Let us turn now to Burundi, a post-colonial state with a history of authoritarian and military dominance by Tutsi (currently 14 per cent of the population) over Hutus (estimated at 85 per cent of the population), with only 1 per cent of its population estimated to be from the Twa (known as

---

3. In negotiations in 1992, unionists had put forward the d'Hondt rule for allocating seats in a future Northern Ireland government. At that juncture, they accepted proportionality, but not power-sharing. After 1994, republicans negotiated for a system in which their mandate would be respected and in which they would have a role in government, as of right. The equilibrium resolution was power-sharing and proportionality according to d'Hondt, and with no party to be excluded from office provided that it endorsed the Mitchell principles of democracy and non-violence: Brendan O'Leary, 'The Nature of the Agreement' (1999) 22 Fordham Journal of International Law 1628.

'Pygmies' by Europeans).[4] A bloody and long-lasting genocidal civil war
(or, strictly speaking, series of wars) broke out between the Hutus and the
Tutsi. These were even worse than the war in Bosnia, as regards the fatalities
caused and the numbers of refugees and internally displaced persons generated.[5] A Burundi peace process, internationally led and mediated by Tan-
zania, South Africa, and the United States, eventually delivered a new
constitution.[6] This was adopted by the Burundi Transitional National

4. Population estimates are from US Central Intelligence Agency (CIA), 'Burundi', in *The World
   Factbook* (2000), available online at <https://www.cia.gov/library/publications/the-world
   -factbook/index.html>. Besides these three ethnic groups, there are very small numbers of
   residents and citizens of European and South Asian extraction.
5. For the scale of genocide in Burundi in 1972, with estimates ranging between 200,000 and
   300,000 dead, see Réné Lemarchand, 'Burundi 1972: A Forgotten Genocide' in *The Dynamics
   of Violence in Central Africa* (Philadelphia, PA: University of Pennsylvania Press 2009), 'Burundi
   1972: Genocide Denied, Revised, and Remembered' in René Lemarchand (ed.) *Forgotten
   Genocides: Oblivion, Denial, and Memory* (Philadelphia, PA: University of Pennsylvania Press
   2011). See also Réné Lemarchand, 'Burundi's Endangered Transition' in *The Dynamics of
   Violence in Central Africa* (Philadelphia, PA: University of Pennsylvania Press, 2009) 162–4
   and *passim*, for a discussion of the costs of the civil war of the 1990s and the scale of Burundi's
   underdevelopment.
6. It is quite remarkable how the South African government led by the African National Congress
   (ANC), which formally rejected consociational devices for the long-run future of South Africa,
   helped to mediate and shape a significantly consociational style settlement in Burundi. There is,
   of course, no fundamental inconsistency in rejecting consociation to protect the beneficiaries of
   past colonialism and racism, and endorsing its use to prevent genocidal conflict among black
   Africans, and nor should we assume that individual South Africans agreed with the outcomes of
   the Burundi peace process. Two South African researchers, funded by the Nelson Mandela
   Foundation, write:

   > Both [Julius] Nyerere [of Tanzania] and [Nelson] Mandela viewed the Burundian conflict
   > in quasi-South African terms, with Tutsis being cast in the role of oppressor whites and
   > Hutus in that of oppressed blacks. Yet Mandela was extremely cautious about being
   > accused of forcing the South African example down Burundian throats; his approach was
   > therefore, 'this is how we did it in South Africa, so draw your own conclusions and
   > borrow what you think might be useful to your situation'. At the same time, he was
   > highly conscious that participants in the talks could not be unaware of the much vaunted
   > success of South Africa's negotiated transition in averting a race war. From this perspec-
   > tive, Mandela was far more prepared than Nyerere to analyse the Burundian conflict in
   > explicitly ethnic terms, and thereby to compel Burundians to face the issue of ethnicity
   > more honestly. Importantly, too, this resulted in his advocating ethnic power-sharing
   > solutions, such as the idea of the presidency revolving between Tutsi and Hutu. His
   > emphasis was on practicality and possibilities. Whilst he insisted that, in principle, the
   > demographic composition of the army should reflect that of the population, he urged
   > pragmatically that, initially, integration of the army should be based on equal representa-
   > tion of Hutu and Tutsi in order to allay the latter's fears of domination. The promotion of
   > such ideas was deemed by many observers as crucial to the eventual construction of the
   > agreement. Mandela was therefore by no means committed to an inflexible South African
   > analogy unless this was helpful.

   > (Kristina A. Bentley and Roger Southall, *An African Peace Process:
   > Mandela, South Africa and Burundi*, Cape Town: Nelson Mandela
   > Foundation HSRC Press, 2005, 75)

Assembly and the Transitional Senate in September 2004, signed by the Burundian President in October of the same year, and ratified by the people in a referendum on 28 February 2005.

Burundi's new constitutional design contains three features of a consociation: the principles of power-sharing on the basis of parity, proportionality, and veto rights are all found, but the formal design lacks any significant component of ethnic autonomy.[7] Aside from the key absence of expressly constituted ethnic autonomy, this constitution is otherwise consociational. René Lemarchand, the authoritative political scientist on the development of Burundi, observes that the Constitution of Burundi 'comes closer than any other African constitution, past or present, to putting into practice Lijphart's model of consociationalism'.[8] It is, however, a case in which parity is prioritized over proportionality. In brief, it is strongly designed to represent Tutsi disproportionally in the executive and the National Assembly (the lower house), and grants Tutsi parity with Hutus in the Senate (the upper house) and the security sector.

In more detail: Burundi's executive consists of a president and two executive vice-presidents: a first and second vice-president. The president is directly elected under a French-style, double-ballot, run-off system.[9] By contrast, the vice-presidents are obliged to 'belong to different ethnic groups and political parties'.[10] This clause is, however, qualified: '[This requirement] notwithstanding, their appointment takes into account the predominant character of their ethnic affiliation within their respective political parties.' This provision is understood to leave the electoral college for the vice-presidents free to choose a Tutsi or a Hutu who is associated with a party of the electors' preference.[11] The mode of election of the vice-presidents makes it extremely unlikely that a non-Hutu or a non-Tutsi

---

7. Hutu and Tutis speak the same language, and are not significantly differentiated by religion, so the institutional demand for separate schooling or college is absent. The territorial mixing of the two groups also inhibits demands for territorial autonomy. Ethnic difference is preserved through endogamous marriage. For a discussion of the absence of autonomy in Burundi's previous experiments with power-sharing, see Daniel P. Sullivan, 'The Missing Pillars: A Look at the Failure of Peace in Burundi through the Lens of Arend Lijphart's Theory of Consociational Democracy' (2005) 43 The Journal of Modern African Studies 75.
8. Lemarchand, 'Burundi's Endangered Transition' (n. 5) 167.
9. See Taagepera and Shugart (n. 2) 20–2.
10. Constitution of Burundi, art. 124. We rely for the English version of the Burundi constitution on Oceana's *Constitutions of the World* database, online at <http://www.oceanalaw.com/>
11. The constitution does not expressly ban ethnic parties, although it requires that parties be open to all and that, at leadership level, they must have a 'national' character: Constitution of Burundi, art. 78.

could be elected to the two posts. If the elected president is a Hutu then the first vice-president will be Tutsi, and the second vice-president Hutu, and vice versa. The president, in consultation with the vice-presidents, appoints the government (the cabinet of ministers), which 'is open to all ethnic components. It is composed of a maximum of sixty per cent Hutu Ministers and Vice-Ministers and a maximum of forty per cent Tutsi Ministers and Vice-Ministers'.[12] Inclusion of parties in the government is guaranteed in proportion to their strength in seats won in the National Assembly, provided that they have won more than 5 per cent of the vote.[13] The Minister of National Defence is obliged to be of a different ethnicity from the Minister of National Police.[14] Again, it is understood, although not expressly stated, that this means that a Tutsi will hold one post and a Hutu the other, even though, formally, the two posts—like all government posts—are 'open to all ethnic components'. Public employment is also guided by ethnic targets: 'The ethnic representation in the public enterprises is fixed at a maximum of sixty per cent for the Hutu and a maximum of forty per cent for the Tutsi.'[15] No proportion, beneficial or otherwise, is specified for 'Others'.

Burundi's legislature has two chambers. The first, the National Assembly, has an express ethnic ratio: 60 per cent of deputies must be Hutus and 40 per cent must be Tutsi. The composition of the Assembly is expressly to be modified and the legislature is to be increased in size if 'the election results do not reflect [these] percentages'.[16] The task of modifying the size and composition of the Assembly is assigned to the Electoral Commission, which must also ensure that a required minimum number of women is elected and that three deputies from the Twa are co-opted.

The second chamber, the Senate, has three components: former heads of state; three Twa; and two 'delegates from each province, elected by an electoral college, composed of members of the local councils of the relevant province, coming from different ethnic communities and elected in distinct

12. Constitution of Burundi, art. 129. Additionally, a minimum of 30 per cent of government ministers must be female. 'Deputy ministers' would be a better translation than 'vice-ministers', but we follow the Oceana translation (n. 10).

13. Constitution of Burundi, art. 129. This provision strongly resembles one found in South Africa's Transitional Constitution of 1994; one former South African President and one future South African President, Nelson Mandela and Jacob Zuma, mediated during the Burundi peace process.

14. Constitution of Burundi, art. 130.

15. Constitution of Burundi, art. 143.

16. Constitution of Burundi, art. 164.

electoral procedures'.[17] The formulation of the third component disguises a clear goal: to achieve parity of Tutsi and Hutu representation in the Senate. Mayors form the provincial electoral college in charge of electing two senators from each province. No more than 67 per cent of the mayoralties are to be held by one ethnic group (understood to be the Hutu), and each province must, in effect, elect one Hutu and one Tutsi senator, thereby creating parity of representation among elected (or co-opted) Hutu and Tutsi in the Senate. The Electoral Commission is again assigned the task of co-opting senators as necessary. Tutsi overrepresentation in the Senate also constitutes a veto power because valid legislation requires a quorum that would not be met if most Tutsi senators were to boycott decisive votes on Bills.

One last provision that is worth mentioning grants special authority to the Senate (in which, we should recall, the Tutsi have the same representation as Hutu). This provision specifies that:

> During a period to be determined by the Senate, the defense and the security forces will not consist of more than fifty per cent of members belonging to a particular ethnic group, taking into account the necessity to ensure ethnic balance and to prevent acts of genocide and coups d'états.[18]

Controversy surrounds whether this provision applies to all ranks of the security forces, or whether the historic dominance of Tutsi among the officer corps is unaffected by this provision.

B. Margin of appreciation and proportionality

With these additional examples of consociations in mind, we can return to consider the implications of the *Sejdić and Finci* judgment. Even though the ECtHR no doubt recognized that it was considering a 'first-order challenge'[19] and that the consequences of mis-judgment would be 'uniquely serious and [could] be highly destabilizing',[20] as Issacharoff put it, the Court did not back away, as it mostly did in the Belgian cases. Many may have

---

17. Constitution of Burundi, art. 160. A minimum of 30 per cent of senators have to be women.
18. Constitution of Burundi, art. 257.
19. Samuel Issacharoff, 'Democracy and Collective Decision-Making' (2008) 6 International Journal of Comparative Law 231, 232.
20. Issacharoff (n. 19) 262.

expected the Court to adopt an 'exit strategy', as had Bosnia's Constitutional Court, 'by means of which [it] could restore a measure of deference
to the institutional realities of politics'.[21] But the ECtHR did not adopt any
of the doctrinal moves available to it to enable it to defer to those who
constructed the consociational arrangements and to their successors
empowered under them. In contrast with the Belgian cases, the Court
took a highly activist and interventionist approach, not only regarding
what constituted the electoral systems covered by Article 3 of Protocol
No. 1 to the European Convention on Human Rights (ECHR), but also
more generally through the weakening of the 'margin of appreciation'
doctrine. The Court was willing, drawing on the Venice Commission's
findings and again in contrast with the Belgian cases, to decide that other
alternatives were available that would satisfy the same objectives as the
impugned measures with less adverse effect on the rights claimed. The
Court was content to second-guess Bosnia's authorities.

Also, again in contrast with the Belgian cases, there was a high-intensity
standard of review adopted in the application of the non-discrimination
norm. This essentially amounted to a test of strict scrutiny, since the Court
regarded ethnic discrimination as being practically impossible to justify. We
accept that the local contexts were different. To be seen to endorse practices
that evidently discriminated against Jews and Roma in a region with an anti-
Roma and anti-Jewish history could have sent signals that the Court had
backtracked in its refusal to tolerate such practices, thereby perhaps giving
aid and comfort to local extremism. But in contrast with the Belgian cases,
little weight was accorded by the Court to the legitimacy of the purposes
sought to be achieved by the impugned measures, as defined by the Bosnian
government.[22] The Court essentially avoided considering whether achieving peace between the groups in conflict after a vicious civil war continued
to be a legitimate purpose. Its method was to hold that, in any event, the
measures were disproportionate.

The Court agreed with the government that:

> ... there is *no* requirement under the Convention to abandon *totally* the
> power-sharing mechanisms peculiar to Bosnia and Herzegovina and that the

---

21. Issacharoff (n. 19) 262.
22. Indeed, it now seems possible that the *Belgian Linguistics* case may no longer be a safe precedent
    to rely on, in general.

time may still not be ripe for a political system which would be a simple reflection of majority rule.[23]

However, the challenged requirements were held not to satisfy the proportionality test for several reasons. The Court confidently relied on the opinions of the Venice Commission to support its conclusion that 'there exist mechanisms of power-sharing which do not automatically lead to the total exclusion of representatives of the other communities' and, therefore, that the state had failed to demonstrate that there were no alternative means of achieving the same end. Not only were there serious alternatives available, but also (and as importantly) the time was ripe for these to be implemented now. While 'progress might not always have been consistent and challenges remain', the Court identified 'significant positive developments in Bosnia and Herzegovina since the Dayton Peace Agreement'. The Court judged that there was progress toward normalization of security, relying on the Venice Commission to support this opinion.

Aspects of this analysis are very troubling—in particular, the Court's assessment of the effects of requiring an immediate change in the basic structure of the constitution. The Court was faced with an argument from the Bosnian government that changes to the rules governing core executive and legislative institutions threatened the whole foundation of the international and inter-ethnic bargain made at Dayton, and risked unravelling it, plunging Bosnia back into civil war. Changes, the Bosnian government argued, should come—but it maintained that the time was not yet ripe and that any changes should be executed under its established procedures for constitutional change, just as Bosnia's own Constitutional Court had suggested. One might, therefore, reasonably have predicted that the European Court would have adopted a cautious, non-interventionist approach. Anyone betting on that prediction would have lost.

Clearly, some politicians and parties in the Bosnian political system have a strong disincentive to change the existing system, either because they benefit from it, as their critics suggest, or because they fear the repercussions that change would set in motion for their constituent people, as they would suggest. A court may sometimes be faced with the request to break a logjam created by self-interested politicians. The question, however, is whether a court of human rights has the standing, or the knowledge, to make such a

---

23. Emphasis added.

judgment. How would a human rights court decide that the likelihood of a return to civil war has sufficiently subsided to allow the court to require a corporate consociational bargain to be unpicked, at least to some degree? Was the Venice Commission's fact-finding process sufficiently rigorous to bear the weight that the ECtHR placed on it? By anyone's standards, it was activism of the highest order for a regional human rights court to require the restructuring of the rules governing the composition and election of a collective presidency and the powerful second chamber of a federal system, to overturn (in practice, if not in theory) the jurisprudence of a domestic constitutional court with a wider remit and with international as well as national judges, to render confident security assessments based largely on the view of an advisory body without security expertise, to presume the most instrumentalist assessment of the motivations governing the conduct of a member state's politicians, and to assume without detailed consideration that there are fully feasible alternatives that will nevertheless keep the same founding constitutional bargain in place.

Steven Wheatley has rightly pointed out that the ECtHR did not hold that *no* justification was ever possible; rather, that justifying ethnic discrimination was *practically* impossible. It was for this reason that the Court went on to consider the issue of proportionality. For Wheatley, even this constrained application of a proportionality test contributed to undermining the legitimacy of the Court's decision, given that examining proportionality meant that the Court was passing judgment 'on complex questions of fact in constitutional and political controversies', on which 'ten of the twenty-six justices that examined the issue at the domestic and international level reached a different conclusion to the majority of the Grand Chamber'. He considers it 'difficult to conclude that a supranational court is better placed than the national constitutional court' to pass judgment on these issues.[24]

Up to this point, Wheatley's assessment is similar to ours, but his legal and policy proposals arising from this assessment are radically different. Wheatley, we understand, views a central function of the Court as being to establish 'the constitutional essentials', which he regards as consisting of 'the minimum requirements of a democratic system of political law-making

24. Steven Wheatley, 'The Construction of the Constitutional Essentials of Democratic Politics by the European Court of Human Rights following *Sejdić and Finci*' in Rob Dickinson, Elena Katselli, Colin Murray, and Ole W. Pederson (eds) *Examining Critical Perspectives on Human Rights* (Cambridge: Cambridge University Press 2012) 163.

at the level of domestic government and the scope and content of fundamental rights'. We agree. He appears, however, to consider that among
these minimum requirements is the political equality of citizens, which he
also appears to consider as excluding 'direct discrimination on grounds of
race or ethnicity'. His conclusion is that the Court 'should have concluded
that direct discrimination in the enjoyment of political rights on grounds of
race or ethnicity could not be justified in any circumstances'.[25] This would
mean that corporate consociational arrangements of any kind should be held
to be in breach of the Convention. We disagree.

Courts have sometimes developed other practices to cope with these
types of situation, in which they think it may not be appropriate for the
court to intervene, but they do not want totally to wash their hands of
consideration of the relevant issue for the future. US legal scholar Alexander
Bickel termed the use of such techniques by the US Supreme Court the
'passive virtues'.[26] He emphasized a fact 'so often missed'—namely, that the
Supreme Court 'wields a threefold power'. It may strike down legislation as
inconsistent with principle; it may, by contrast, legitimate legislation as
principled; or '[i]t may do neither, and therein lies the secret of its ability
to maintain itself in the tension between principle and expediency'.[27]
A court has many ways of 'not doing'. It may deny that it has jurisdiction
to hear a case or argue that the plaintiff lacks standing to bring it; it may
dismiss a case for lack of ripeness or refuse to hear it on the ground that it
raises a 'political question' best decided by the legislature; or it may decide a
case on a narrower basis than that proposed by the parties and carefully avoid
key constitutional issues, for example avoiding deciding between corporate
consociational principles and universal human rights.

The main doctrinal resource that the ECtHR currently has available to it,
should it wish to exercise the passive virtues, is the 'margin of appreciation'.
This margin is, however, perhaps not quite subtle enough to deal with the
tension between corporate consociations and human rights when both have
been embedded in a constitution that gives jurisdiction to the Court.
Perhaps what is required is a 'political question' doctrine—one that encour-
ages political and legislative resolution of controversial questions, and which

25. Wheatley (n. 24) 173.
26. Alexander Bickel, 'The Supreme Court, 1960 Term: Foreword—The Passive Virtues' (1961)
    75 Harvard Law Review 40 and *The Least Dangerous Branch: The Supreme Court at the Bar of
    Politics* (Indianapolis, IN: Bobbs-Merrill 1962).
27. Bickel, 'The Supreme Court' (n. 26) 69.

urges modest restraint upon future courts. Unfashionable though it has recently seemed in the country of its birth, this doctrine might be profitably emulated in Strasbourg in these cases.

We may, however, be placing too much emphasis on the failure of the Court to exercise the 'passive virtues' in its development of *substantive* legal doctrine in political matters: it is able, for example, to limit access to the Court through the use of more *procedural* methods. One obvious example is the use of the requirement that the applicant must be a 'victim' of the violation and not simply a concerned bystander. This method of restricting access is transparent and included in reasoned judgments on admissibility or the merits of the case.

There appears to be a somewhat different process method available to the Court, however, one that is somewhat less transparent: the ability of the Court simply to accelerate or to slow down the progress of a case through the system.

The *Sejdić and Finci* case is a good example of a case that was accelerated through the system. The initial application to the Court through to final decision by the Grand Chamber took just over three-and-a-half years, which was remarkable speedy in comparison with many other cases. Applications against Bosnia by Mr Sejdić and Mr Finci were made to the Court on 3 July and 18 August 2006, respectively. The applications were then allocated to the Fourth Section of the Court. On 11 March 2008, a Chamber of that Section decided to give notice of the applications, to 'communicate' the cases, to the government. On 10 February 2009, the Chamber relinquished jurisdiction in favour of the Grand Chamber, none of the parties having objected, and a hearing took place in public in Strasbourg on 3 June 2009. The Court then deliberated in private on 3 June and 25 November 2009, and delivered its judgment on 22 December 2009. At each stage, the Court had the discretion whether to delay or to accelerate; at several stages, the Court appears to have accelerated the process, notably in relinquishing the case to the Grand Chamber.

If the Court has the discretion to accelerate, it also has the ability *not* to accelerate. Given the backlog of cases before the Court, a system has been introduced to permit the Court to define priority cases. If a case is not given this priority status, it is likely to languish unaddressed. This appears to be what has happened to the *Pilav* case, first discussed in Chapter 6,[28] involving what may be thought to be an even more fundamental challenge to the

---

28. See 'C. Challenges to the presidency election arrangements'.

Bosnian consociational arrangements than that presented in *Sejdić and Finci*.[29] Following the Bosnian Constitutional Court's rejection of his application, Mr Pilav applied to the ECtHR on 24 September 2007—just over a year after Mr Sejdić and Mr Finci. As with their cases, Mr Pilav's application was allocated to the Fourth Section of the Court. Other than acknowledging the receipt of the application, it appears that the Court has taken no further action regarding the case since then. Applications were made to the Court by Mr Pilav's legal representative in 2009 and 2010 to give priority treatment to the application, and in both instances the President of the Chamber refused these applications on the grounds that priority treatment was not necessary.

Five years after the application was first made, the *Pilav* case has not (at the time of writing) even been communicated to the Bosnian government (effectively the first stage after making an application), let alone decided by the Grand Chamber. It is unclear whether the Court is here exercising Bickel's 'passive virtues', neither deciding nor not deciding, but that is a reasonable interpretation of what has happened. In the absence of more substantive doctrines, such as a 'political question' doctrine, the Court may have adopted somewhat less transparent methods of avoiding hard cases.

C. What is the significance of overt discrimination?

Neither Pildes nor Issacharoff distinguished between different types of discrimination in considering whether courts would intervene. The ECtHR has now appeared to make this distinction critical—or at least has muddied the waters as to whether covert discrimination matters as much as overt (which Americans sometimes call 'facial') discrimination in constitutional design. The Court seemed most concerned with the fact that the discrimination in the Bosnian context was apparent on the face of the constitution and the Election Law. Would the Court have been as anxious to strike down provisions if they had been more covert, but had identical consequences? That is, would other approaches to constitutional design be permissible, which would have the same effect, perhaps based on the same motivation, but which would not be facially discriminatory? Is it permissible,

---

29. This discussion is based on the file relating to the *Pilav* case, Application no. 41939/07, provided to us by the Registry of the ECtHR in September 2012.

under the Court's approach, to achieve racial or ethnic shares as long as that is not overtly expressed? We do not know the answers to these questions because the Court expressed no opinion on which of the Venice Commission's options it considered acceptable, let alone *most* acceptable—and several of them appear to continue to rely on discrimination on their face. But the answer to this issue is critical for assessing the implications of the Court's judgment for other consociations.

Regarding Northern Ireland,[30] we have shown that the application of the d'Hondt rule to the allocation of ministerial portfolios is intended to ensure proportional representation of ethno-national blocs in the Northern Ireland Assembly (as well as those who do not identify with such blocs) and to prevent any party from having the ability to veto the participation of another in government. The d'Hondt rule achieves its goals, but not explicitly at the expense of 'Others'. Therefore, on a narrow reading of the Court's judgment, it should not be suspect: it is a liberal consociational device that would pass strict human rights scrutiny. Now, however, consider the method of selection of the First and Deputy First Minister of Northern Ireland's executive. Remember that the system first adopted was explicitly based on selection by identity. Unless and until the United Kingdom ratifies Protocol No. 12, these rules would clearly not fall foul of the ECHR because the First and Deputy First Minister would not constitute a 'legislature' for the purposes of Article 3 of Protocol No. 1. Assume, however, that the UK had ratified Protocol No. 12 (or that it does so in the future): would Northern Ireland's dual premiership then be acceptable under the Court's approach in *Sejdić and Finci*? We cannot be at all certain, since the manifest and express intent of the rules choosing the two premiers, negotiated by the more moderate nationalist and unionist parties, was to share the two posts among Irish nationalists and British unionists—with no place for the others. We may reasonably ask, however, whether the ECtHR, or the Venice Commission, would have considered it wise to adjudicate the merits of the first method of election when the parties were negotiating over modifications of the 1998 Belfast Agreement.

We may ask the same question about the rules governing the passage of *legislation* in Northern Ireland. Either of the two procedures that we discussed arguably renders the legislative vote of those self-designating as 'Others' less

---

30. See Section A, '1. Northern Ireland'.

likely to be pivotal.[31] Would a future ECtHR or the Venice Commission consider it wise to judge the merits of these legislative decision-making rules because there are alternative ways of achieving the same goals that do not violate the right to equality of the 'Others'?[32]

Inevitably, our unease about the possible application of the *Sejdić and Finci* judgment is somewhat speculative, but some extrapolation from the case is useful as a way of evaluating the Court's decision and its trajectory. Let us be even more speculative: what would non-European human rights bodies, influenced by the ECtHR, make of the consociational provisions of the Constitution of Burundi? Are these arrangements suspect on human rights grounds, analogous to those in the *Sejdić and Finci* judgment? Burundi's constitution does not specify that the presidency must consist of two Hutu and one Tutsi, although that is the transparent effect of its rules. It does not specify an exact ratio of Hutu and Tutsi to be allocated to ministerial portfolios. Yet in setting, permanently, a maximum target for the Tutsi and a maximum for Hutu representation in the government and in the Assembly, it makes Tutsi voters (or voters for Tutsi candidates) more powerful than Hutu voters (or voters for Hutu candidates). The 'Others', although not named as such, are not strictly speaking neglected. A Twa may aspire to be president or vice president, although he or she is incredibly unlikely to be successful. Those of European or Asian origin who hold Burundi citizenship can presumably be regarded as being part of 'all ethnic components'. But the provisions indirectly treat Hutu and Tutsi as distinct corporate groups for the purposes of representation, while dressing the rules of office-holding in formally nationally and inclusive terms. The role assigned to the Electoral Commission in shaping the composition of both the first and the second

---

31. See Alex Schwartz, 'How Unfair is Cross-Community Consent? Voting Power in the Northern Ireland Assembly' (2010) 61 Northern Ireland Legal Quarterly 349.

32. To be clear, one of us advocated rule changes that would have reduced (not eliminated) the corporate character and increased the liberal character of Northern Ireland's consociational rules: John McGarry and Brendan O'Leary, 'Introduction: Consociational Theory and Northern Ireland' in Joanne McEvoy and Brendan O'Leary (eds) *Essays on the Northern Ireland Conflict: Consociational Engagements* (Oxford: Oxford University Press 2004); John McGarry and Brendan O'Leary, 'Stabilising Northern Ireland's Agreement' (2004) 75 Political Quarterly 213; revised and updated in John McGarry and Brendan O'Leary, 'Stabilising Northern Ireland's Agreement' in Paul Carmichael and Colin Knox (eds) *Devolution and Constitutional Change in Northern Ireland* (Manchester: Manchester University Press 2007). However, these proposals, consistent with the changes that have since occurred, were advocated for resolution through political negotiations and agreements, not Court decisions.

chambers of the legislature, to ensure either that ethnic targets (in the Assembly) or ethnic quotas (in the Senate) are met, certainly weakens the formal equality of individual voters and constrains the power of the Burundi demos to choose its representatives. Throughout the constitution, indirect provisions are used to achieve positive, but discriminatory and explicitly ethnic, effects.

D. What makes the use of a 'suspect classification' suspect?

The hypotheses of Issacharoff and Pildes may also need to be modified by distinguishing between courts' expected reactions to political bargains involving ethnic, as opposed to other, preferences—although, as we shall show, the ECtHR has rendered even more uncertain the always problematic boundaries between the 'ethnic' and the 'non-ethnic'. The Court, in one of its most important moves, identified ethnic discrimination as akin to racial discrimination, which is a type of discrimination of such danger as to be almost impossible to justify. In future, it would therefore appear that the Court (and other regional or international courts, if they follow the Court's approach) will be less willing to accept some types of consocation than others—especially those based, on their face, on racial or ethnic criteria.

At least two significant problems may be identified with the Court's approach. The first was the Court's inattention to local context in pronouncing on 'ethnicity'. It is well known, and not only to scholars, that the major protagonists to the conflict in Bosnia, and more widely in the Balkans, have historically often used the language of 'nation'[33] rather than 'ethnicity' to describe themselves and their opponents. The expressions 'ethnic', 'multi-ethnic', and 'multicultural' were not widely used in Bosnia before international intervention there.[34] The use of these expressions in international

---

33. The term used in Bosnian/Serbian/Croatian is *narod*, on the significance of which see, in particular, Robert M. Hayden, *Blueprints for a House Divided: The Constitutional Logic of the Yugoslav Conflict* (Ann Arbor, MI: University of Michigan Press 1999).
34. This is common ground among scholars of Bosnia, even among those whom we would expect to disagree with the overall argument of this book: see e.g. Gerard Toal and Carl Dahlman, *Bosnia Remade: Ethnic Cleansing and its Reversal* (Oxford: Oxford University Press 2011) e-book loc. 72.

circles was often accompanied by unnoticed American assumptions (such as that ethnicities are minorities and that 'the majority' is non-ethnic). The former Yugoslavia, by contrast, had organized itself under a particular Marxist-Leninist approach to the subject of national self-determination.[35] Its vocabulary was still dominant when the Dayton Peace Agreement (DPA) was negotiated. That explains why the leaders of Bosniaks, Croats, and Serbs in Bosnia vested such significance in the expression 'constituent peoples', why Croats and Serbs insisted on this status as an absolute minimum, and why Bosniaks were reluctant to concede a triple constitution of Bosnia. Constituent nations in the former Yugoslavia had the (ambiguous) right to self-determination, whereas minority groups did not. In the former Yugoslavia, Roma, Jews, Vlachs, Hungarians, and Albanians were not constituent nations; rather, they were either national minorities (whose national homelands were elsewhere) or ethnic minorities. Had it chosen to do so, the Court could have chosen to treat Bosnia's foundation (or re-foundation in 1995) as an act of 'nationalities' rather than of 'ethnicities'. If it had done so, then it would, as we shall suggest in this section, have been able to ask whether anything in the constitution or the law excluded Roma, Jews, or other minorities from membership of one of the three constituent peoples.

The second problem arising from the *Sejdić and Finci* judgment is precisely what makes ethnicity suspect, and how we should clarify the boundaries between ethnic discrimination and other forms of presumably acceptable, objective, or reasonable discrimination. Trying to explain why some grounds are potentially suspect, and why their use occasions heightened scrutiny while others do not, has generated a substantial debate in different jurisdictions. Before the *Sejdić and Finci* judgment, Gro Nystuen's 2005 assessment of the compatibility of the ethnic differentiation rules in Bosnia's constitution with the ECHR sought to distinguish the language issue at the heart of the Belgian *Mathieu-Mohn and Clerfayt* case from the 'ethnic' criteria at issue in the Bosnian constitutional arrangements. In the Belgian case, she argued, 'the candidates could freely choose the language they wanted to use. In Bosnia and Herzegovina, the persons who are excluded from the House of Peoples cannot choose to alter the exclusion criteria'. In particular, she

---

35. Walker Connor, *The National Question in Marxist-Leninist Theory and Strategy* (Princeton, NJ: Princeton University Press 1984) 128–71, 430–3. In interview with Brendan O'Leary, in Townshend, VT, 17 August 2012, Ambassador Galbraith emphasized the importance of existing constitutional provisions and of previous Marxist assumptions on national questions among the parties leading up to the Dayton Agreement.

asserted, the ethnicity of those in Bosnia 'is something they are born with, which cannot be easily changed'.[36]

Mr Finci's counsel took a similar approach, following that also adopted by the US Supreme Court—namely, that the common element that linked those grounds that were most highly protected was that they involved 'immutable traits', meaning that these characteristics were not chosen and could not be altered by an individual:

> The [ECtHR] has never found that restrictions in voting and election rights based upon immutable traits such as ethnicity to be a proportionate response to what might otherwise be a legitimate consideration . . . [T]he Applicant can do nothing to overcome the restrictions that prevent him from standing for office. The restrictions are based on his being born a Jew.[37]

Note immediately that this argument, like the Court's, treats race and ethnicity as equivalently exogenous, given, and externally determined, and treats Jewishness as a racial or a descent-based ethnicity. The argument cannot, however, have been meant to apply to the applicant's religion, which he is free to choose and, in any case, there is no religious test for office in Bosnia.

The Court was not overly concerned to explain why the use of 'ethnicity' should produce heightened scrutiny. There was, in fact, remarkably little discussion of the issue. Heightened scrutiny, however, cannot have been warranted because the ethnicity of the applicants was deemed 'immutable'. We have shown that, in the constitutional arrangements put in place in Bosnia, individuals themselves decide whether to affiliate with one of the constituent peoples. Judge Mijović analysed in detail in her partial dissent the use to which ethnic affiliation is actually put in the consociational arrangements, its legal status, and the method by which a person's ethnic affiliation is determined. Ethnic affiliation in Bosnia, she argued, 'is not to be taken as a legal category, since it depends exclusively on one's self-classification, which represents *stricto sensu* a subjective criterion'. It means that 'everyone has a right to declare (or not) his or her affiliation with one ethnic group. It is not obligatory to do so'. There is neither 'a legal obligation to declare one's ethnic affiliation, nor objective parameters for establishing such affiliation'. Ethnic affiliation therefore becomes an

---

36. Gro Nystuen, *Achieving Peace or Protecting Human Rights? Conflicts between Norms Regarding Ethnic Discrimination in the Dayton Peace Agreement* (The Hague: Martinus Nijhoff 2005) 169.
37. Finci, Application to ECtHR, [99].

important issue 'only if an individual wishes to become involved in politics'. A declaration of ethnic affiliation 'is thus not an objective and legal category, but a subjective and political one'.

The implications of this analysis might be taken in two (rather different) directions. One reasonable consequence of this analysis might be to say that because the applicants were able to self-designate as affiliated with one of the constituent peoples, then they should bear the consequences of their choice not to do so. There is no incompatibility between being Roma or Jewish and self-identifying as Bosniak, Serb, or Croat (by nationality, or as constituent people).[38] Self-identifying with one of the three designations does not require any repudiation or denigration of any other identity. On the other hand, Edin Hodžić and Nenad Stojanović have suggested that any such requirement 'can constitute an insurmountable (moral) obstacle' for some, threatening their dignity.[39] The European Roma Rights Centre (ERRC) has gone further, claiming that to accept this reasoning would be contrary to Article 3 of the Framework Convention for the Protection of National Minorities, which provides:

> Every person belonging to a national minority shall have the right freely to choose to be treated or not to be treated as such and no disadvantage shall result from this choice or from the exercise of the rights which are connected to that choice.

The ERRC's argument in turn raises the question of whether choosing to affiliate to a constituent people requires one to say that one does not wish to be treated as a national minority.

It also raises the question of how far it is appropriate in the consociational context for negotiators to seek to prevent the agreement being undermined by individuals choosing to identify with one of the primary groups even though those individuals are not seen as 'representative' of that group. The history of the negotiations over Burundi's constitution is importantly suggestive on this issue. On our reading, nowhere does the Burundi constitution specify how ethnic identification is established for purposes of

---

38. There would, of course, be an incompatibility if a Jew thereby had to choose to be a Muslim, or a Roman Catholic, or of the Orthodox faith.

39. Edin Hodžić and Nenad Stojanović, *New/Old Constitutional Engineering? Challenges and Implications of the European Court of Human Rights Decision in the Case of* Sejdić and Finci v BiH (Sarajevo: Analitika 2011) 85.

representation, which may mean that Hutus could self-identify as Tutsi to overturn the ethos of the power-sharing settlement:

> [The] critical issue during the constitutional debates hinged upon the political affiliation of Tutsi representatives. Could any Tutsi candidate qualify, irrespective of party affiliations, or only those Tutsis who belonged to all-Tutsi parties? After much wrangling, it was agreed that Tutsi members of predominantly Hutu parties . . . could indeed qualify as representatives of the Tutsi community, contrary to what Tutsi hardliners advocated.[40]

We may detect in this negotiating victory for the Hutu majority and the rational fears of the minority of Tutsi hardliners, the basis through which disguised majoritarianism may conceivably displace power-sharing in the future in Burundi. Only small numbers of socially co-opted Tutsi would be required to ensure Hutu dominance in Burundi politics.[41] Sometimes, corporate or designation provisions may be required to protect against the abuse of measures intended to represent minorities.

But it is not necessary to take the consequences of Judge Mijović's analysis so far. A more minimalist approach suggests that, whatever other consequences may or may not flow, the 'immutability' theory of ethnicity cannot be a convincing explanation of why the ECtHR decided as it did in *Sejdić and Finci*, given the extent to which 'ethnicity' in Bosnia is potentially quite alterable. Indeed, the immutability approach has long been regarded sceptically by many legal academics in the home of its birth as being both under- and overinclusive.[42]

While the 'immutability' theory may be unconvincing, no *alternative* theory has yet emerged as a replacement, explaining why the Court regards some grounds of discrimination as particularly protected and other not.[43]

---

40. Lemarchand, 'Burundi's Endangered Transition' (n. 5) 169.
41. As we noted in Chapter 2, n. 22, analogous arrangements have produced deep dissatisfaction among Croats over elections to the Bosnian presidency since 2006, and elsewhere within the institutions of the Federation of Bosnia and Herzegovina. We may hypothesize that the smaller a minority is, the less territorially concentrated it is, and the more it fears a diminution in its electoral weight, then the more likely it is to insist on corporate consociational arrangements.
42. Jack M. Balkin, 'The Constitution of Status' (1997) 106 Yale Law Journal 2313. Lawrence Tribe argues that it is overinclusive. 'Intelligence, height, and strength are all immutable for a particular individual but legislation that distinguishes on the basis of these criteria is not generally thought to be constitutionally suspect': Lawrence H. Tribe, 'The Puzzling Persistence of Process-Based Constitutional Theories' (1980) 89 Yale Law Journal 1063, fn. 51.
43. An elegant attempt to do so is Wojciech Sadurski, *Equality and Legitimacy* (Oxford: Oxford University Press 2008) 93–145.

Identifying an alternative is not made any easier given that the Court seldom, if ever, makes explicit its grounds for deeming some classifications as suspect. Attempting to isolate a principled reason why certain groups are particularly protected brings us face to face with the major unresolved issue in the approach that the Court takes in its recent anti-discrimination jurisprudence: what is it that ECHR anti-discrimination law is attempting to do? Of the alternatives available, probably the most popular theory is that the Court chooses those categories of protected characteristics closest to an individual's *identity*. Not all identity groups are protected, however, and therefore 'identity' in itself is significantly overinclusive as an explanation. Most often, there is a sense that, to become specially protected identities, the identity group also has to be seen as in some way 'vulnerable'—but in what does the vulnerability of the groups protected in *Sejdić and Finci* lie? The Court's opinion provides no clear answer. European history in the twentieth century presumably led the Court to believe that there was no need to declare that Jews or Roma are people vulnerable to racial and ethnic bigotry and life-threatening hatred. But if that was the basis for its judgment, then we think that should have been made clear, not least because of the Court's responsibility to set out its reasoning clearly.

The possible difficulties in future reviews of other consociational arrangements should now be obvious: the Court has placed much importance on whether the groups are classified in ethnic terms; the Court has conflated race and ethnicity—or at least has ranked them as equally suspicious categories, although on what basis is not clear; and, compounding all of these difficulties, we do not know on what *basis* the Court classifies treatments as ethnic. Given these uncertainties, would the *Belgian* consociation be classified as involving 'linguistic' rather than 'ethnic' distinctions, and would this mean that they are more acceptable? Would Northern Ireland's executive and legislative arrangements be classified as involving 'national' (or indirect 'religious') rather than 'ethnic' criteria, and would that also be more acceptable?[44] Would its (now repealed) employment legislation establishing a quota of Catholics for the filling of posts in the police force have been

---

44. The Belfast Agreement's executive and legislative provisions do not refer at all to religious opinion or designations; they do refer to the designations that Assembly members make regarding whether they share national identification with the United Kingdom (unionists) or with Ireland (nationalists).

classified as 'ethnic' rather than 'religious', and would that mean that it was less acceptable under the Convention?[45]

These matters, as we have already suggested, are highly pertinent in the case of Bosnia itself. One way of viewing the major groups involved in Bosnia is in 'national' terms—the way in which they themselves have reliably been reported to see matters. One of the arguments for the Dayton arrangements was that they helped to deliver self-determination for different 'peoples', as provided for in international human rights law itself. Instead, therefore, of a clash between consociational principles and human rights principles, arguably two different rights—self-determination and equality—have to be balanced. After all, each of the 'constituent peoples' of Bosnia is, under this approach, a nation, each of which merits self-determination. Seen from this perspective, differentiating whether one person is a member of one of these 'peoples' means preferring 'co-nationals' rather than dis-crimination on grounds of ethnic origin.[46] One person's 'national' conflict may be another's 'ethnic' conflict[47] and, in conflicts of these kinds, there may indeed always be a 'meta-conflict'—that is, a conflict about what the conflict is about. We are not alone in asking whether courts can always judge expertly and objectively on these matters. Because the ECtHR did not explain why, in this case, it was 'ethnicity' rather than 'nation' that was in issue, it has made future cases even more difficult to predict.

Will the Court be more willing to uphold the constitutional arrange-ments in Bosnia faced with a challenge from a Bosnian *Serb* resident in the *Federation* who wants to participate in elections for the Federation candi-dates for the presidency and the House of Peoples, or a Bosniak who wants to stand for the Serb Republic's presidency position? The Court may be in the position of deciding just this issue in the application that Ilijaz Pilav made to the Court following the rejection of his case by the Bosnian Constitutional Court—the third of the three cases by that Court that we discussed in Chapter 6. As we have shown,[48] when, or whether, the Court will determine these issues is uncertain at the time of writing, but if the case

---

45. For a discussion of these arrangements, see Christopher McCrudden, 'Consociationalism, Equality, and Minorities in the Northern Ireland Bill of Rights Debate: The Role of the OSCE High Commissioner on National Minorities' in John Morison, Kieran McEvoy, and Gordon Anthony (eds) *Judges, Transition and Human Rights* (Oxford: Oxford University Press 2007) 315.
46. See Nystuen (n. 36) 202–3. For the right to self-determination. See ICCPR, art 1.
47. Don Horowitz to Christopher McCrudden, personal communication.
48. See 'B. Margin of appreciation and proportionality'.

proceeds, the Court will likely be called on to consider whether any of the three differences between the *Pilav* case and the *Sejdić and Finci* case are sufficiently significant for the Court to reach a different result. First, will the Court consider exclusion of Bosniaks to be different from exclusion of Jews and Roma, and if so, on what grounds? The second difference is that whereas Mr Sejdić and Mr Finci were both unable to stand for election to the presidency from anywhere in Bosnia, Mr Pilav could stand for election for one of the Federation's presidency seats. These two differences might be thought likely to influence the Court to find in favour of the existing arrangements. On the other hand, a third difference might influence the Court to be even more hostile to the 'ethnic' arrangements in the *Pilav* case: the extent to which these arrangements tend to undermine attempts to encourage the return of Bosniaks and Croats to their previous homes in the Serb Republic, and Serbs to return to the Federation. As Gro Nystuen has observed, it is 'a paradox that the more successful this reintegration policy becomes, the fewer people will be entitled to full political participation'.[49]

More generally, the different levels of scrutiny that may be applied to discrimination on different grounds raises several questions about the stability of other consociations, current and future. Several consociations have been established to manage religious, as well as other, disputes (such as in the Netherlands and Cyprus). How are these to be treated? There are close connections, on occasion, between religion and ethnicity. Indeed, it can be difficult to draw a distinction between the two, as is famously true of Jews[50] and, say some, of Croats. Ethnic discrimination may be interwoven with discrimination because of a person's adherence to a particular religion. Indeed, the Court itself, in defining what constitutes 'racial' discrimination in previous cases, has not only explicitly included 'ethnic' discrimination within the concept of 'racial', but has also defined 'ethnic' as including 'religious faith'.[51] In *Cyprus v. Turkey*, the Court found discrimination on

---

49. Nystuen (n. 36) 158.
50. See the discussion in Christopher McCrudden, 'Post-Multiculturalism, Freedom of Religion, and Antidiscrimination Law: The *JFS* Case Considered' (2011) 9 International Journal of Constitutional Law 200.
51. *Timishev v. Russia* (2007) 44 EHRR 37, [55]:

> Ethnicity and race are related and overlapping concepts. Whereas the notion of race is rooted in the idea of biological classification of human beings into subspecies according to morphological features such as skin colour or facial characteristics, ethnicity has its origin in the idea of societal groups marked by common nationality, tribal affiliation, religious faith, shared language, or cultural and traditional origins and backgrounds.

the basis of 'ethnic origin, race *and religion*'.[52] The judgment in that case primarily confirms the gravity of discrimination based on race, but it also suggests that religious discrimination should be strictly reviewed. The Council of Europe's European Commission against Racism and Intolerance (ECRI) recommends that the member states of the Council of Europe enact legislation against racial discrimination. Under 'racial discrimination', the Recommendation includes 'differential treatment based on grounds such as race, colour, language, *religion*, nationality or national or ethnic origin'.[53] Does this mean that all of these grounds should be subjected to the strictest scrutiny?

A somewhat similar issue arises regarding policies seeking to secure the participation of women in legislative and executive arrangements. This is not the place in which to explore fully the implications of *Sejdić and Finci* for gender quotas in electoral law, but a suggestion of the contours of the issue may be useful. Such electoral quotas have proven immensely popular in Europe and in several other regions among those campaigning for women's equality. Indeed, as we saw in relation to Burundi,[54] such policies have not infrequently been developed alongside the consociational arrangements that we have discussed in this book.[55] Under the jurisprudence of the ECtHR, gender is a 'suspect qualification' and, applying the approach set out in *Sejdić and Finci,* these gender quota arrangements would therefore seem to be candidates for a rigorous application of Article 14 ECHR and Protocol No. 12. However, in the one case in which the Court has examined the question, a little-known admissibility decision by the Third Chamber of the Court (not the Grand Chamber, in other words), the Court appears to have adopted a distinctly light-touch approach.

In this case, *Méndez Pérez v. Spain*,[56] the Court was asked to consider the legality under the ECHR of Spanish gender quota arrangements. The president of a local policy committee of the Popular Party had invited

52. (2002) 35 EHRR 30, [309], emphasis added.
53. European Commission against Racism and Intolerance (ECRI), *General Policy Recommendation No. 7 on National Legislation to Combat Racism and Racial Discrimination,* CRI(2003)8, 17 February 2003, para. 1(b), emphasis added. National courts have also accepted that religion is included as one of the list of grounds that are regarded as '*suspect*' under Article 14 ECHR. The (former) UK House of Lords considered the issue: see in particular *R v. Secretary of State for Work and Pensions, ex p Carson* [2005] UKHL 37, [58] *per* Lord Walker.
54. See Section A, '2. Burundi'.
55. Quotas in favour of women were also adopted in Iraq: John McGarry and Brendan O'Leary, 'Iraq's Constitution of 2005: Liberal Consociation as Political Prescription' (2007) 5 International Journal of Constitutional Law 670.
56. *Méndez Pérez v. Spain,* Application no. 35473/08, 4 October 2011.

those interested to become candidates for local elections in 2007. All potential candidates were female, which may have been in conflict with Spanish legislation, which requires a balanced composition of men and women on all of the candidate lists, so that there are at least 40 per cent of candidates of each sex. The Party argued that the provision on quotas was unconstitutional and discriminatory, and took the case to the Spanish Constitutional Court, which was of the opinion that the quota provision was in compliance with the constitution. The ECtHR, ostensibly applying *Sejdić and Finci*, reiterated that discrimination means treating differently those in similar situations without a reasonable justification. The Court held, however, that the application of the Spanish quota requirements did not even engage Article 14 ECHR because there was no difference in treatment. The legislation also disqualified a list of candidates consisting only of men, since it would not conform to the legal requirement that there must be 40 per cent of candidates of each sex. The statute therefore established a system of percentages that applied equally to candidates, to ensure the balanced participation of women and men to elected office. Would a similar interpretation of Article 14 have been forthcoming had an ethnic or racial quota been in issue? Indeed, the Court, without citing *Belgian Linguistics*, appears to have accepted in *Méndez Pérez* exactly the 'parallelism' interpretation of Article 14 that the Court had rejected in the former case: remember that the Belgian government failed to convince the Court that the fact that the same situation would occur to Dutch-speaking children in Wallonia, but in reverse (so-called 'parallelism'), meant that there was no discrimination against the French-speaking children.

E. Civic versus ethnic models, or why the civic model is not neutral

The Court's judgment in *Sejdić and Finci* may reasonably be read as requiring limited changes in the short term, but also as casting doubt on any consociational model of express ethnic difference reservation and protection in the longer term. The Court's broader unease about such arrangements appears to be based on a belief that a civic integrationist and majority-rule model of democracy both represents the European norm and is the best way of transcending historic divisions—and the Venice Commission agrees. The civic integrationist model is thus perceived by the Court and the Commission as a neutral way forward for all in the longer term.[57] To make this judgement is, however, to underestimate three facts of life.

1. First, as we observed in Chapter 1, consociations are recurrent features on the European political landscape.

2. Second, what is deemed to be civic is rarely devoid of ethnic content and therefore rarely neutral. The civic is rarely a true fusion of diverse ethnic influences; it is more usually a 'secularized' version of the culture of the dominant group (or dominant coalition of groups).

3. Lastly, and relatedly, the dominant group, or the most likely dominant group, tends to define itself as civic and to deem its minority challengers as ethnic. Differently put, when the dominant ethnic group controls public institutions, it is able to define what is 'civic'.

Applied to the Bosnian context, these insights have particular importance. As Joanne McEvoy observes: 'Bosniaks, by virtue of being the plurality, would like to see the abolition of the entities and a move towards a citizen- rather than group-based democracy.'[58] Eldar Sarajlić goes further, describing the dichotomy between civic and ethnic as 'analytically false' when applied to Bosnia.[59] He continues:

> The problem with the 'civic' versus 'ethnic' understanding of nationalism in Bosnia . . . is . . . [that] it is essentially embedded in a particular Bosniak political discourse and has few supporters outside political and intellectual circles of this ethnic group. . . . Consequently, the notion of civic belonging in Bosnia and Herzegovina is often identified with Bosniak political discourse and does not resonate in areas dominated by Serbs and Croats.[60]

57. Compare with Fionnuala Ní Aoláin 'The Fractured Soul of the Dayton Peace Agreement: A Legal Analysis' (1998) 19 Michigan Journal of International Law 957, 1004: 'Rebuilding Bosnia in a meaningful way requires modalities of transition from the starting point of a settlement premised on the cohesion of the group, to a society that nurtures the individual and celebrates its multi-ethnicity, multiculturalism, and diversity.'

58. Joanne McEvoy, ' "We Forbid!" The Mutual Veto and Power-Sharing Democracy' in Joanne McEvoy and Brendan O'Leary (eds) *Power-Sharing in Deeply Divided Places* (Philadelphia, PA: University of Pennsylvania Press, in press).

59. Eldar Sarajlić, 'Bosnian Elections and Recurring Ethnonationalisms: The Ghost of the Nation State' (2010) 9 Journal on Ethnopolitics and Minority Issues in Europe 66, 67. It is certainly empirically false if one tries to suggest that western nationalisms are civic, whereas Eastern are ethnic: see Brendan O'Leary, 'Gellner's Diagnoses of Nationalism: A Critical Overview—or What is Living and What is Dead in Gellner's Philosophy of Nationalism?' in John A. Hall (ed.) *The State of the Nation: Ernest Gellner and the Theory of Nationalism* (Cambridge: Cambridge University Press 1998) 86, n. 76.

60. Sarajlić (n. 59) 72.

Plainly put, the decision of the Court in *Sejdić and Finci* is one that appears to attempt to move Bosnia decisively in the direction of the preferred Bosniak position, because a central element of Bosniak parties' and politicians' political objectives is to move towards majority rule.[61] This is not to claim that Mr Finci's or Mr Sejdić's real strategy was intentionally to engineer a judgment that would favour the Bosniak position.[62] Intentional or not, however, a pro-Bosniak outcome has been the effect of their litigation. The motives of those engaged in future litigation seeking to unwind consociations may be less benign. Any revised assessment of the role of courts in consociations should take into account the possibility that the parties before the courts are engaging in something akin to 'lawfare', which Charles Dunlap defined as 'the use of law as a weapon of war'.[63]

F. Uncertainty for future negotiators in other conflict zones

Perhaps the most troubling future dimension of the decision in *Sejdić and Finci* is the uncertainty that the Court's approach has generated for past, present, and future conflict sites, and for efforts to resolve conflict. Remember that the Court's approach in the Belgian cases was seen to express international human rights standards generally. The Court's new approach therefore brings with it significant uncertainties, not only in Europe, but

---

61. Bruce R. Hitchner, 'From Dayton to Brussels: The Story Behind the Constitutional and Governmental Reform Process in Bosnia and Herzegovina' (2006) 30 The Fletcher Forum of World Affairs 125, 132.

62. We do not have the requisite evidence to make or reject such a judgment. There is, however, some evidence of Bosnian Jewish support for Bosniaks in the past and present. A non-governmental organization (NGO) called 'Bosniak and Jewish Solidarity' (online at <http://www.bosniakandjewishfriendship.wordpress.com>), for example, promotes friendship between Jewish and Bosniak people. It argues that they share a common historical bond: they both suffered genocide at the hands of Serbian Nazi collaborators in the Second World War.

63. Charles J. Dunlap Jr, 'Law and Military Interventions: Preserving Humanitarian Values in 21st Century Conflicts' (Humanitarian Challenges in Military Intervention Conference, Carr Center for Human Rights Policy, Kennedy School of Government, Harvard University 2001). We are aware that the term 'lawfare' is sometimes used to refer to the use of armed force for the purpose of advancing a human rights agenda—David Kennedy, *The Dark Side of Virtue: Reassessing International Humanitarianism* (Princeton, NJ: Princeton University Press 2004) 262—but we use the term here in the sense specified by Dunlap. See further Richard Mullender, 'Lawfare and the International Human Rights Movement' in Rob Dickinson, Elena Katselli, Colin Murray, and Ole W. Pederson (eds) *Examining Critical Perspectives on Human Rights* (Cambridge: Cambridge University Press 2012) 248.

also internationally over how courts will react to consociations (whether corporate or liberal)—hence our suggestion that the Burundi arrangements are relevant. Remember, too, that one of the defining features of consociational arrangements is the expectation of the parties that the arrangements entered into are *durable*—that is, that the arrangements will operate until the contracting parties renegotiate the arrangements in ways provided for under the agreement itself. 'Durable' does not necessarily mean 'forever'—but it does not mean 'until tomorrow'.

Samo Bardutzky raises this issue in his discussion of the *Sejdić and Finci* case, but is unclear how best to view it:

> It is difficult to assess the relevance of the fact that the Court deals with a transitional constitutional order ... May restrictions be more easily justified shortly after the establishment of the new constitutional order, whereas the burden of the respondent may also be higher when enough time has passed?[64]

Others are considerably less tentative, answering Bardutzky's question strongly in the affirmative.[65] Indeed, one of the pervasive aspects of the 'new' approach is the sense that consociations are appropriate *only* in the immediate *aftermath* of the dispute, and only for a *temporary* period.

The model, in some ways, for what is deemed acceptable by the Court and others seems to be an overgeneralization from the South African transition from apartheid. For Timothy Sisk, for example, who has extensively studied South Africa,[66] 'power sharing may be appropriate as a transitional, confidence-building mechanism but not as a permanent solution to ethnic conflict management through democratic institutions'.[67] Likewise, for Steven Wheatley, power-sharing 'is appropriate only in the

---

64. Samo Bardutzky, 'The Strasbourg Court on the Dayton Constitution: Judgment in the case of *Sejdić and Finci v. Bosnia and Herzegovina*, 22 December 2009' (2009) 6 European Constitutional Law Review 309, 328.

65. There is some evidence that the Court regards the ongoing nature of a peace process as a reason for judicial restraint, for example, in dealing with aspects of the Northern Ireland peace agreement. In *Murdock v. United Kingdom*, Application no. 44934/98, 25 January 2000, the Court accorded the United Kingdom a significant decree of discretion in distinguishing between prisoners. A prisoner complained about his treatment compared with those released under the Good Friday Agreement. In holding that the UK enjoyed a wide margin of appreciation, the Court referred, at 3, to the 'sensitive nature of the ongoing peace process and the complexity of the security situation which it [sought] to resolve'.

66. Timothy D. Sisk, *Democratization in South Africa: The Elusive Social Contract* (Princeton, NJ: Princeton University Press 1995).

67. Timothy D. Sisk, *Power Sharing and International Mediation in Ethnic Conflicts* (Washington, DC: United States Institute of Peace 1996) 116.

initial transition from conflict to democracy. Consociational democracy can only be justified by reference to ideas of transitional justice'.[68]

How long a 'transition' should last, however, is not spelled out by those who favour consociation solely for transitional purposes. As Bruce Hitchner says, regarding Bosnia:

> Some will say that ten years is plenty of time to draft a replacement for the old constitution … But an equally powerful argument could be made that the current process has *only* taken ten years—less than half a generation since the end of the war, hardly enough time for full trust and reconciliation to have developed on all sides.[69]

We think he is right in this respect, but that is not the point that is of most importance for our purposes. Whether a transition should be judged by the numbers of general elections since the point of transition or built into a settlement, with a review period, is less important than asking who should be in charge of changing consociational arrangements.[70]

Given how it had approached previous cases of transition to democracy in Europe, it might have been predicted that the ECtHR would accord significant weight to the inevitable problems of transition in Bosnia too, whilst perhaps commenting adversely about the permanency of the Bosnian arrangements. In *Ždanoka v. Latvia*,[71] the Grand Chamber had concluded that there has been no violation by Latvia of Article 3 of Protocol No. 1 in excluding certain persons from being able to stand for election, based in part on the Court's unwillingness to second-guess the Latvian authorities as to what was necessary in the circumstances of transition to democracy.[72] In particular, the Court accepted, in that case:

---

68. Steven Wheatley, *Democracy, Minorities, and International Law* (Cambridge: Cambridge University Press 2005) 167.

69. Hitchner (n. 61) 133.

70. We are conscious, of course, that creating an inflexible and permanent corporate consociation may be politically unwise, and that its permanence and inflexibility may contribute to its ultimate destruction, as arguably occurred in Lebanon in the 1970s, where shifts in the relative proportions of the groups over time meant that the original proportions specified in the consociational agreement overrepresented one group (the Christians), a situation that that group was unwilling to alter, contributing to the outbreak of civil war in 1975. See Theodor Hanf, *Coexistence in Wartime Lebanon: Decline of a State and Rise of a Nation* (tr. J. Richardson, London: I.B. Tauris & Co 1993).

71. *Ždanoka v. Latvia*, Application no. 58278/00, 16 March 2006 (Grand Chamber), (2007) 45 EHRR.

72. See also the cases dealing with the transition in Germany: *Jahn and others v. Germany*, nos 46720/99, 72203/01, and 72552/01, 30 June 2005 (Grand Chamber), (2006) 42 EHRR 49, [116]; *Von Maltzan v. Germany*, nos 71916/01, 71917/01, and 10260/02, 2 March 2005 (Grand Chamber) (admissibility decision) (2006) 42 EHRR SEII [110].

that the national authorities of Latvia, both legislative and judicial, are better placed to assess the difficulties faced in establishing and safeguarding the democratic order. Those authorities should therefore be left sufficient latitude to assess the needs of their society in building confidence in the new democratic institutions, including the national parliament, and to answer the question whether the impugned measure is still needed for these purposes, provided that the Court has found nothing arbitrary or disproportionate in such an assessment. In this respect, the Court also attaches weight to the fact that the Latvian parliament has periodically reviewed [the contested provision] ... Even more importantly, the Constitutional Court carefully examined ... the historical and political circumstances which gave rise to the enactment of the law in Latvia, finding the restriction to be neither arbitrary nor disproportionate at that point in time, that is, nine years after the events in question ...[73]

In the Bosnian case, however, the ECtHR sought to achieve a degree of liberalization mostly hoped for only by Bosniaks, who had earlier failed to persuade their negotiating partners or US and European Union diplomats to their point of view, and in ways that require change beyond that envisaged by the founding bargain itself. In so doing, the Court has sent a clear signal that a foundational aspect of a consociation can be reversed *by judges*, even, or especially, when the parties themselves have not, or cannot, agree to change the arrangements.

The message that the case sends to the world, intentionally or not, is that courts can and may well unpick highly sensitive national, ethnic, religious, or linguistic bargains in some future, unpredictable, circumstances. Perhaps that is not the most helpful message to filter into the latest or any future UN-led negotiations to reunify Cyprus. As Nystuen suggests would have been the case in Bosnia, 'none of the parties would make any effort to implement [the resulting agreement], but rather position themselves and wait for the next "round". This was the political "reality" to which the mediators had to relate'.[74] The Court's message may lead, in the future, to negotiators being much less open to persuasion that the arrangements they are being offered as protection for their interests will be stable for the foreseeable future—that is, that they will not be subject to change without their consent. The blunt choice between a continuation of war or agreeing to a heavily compromised power-sharing agreement to end hostilities,

73. *Ždanoka v. Latvia* (n. 71) [134].   74. Nystuen (n. 36) 216.

always highly uncertain, may now hang even more in the balance than it has in the past.

Lawyers and political scientists will immediately reflect on a related repercussion: should wise advisers to the parties to a future consociational bargain counsel them to exclude domestic, regional, and international courts from having the right to review their bargain? Should they suggest that bills of rights be written that expressly exclude the application of the rights in question to the composition and decision-making rules of executive, legislative, and judicial bodies? For those in Europe, should they advise that accession to the Council of Europe, let alone the European Union, will jeopardize any consociational bargain? There are, of course, mechanisms that may be drawn on to prevent the judicial reversal of a consociational agreement from occurring, such as creating exceptions, making derogations, entering reservations, and specifying the durations of agreements, and the rules under which they may be reviewed or modified. One indication that negotiators of consociational arrangements are already aware of the potential for judicial unwinding is to be found in Northern Ireland. In 2000, under pressure from local parties and supported by the government of Ireland, the European Union amended one of its principal anti-discrimination directives specifically to protect aspects of the consociational arrangements in Northern Ireland from challenge on equality grounds.[75]

There is another possibility provided by the ECHR itself. Article 57(1) ECHR provides that any state may, when signing the Convention or when depositing its instrument of ratification, make a reservation in respect of any particular provision of the Convention to the extent that any law then in force in its territory is not in conformity with the provision. The parties to the agreement might have specified that Bosnia should enter a reservation to preserve the special and controversial aspects of the architecture of that agreement. It is certainly arguable that such reservation to Article 3 of Protocol No. 1 and Article 14 ECHR would have been compatible with Article 57 (or Article 64, as it then was), as would a reservation to Protocol No. 12. It is true that reservations 'of a general character' are not permitted under this Article, but, as interpreted by the Court,[76] an appropriately

---

75. See Council Directive 2000/78/EC of 27 November 2000 establishing a general framework for equal treatment in employment and occupation, OJ L 303/16, 2 December 2000, Art. 15. However, in other respects, legal challenges to aspects of consociation may still be possible under EU law: see e.g. Case C-274/96, *Bickel and Franz* [1998] ECR I-7637.

76. *Belios v. Switzerland* (1988) 10 EHRR 466.

drafted Bosnian reservation (one drafted with 'precision and clarity,'[77] and in terms not 'too vague or broad for it to be possible to determine their exact meaning or scope'[78]) would be unlikely to have been considered a general reservation. That is because the potential incompatibility would be enshrined in constitutional arrangements that were clear and unambiguous, and therefore could be specified with precision.

Such approaches seem superficially attractive, but have several significant problems. Even assuming that specific derogations or reservations are legally permitted, which is a technical question of some complexity,[79] such a move may well prove itself to be a barrier to successfully concluding a negotiation. Nystuen recounts how, in the Dayton negotiations, the question of derogating from the ECHR or the international human rights instruments 'was never considered . . . primarily for political reasons'. She continues:

> Some of the western politicians and diplomats who had been involved in the negotiations knew that the ethnic privileges were highly doubtful from a human rights perspective, but the tendency was rather to play this aspect down than to highlight it. Bringing up the issue of derogation . . . would, in all likelihood, have been counter-productive in terms of reaching an agreement at all.[80]

Indeed, she suggests, it 'is entirely possible that such a move in itself could have ruined the negotiations'.[81] In other negotiations, the political difficulty of going down the route of using derogations from particular treaties as a way out of potential problems is likely to be exacerbated when negotiators are advised that such derogations for reasons of emergency are also typically *temporary* arrangements.[82] There is, finally, a significant danger that, in following this route, trying to close off the availability of judicial review completely may result in the new arrangements becoming even more complex, being filled with even more veto points, and preventing courts from doing what they are often good at. They may even encourage lawyers and courts to find ways around these exclusions and limits. There is often nothing more determined than a court faced with an exclusion clause restricting its jurisdiction, adding an added layer of legal complexity.

---

77. *Belios v. Switzerland* (n. 76) [55].   78. *Belios v. Switzerland* (n. 76) [55].
79. Nystuen (n. 36) ch. 8.   80. Nystuen (n. 36) 184.   81. Nystuen (n. 36) 186.
82. See e.g. Jamie Oraá, *Human Rights in States of Emergency in International Law* (Oxford: Oxford University Press 1992) 237.

G. Underestimating democratic ratification by the consociational partners

It is surprising and somewhat troubling that there was an obvious distinction between the Bosnian and the Belgian consociation cases that the Court did *not* stress. A much narrower basis for its decision was available to the Court. One of the most significant differences between the Belgian and the Bosnian cases is that the consocational measures in Bosnia were not supported by any recognizably democratic ratification process. This was in marked contrast with Belgium, where the democratic and inclusive nature of the support received for the arrangements across the different communities was clear. Not only is it arguable that the United States, and the international community, foisted the Dayton Accords on Bosnia,[83] but it is also apparent that the minority groups that make up the 'Others' were not even invited to the negotiating table, and had no opportunity subsequently to accept or reject the package that was agreed by the negotiators on behalf of the three 'constituent peoples'.[84] The DPA was not only created through the full vigour of coercive US diplomacy, but it was also not ratified by any referendum that enabled the relevant groups to endorse it. Northern Ireland's 1998 Belfast Agreement, which secured majority support in both jurisdictions in Ireland (and also achieved, just, a concurrent majority of unionists and nationalists within Northern Ireland), stands in marked contrast, as does the Burundi constitution, also ratified in a referendum. The Constitution of Iraq of 2005—ratified in fifteen of its eighteen governorates, as well as by a majority overall, thereby meeting the ratification criteria established in the negotiation of Iraq's transitional administrative law—provides a third recent example.[85]

83. See Richard Holbrooke, *To End a War* (London: Random House 1998); Daniel Curran, James K. Sebenius, and Michael Watkins, 'Two Paths to Peace: Contrasting George Mitchell in Northern Ireland with Richard Holbrooke in Bosnia-Herzegovina' (2004) 20 Negotiation Journal 513.
84. Florian Bieber observes that none of the power-sharing arrangements and the political units have been legitimized by referendum: Florian Bieber, 'The Balkans: The Promotion of Power-Sharing by Outsiders' in Joanne McEvoy and Brendan O'Leary (eds) *Power-Sharing in Deeply Divided Places* (Philadelphia, PA: University of Pennsylvania Press, in press).
85. Brendan O'Leary, *How to Get out of Iraq with Integrity* (Philadelphia, PA: University of Pennsylvania Press 2009) 145, table 7.1. On the Constitution of Iraq, see John McGarry and Brendan O'Leary, 'Iraq's Constitution' (n. 55); Ashley S. Deeks and Matthew D. Burton,

We noted earlier in this chapter that Issacharoff argued that courts should be more willing to intervene where corporate consociational arrangements are *maintained* because of 'a lock up of power by self-interested incumbents' rather than because of 'a genuine compromise'. We would go further, but in a rather different direction. In general, as we hope we have made clear, we favour consociational bargains being unwound only by the parties to that bargain themselves, according to their agreed rules—and there is certainly a role for courts, including constitutional courts, in ensuring that they comply with such rules. But, that said, we also favour making the democratic inclusiveness of the process under which the bargain was arrived at a key test of its political acceptability *and* a key element in deciding whether a particular consociational arrangement should pass muster under human rights scrutiny. The absence of any significant reliance by the ECtHR on the absence of democratic ratification procedures in the Bosnian case is troubling because it renders uncertain those European consociational arrangements that *have* a significant democratic mandate (in Belgium, Northern Ireland, Macedonia, and, perhaps in the future, Cyprus). Perhaps it is necessary to add that such democratic mandates are likely to be defensible only when they are concurrent—that is, only when supportive majorities are elicited from each of the consociational partners respectively.

Our suggestion is not without difficulties, however. The DPA was intended to make peace among warring parties and set in place arrangements that were deemed necessary to do that. The 'Others' were not among the warring parties. What if they had been present during the negotiations and had raised their objections, and the overwhelming majority, including the representatives (such as they were) of the three main groups, had then rejected their arguments? Would their unsuccessful participation have been sufficient to justify affirming the arrangements that resulted? We can also imagine analogous circumstances in which the 'Others' participate and agree to provisions that they dislike under the threat that conflict will continue if they do not.[86] What effect should such consent have? Are

---

'Iraq's Constitution: A Drafting History' (2007) 40 Cornell International Law Journal 1. For the Transitional Administrative Law, see Karna Ekland, Brendan O'Leary, and Paul R. Williams, 'Negotiating a Federation in Iraq' in Brendan O'Leary, John McGarry, and Khaled Salih (eds) *The Future of Kurdistan in Iraq* (Philadelphia, PA: University of Pennsylvania Press 2005) and see the Bibliographical guide at the end of this book.

86. Such, arguably, was the perspective of Northern Ireland's Alliance Party and its Women's Coalition: see (for the Alliance Party) Stephen Farry and Sean Neeson, 'Beyond the "Band-

international or regional courts obliged to be suspicious of any negotiation result, constitutional or otherwise, reached on the basis of rights being balanced or traded for peace, on the analogy of viewing agreements made under duress as unacceptable? The ECtHR has only just begun to engage with these questions and its answers are, again, somewhat ambiguous. The Grand Chamber, in *DH*,[87] held that individuals were unable to waive the right not to be subject to racial discrimination because 'it would run counter to an important public interest'.[88] In any event, the Grand Chamber stated that, even in so far as such a waiver is permissible, it 'must be established in an unequivocal manner and be given in full knowledge of the facts, that is to say on the basis of informed consent and without constraint'.[89]

H. Undermining judicial legitimacy

Neither Pildes nor Issacharoff, despite their insightfulness, appear to have envisaged the possibility that, were courts to strike down aspects of an ethnic consociational bargain, their judgment might simply be ignored. Yet, to date, that is what appears to be happening following the Bosnia decision, with potential damage to the Court's own long-term credibility and the legitimacy of the Bosnian Constitutional Court.

Wojciech Sadurski usefully distinguishes between four different types of legitimacy applicable to courts.[90] 'Sociological legitimacy' relates to the legitimacy of the courts judged against the 'standards adopted in a given community'; 'normative legitimacy' refers to procedural 'factors such as rationality, reasonableness, consistency', among others. He also distinguishes 'input legitimacy' from 'output legitimacy'. The former is focused on pedigree: are constitutional courts set up in a way that properly confers legitimacy on them? The latter addresses what the courts deliver: the consequences of

Aid" Approach: An Alliance Party Perspective upon the Belfast Agreement' (1999) 22 Fordham Journal of International Law 1221, and (for the Women's Coalition) Kate Fearon and Monica McWilliams, 'The Good Friday Agreement: A Triumph of Substance over Style' (1999) 22 Fordham Journal of International Law 1250.

87. *DH v. Czech Republic* (2008) 47 EHRR 3, [204].
88. See also *Sampanis v. Greece*, Application no. 32526/05, 5 June 2008, [95].
89. *DH* (n. 87) [202].
90. Wojciech Sadurski, *Constitutional Courts in Transition Processes: Legitimacy and Democratization*, Sydney Law School Research Paper No 11/53 (Sydney: University of Sydney, Faculty of Law 2011).

their actions are judged according to the broad political values espoused by the society.

We can say, at the moment at least, that the sociological, normative, and output legitimacy of the ECtHR's judgment is low among Bosnian Serb and Bosnian Croat politicians, whereas it is high among many academic Court-watchers and human rights activists. Marko Milanovic captures this gap in perceptions well:

> From the Strasbourg perspective, the result in *Sejdić* . . . could hardly have been different. Ethnic discrimination is repugnant to any form of liberalism, and the Court would simply not set a precedent that would potentially open the door to future cases seeking further exceptions to the Convention's prohibition on such discrimination. Viewed from Sarajevo, however, the clarity of the law does not sit very comfortably with the messy facts on the ground.[91]

The *Pilav* case pending before the Court at the time of writing may further complicate matters.[92]

Formally, Bosnia has a legal obligation to 'abide by the final judgment of the Court'. The Committee of Ministers of the Council of Europe is tasked with supervising the execution of final judgments of the Court.[93] The decision of the Court was referred to the Committee of Ministers to supervise compliance in *Sejdić and Finci*.[94] A group of human rights non-governmental organizations (NGOs)—the Benjamin N. Cardozo School of Law, Human Rights Watch, and Minority Rights Group International (MRG), which included those who represented Mr Finci before the Court—continued their involvement by making submissions to the Committee of Ministers on how the judgment should be implemented.[95] According to a declassified information document of the Ministers' Deputies,[96] there has

---

91. Marko Milanovic, '*Sejdić & Finci v. Bosnia and Herzegovina*' (2010) 104 American Journal of International Law 636, 638.

92. See the discussion concerning the *Pilav* case: Chapter 6, 'C. Challenges to the presidency election arrangements'.

93. Article 46(1) and (2) ECHR.

94. See Hodžić and Stojanović (n. 39) 27–33 for a detailed account of the discussions within Bosnia on the implementation of the decision, until late 2010.

95. See *Submissions under Rule 9 of the Rules of the Committee of Ministers by Benjamin N. Cardozo School of Law, Human Rights Watch and Minority Rights Group International (MRG) on Execution of Judgment, 26 May 2010*, DH-DD(2010)307E, 9 June 2010; and *Submissions under Rule 9 of the Rules of the Committee of Ministers by Benjamin N. Cardozo School of Law, Human Rights Watch and Minority Rights Group International (MRG) on Execution of Judgment, 16 November 2011*, DH-DD(2011)1065, 24 November 2011.

96. *Memorandum: Sejdić and Finci*, CM-INF/DH(2011)6, 8 February 2011.

been a flurry of diplomatic activity attempting to secure the constitutional changes necessary to bring Bosnia into compliance with the Convention, but so far, at the time of writing, without success. Ms Micheline Calmy-Rey, chairperson of the Committee of Ministers, visited Sarajevo in April 2010, where she stressed that the authorities should speed up the required process of constitutional reform and amend the Electoral Code in compliance with the judgment. In May 2010, the outgoing and incoming chairpersons of the Committee, Ms Calmy-Rey and Mr Antonio Milošoski, reminded Bosnia of the importance of implementing the Court's judgment. In May and November 2010, Mr Milošoski discussed constitutional reform in Bosnia in Sarajevo with Bosnia Foreign Minister Sven Alkalaj. The Committee urged the Bosnian authorities to bring the country's constitution in line with the Convention, in July, September, and December 2010. The chairman encouraged the political parties to incorporate the question of constitutional reform in their coalition-building discussions. In addition, in 2010, the Council of Europe's Parliamentary Assembly stressed the need to accord to the 'Others' an effective opportunity to participate fully in political life, by running in elections to the presidency and participating in the designation of delegates to the House of Peoples.[97] In March 2010, the president of the Parliamentary Assembly visited Sarajevo, and urged the political leaders and members of the Bosnia Parliament to comply with the judgment.

Nor has the involvement of the European Union and arm-twisting by the United States yet broken the logjam. In January 2010, then EU Commissioner for Enlargement Ollie Rehn wrote to the chairman of the Council of Ministers of Bosnia, requesting information on measures envisaged in this case. In March 2010, the subsequent EU Commissioner for Enlargement, Štefan Füle, stated that it would be very important to execute this judgment before the October general elections. In April of that year, US Deputy Secretary of State James B. Steinberg and Spanish Foreign Minister Miguel Ángel Moratinos discussed constitutional amendments with the political leaders of Bosnia in Sarajevo. In June 2010, the European Parliament called on the Bosnian authorities, in the context of comprehensive constitutional reform, to amend the relevant constitutional provisions and provisions of

---

97. Resolution 1626 (2008) on the Honouring of Obligations and Commitments by Bosnia and Herzegovina; Resolution 1701 (2010) on the Functioning of Democratic Institutions in Bosnia and Herzegovina.

the Bosnia Electoral Code as soon as possible to comply with the Grand Chamber judgment.[98]

None of this activity led to any changes to meet the requirements of the Grand Chamber's judgment. The hope that changes would be introduced to enable the October 2010 elections to be conducted under new rules was not realized. Assessing developments up to late 2010, Edin Hodžić and Nenad Stojanović identified an 'absence of political will among the key actors to seriously address the issue'.[99]

The fragility of the Bosnian government added to the difficulties in implementation. Following the October 2010 elections, fourteen months elapsed before a coalition government could be formed—a coalition that collapsed only six months later, in May 2012. During this period, external pressure continued, but to little effect. In March 2011, the Council of Europe's Ministers' Deputies formally rapped Bosnia over the knuckles for its failure to implement.[100] The Resolution noted the continuing failure to reach a political consensus on the content of the constitutional and legislative amendments necessary to execute the Grand Chamber judgment, despite the Committee's repeated calls to do so, and regretted that 'no information has been provided on developments regarding the procedural steps taken to implement this judgment as well as the different proposals made in this respect'. In April 2012, the chairman of the Committee of Ministers of the Council of Europe stressed the need to ensure full implementation of the judgment, stressing the linkage between implementation and future membership of the European Union.[101]

The perception of observers as to the likelihood of agreement is mixed. Rudi Kocjančič believes that Bosnia 'will not adopt the constitutional amendments without an authoritative and intense intervention by the international community, especially the European Union'.[102] Céline Tran argues that there is some consensus among the local parties to introduce the necessary changes, in contrast to wider constitutional change, and that

98. *Memorandum* (n. 96).

99. Hodžić and Stojanović (n. 39) 33.

100. *Memorandum* (n. 96); *Case of Sejdić and Finci against Bosnia and Herzegovina (Application No. 27996/06): Communication from the Delegation of Bosnia and Herzegovina*, DH-DD(2010)108E, 26 February 2010; *Submissions* (n. 95).

101. Declaration of the Chairman of the Committee of Ministers of the Council of Europe on the *Sejdić and Finci* case, 25 April 2012.

102. Rudi Kocjančič, 'Bosnia and Herzgovina between Dayton and Brussels' (2011) 4 Journal of Comparative Politics 67, 86.

'there is a greater chance that a constitutional reform limited to the discriminatory electoral rules will be carried out due to political consensus, the
Council of Europe reprimand, and the lure of EU accession'. There are
various factors 'motivating Bosnia to adhere to the Court's judgment', in
particular that compliance is 'a prerequisite for EU integration' and that EU
accession 'is one of the few common grounds that Bosnian political leaders
share'.[103] The European Union, as we have seen, has used Bosnia's desire to
become a member to pressure local politicians to introduce constitutional
changes. In March 2012, for example, Herman van Rompuy, President of
the European Council, reiterated that the European Union 'look[s] forward
to and expect[s] credible steps in bringing the Constitution in line with' the
ECHR.[104] In June 2012, an EU-hosted meeting in Brussels of Bosnia's
senior politicians resulted in an agreement 'to amend the Constitution by
30 November 2012 and, to this end, to present draft constitutional amendments to the Parliamentary Assembly of Bosnia and Herzegovina by
31 August 2012'.[105]

By July 2012, however, some respected observers were doubtful whether
this agreement was likely to result in an agreed solution and were becoming
more sceptical of the EU's strategy of linking future membership with
implementation of the judgment. The International Crisis Group concluded that the 'EU should not make implementing the ECtHR decision
a prerequisite for a credible membership application if it seeks through
comprehensive reform to put the country on a firm footing'.[106] The danger
is, of course, that the non-implementation of the Bosnian judgment not
only weakens the sociological output legitimacy of the ECtHR in Bosnia,
but may further weaken the Court's legitimacy elsewhere. A court that is
disobeyed begins to lose its credibility.

Turning now to the impact of the Court's decision on judicial 'input
legitimacy', the main issue relates to the effect of its decision on the

---

103. Céline Tran, 'Striking a Balance between Human Rights and Peace and Stability: A Review
    of the European Court of Human Rights Decision *Sejdić and Finci v. Bosnia and Herzgovina*'
    (2011) 18 Human Rights Brief 3, 7. See further Nicola Sibona, 'BiH From Dayton to the
    European Union' (2010) 1 International Journal of Rule of Law, Transitional Justice and
    Human Rights 150, on prospective moves towards EU membership negotiations.
104. Press statement by the President of the European Council, Herman van Rompuy, following
    the meeting with the chairman of the Council of Ministers of Bosnia and Herzegovina,
    Mr Vjekoslav Bevanda, PCE EUCO 45/12, Brussels, 9 March 2012.
105. Council of Europe, Committee of Ministers, 1147th Meeting, 4 and 6 July 2012.
106. International Crisis Group, *Bosnia's Gordian Knot: Constitutional Reform*, Europe Briefing
    No. 68, (2012) 1.

legitimacy of the Constitutional Court of Bosnia. Bardutzky has raised the issue of whether, under the approach adopted in *Sejdić and Finci*, the composition of the Constitutional Court could itself be seen as question-able.[107] If so, it would be profoundly ironic if the carefully negotiated rules to ensure equal presence in the Constitutional Court for the three constitu-ent peoples were in future deemed illegitimate, whereas the position of foreigners on the Court was not regarded as suspect.

I. Different readings of the Court's judgment

In this chapter, we have identified difficulties with the Court's judgment, but it has not been possible to be definitive in assessing the effect of the case, not least because the reasoning presented by the Court to justify its decision is surprisingly sketchy and somewhat ambiguous. On one reading, what the Court was doing was casting a sceptical gaze on consociations generally (the broad interpretation). Taken to an extreme, the logic of the Court's position (although not its actual words) might be seen as 'a prelude to a complete shift from ethnocracy to full affirmation of citizens as individuals in the organisa-tion of the state'.[108] If the Court's decision indicates that this is the likely trajectory of human rights courts' reactions to consociations in general, we consider this to be deeply unfortunate, for the reasons that we have outlined.

But, on another view, the case may have less dramatic effects on other consociational agreements than we fear. First, the decision deals only with who can be a candidate for office rather than with who can define the voting constituency that chooses among the candidates. Second, there is more than a hint in some of the scholarly commentary on the case that the Dayton Agreement was viewed more negatively than any other consociational agree-ment would be. Thomas Burri, for example, has surmised that what he terms the 'Dayton Constitution' 'probably does not enjoy the same pristine standing as other, non-imposed constitutions' and that the Court's decision might not,

---

107. Bardutzky (n. 64) 328. The Human Rights Committee, which adjudicates applications under the UN International Covenant on Civil and Political Rights, rejected on its merits a claim that the introduction in Belgium of a gender quota for male and female judges was contrary to the Convention on the grounds that the use of the criterion of gender was justified: *Jacobs v. Belgium*, Communication No. 943/2000, UN Doc. CCPR/C/81/D/943/2000, 17 August 2004.

108. Hodžić and Stojanović (n. 39) 15.

therefore, create 'a precedent'.[109] That, perhaps, is good news, although the Court hardly made this conclusion evident in its judgment.

A third reason to regard the decision as of possibly limited effect on Bosnian arrangements and on consociations generally is that perhaps all that the Court was aiming to achieve was to require the parties to liberalize the existing Bosnian consociational arrangements by specifying that the 'Others' should have the opportunity to be elected to the presidency and the House of Peoples. On this latter reading (the more restrictive interpretation), the Court aimed to reform the consociational arrangements rather than to abolish them—what Edin Hodžić and Nenad Stojanović have described as 'opening up room for something akin to a *pluralisation of ethnocracy* by merely including minorities in the state's tripartite structure and in the formula of power-sharing among the constituent ethnicities applied so far'.[110] That more restrictive interpretation is, we suggest, the most constructive reading.

This more restrictive interpretation of the judgment clearly gives rise to fewer problems than the broader interpretation, but even the more restrict-ive interpretation is, we consider, problematic in two respects. It would be hard to argue that liberalizing the Bosnian consociation would not, overall, lead to a better system, but the key issues are when to make the changes, how, and who has the legitimate authority to do so. In the Belgian cases, the opportunity for the Court to 'unwind' the political bargain was mostly avoided—wisely in our view—whereas in *Sejdić and Finci* the Court appears much more prominently in the role of an 'unwinder'. More generally, although we have suggested that liberalizing the Bosnian constitution, moving towards a more liberal and away from corporate consociational arrangements, would lead to a better system overall, we do so only with reservations. Our principal reservation is simple. Protagonists to a conflict may well consider that it is necessary to bind themselves to corporate arrangements to ensure their mutual protection and this perceived need may well, in the circumstances, be an entirely rational choice.

109. Thomas Burri, 'The Rigidity of Structures to Protect Minorities: Hidden Facets of the Strasbourg Court's Judgment in *Sejdić* and the Banjul Commission's Decision in *Endorois*' in Daniel Thürer (ed.) *The Rigidity of Structures to Protect Minorities, Vol. 3* (Zurich: Schulthess forthcoming).
110. Hodžić and Stojanović (n. 39) 15, emphasis original.

Conclusions and policy implications

The European Court of Human Rights' decision in *Sejdić and Finci* has, we have argued, significantly altered the approach that it previously took to judicial review of key consociational arrangements in Belgium. We have sought here to account for this change and to assess its major implications. We have considered how far the Court's decision challenges previous well-reasoned academic hypotheses about how courts are likely to react to being asked to unpick the profound political compromises that consociations inevitably involve and we have suggested that the new approach adopted by the Court requires the modification of these theories.

The Court's decision is ambiguous and can be given either a broader or narrower interpretation (the former being more sceptical of consociations than the latter). If the broader interpretation subsequently proves to be the correct interpretation, and indicates the likely trajectory of this and other human rights courts' reactions to consociations, we have suggested that this may have several problematic consequences for courts themselves. We are able, first, to make an informed prediction about how future legal and political advisers are likely to counsel the makers of future power-sharing agreements with consociational components: they will advise on the exclusion of bills of rights with wide application, and seek to exclude regional courts and the jurisprudence of international human rights law. We fear, also, that future international or cosmopolitan courts that follow in the path of the European Court of Human Rights may suffer from reduced legitimacy, as a result of the political rejection of their judgments.

We fear that any deepening of the trend of judicial scepticism of consociations will be deeply unfortunate in another critical respect, because it will leave future diplomats, delegates, and peace negotiators in other places riven by bloody ethnic conflicts with considerably less flexibility in reaching either a transitional or durable political settlement, and may therefore unintentionally contribute to prolonging such conflicts.

To avoid these unfortunate consequences, we have also argued for two key principles that constitutional, regional, and international courts would be well advised to consider, as and when they hear future analogous cases. The first of these is that consociations in states or regions of states that have been ratified through referendums, especially with the concurrent assent of the affected groups or peoples, deserve a higher margin of appreciation from courts than do those that have not. This is not an idle recommendation, given that any Cyprus settlement will be conditional on concurrent assent from Greek and Turkish Cypriots, and given also that the Belfast (or Good Friday) Agreement was endorsed by majorities in both parts of Ireland and by 71 per cent of the voters within Northern Ireland.

The second is that consociations are best unwound, as and when that is thought to be required, by the parties who made the relevant bargain, with or without mediators (not arbitrators). If that bargain was initially broadly inclusive in its negotiation and produced with relatively little overt great power, regional, or local coercion, then its provisions for its own review and amendment deserve the profound respect of courts, whether they are specialized human rights courts or otherwise.

We have implicitly suggested two more conclusions, which we shall flesh out a little further. The first is practical. Courts are well advised to weigh more than the judgments of legal advisory bodies, however distinguished, and human rights non-governmental organizations (NGOs), however committed, when they evaluate whether critical human rights are adversely affected by consociational bargains. They should also take greater care to hear the general, and not only the particular, case for consociational arrangements. They also minimally need accurate surveys of public opinion and professionally credible evaluations of what group members themselves regard as vital national, ethnic, religious, or linguistic concerns, as well as international and local security assessments by experts on civil wars.

The second implicit conclusion is more political, but it also has implications for the way in which courts approach consociational bargains. Although a move from corporate to more liberal principles of consociation may, other things being equal, indeed be better for all citizens, especially 'others', there should be no presumption that there are always feasible institutional alternatives to corporate principles. Difference-blind rules for making and running institutions can always be imagined that will protect more than the largest group. We can all think of them. Yet the fact that they can be formulated proves nothing about their feasibility. All such rules will have advantages and disadvantages for key groups, and their leaders and followers will not be slow to deduce their implications, material and symbolic. If the parties to negotiations do not agree on difference-blind rules, it may not be because those parties are illiberal, or contemptuous of human rights provisions, or lacking in expertly provided knowledge of alternatives, but rather because they are existentially anxious about the future of their group and have no reason to trust cosmopolitan rules to protect them from their often equally anxious co-negotiators.

Liberalizing some features of the Bosnian consociation would likely lead to a better political system for all Bosnians, but we have argued that deciding when to make such changes, who is to make them, and how they should be made should not be in the hands of a court. We have argued that the majority of the European Court of Human Rights' answers to these questions are troubling and its reasoning unpersuasive. The judges of Europe's most distinguished human rights institution have made the tasks of diplomats and peacemakers much harder than was once the case. Unintentionally, but imprudently, they may have endangered too many humans' rights to existence and cast doubt on forms of political practice with a strong track record of helping to terminate violent conflicts.

Bibliographical guide

This guide is not comprehensive, but it will enable the reader to follow up matters of interest in English. Only items cited in the main text are found in the Bibliography at the end of the book.

* * *

For commentary on *Sejdić and Finci v. Bosnia and Herzegovina*, see: Samo Bardutzky, 'The Strasbourg Court on the Dayton Constitution' (2010) 6 European Constitutional Law Review 309; Lucy Claridge, 'Protocol 12 and *Sejdić and Finci v Bosnia and Herzegovina*: A Missed Opportunity?' (2011) 1 European Human Rights Law Review 82; Lindsey E. Wakely, 'From Constituent Peoples to Constituents: Europe Solidifies Fundamental Political Rights for Minority Groups in *Sejdić v Bosnia*' (2010) 36 North Carolina Journal of International Law and Commercial Regulation 233; Marko Milanovic, 'Case Note' (2010) 104 American Journal of International Law 636; Steven Wheatley, 'The Construction of the Constitutional Essentials of Democratic Politics by the European Court of Human Rights following *Sejdić* and *Finci*', in Rob Dickinson, Elena Katselli, Colin Murray, and Ole W. Pedersen (eds) *Examining Critical Perspectives on Human Rights* (Cambridge: Cambridge University Press 2012).

In addition, Edin Hodžić and Nenad Stojanović offer a book-length discussion of possible models for implementing the judgment: *New/Old Constitutional Engineering? Challenges and Implications of the European Court of Human Rights Decision in the Case of* Sejdić and Finci v BiH (Sarajevo: Analitika 2011).

* * *

On Arend Lijphart's work on consociations, begin with four especially important book-length collections by Lijphart on consociation: *The Politics of Accommodation: Pluralism and Democracy in the Netherlands* (2nd edn, Berkeley, CA: University of California Press 1975); *Democracy in Plural Societies: A Comparative Exploration* (New Haven, CT: Yale University Press 1977); *Power-Sharing in South Africa* (Berkeley, CA: University of California Press 1985); and *Thinking about Democracy: Power Sharing and Majority Rule in Theory and Practice* (London: Routledge 2008).

For criticisms of Lijphart's work, see Brian Barry, 'The Consociational Model and its Dangers' (2006) 3 European Journal of Political Research 393 and 'Review Article: Political Accommodation and Consociational Democracy' (1975) 5 British Journal of Political Science 477; Adriano Pappalardo, 'The

Conditions for Consociational Democracy: A Logical and Empirical Critique'
(1981) 9 European Journal of Political Research 365; Rinus van Schendelen,
'The Views of Arend Lijphart and Collected Criticism' (1984) 1 Acta Politica 19;
and Ian Steven Lustick, 'Lijphart, Lakatos and Consociationalism' (1997)
50 World Politics 88.

For defences, see Arend Lijphart, 'Consociational Theory and its Critics' in
Power-Sharing in South Africa (Berkeley, CA: University of California Press 1985);
Brendan O'Leary, 'Debating Consociation: Normative and Explanatory Argu-
ments' in Sid Noel (ed.) *From Power-Sharing to Democracy: Post-Conflict Institutions
in Ethnically Divided Societies* (Montreal, QC: McGill-Queens University
Press 2005).

For both pro- and anti- positions, see the essays in Rupert Taylor (ed.) *Consocia-
tional Theory: McGarry and O'Leary and the Northern Ireland Conflict* (London:
Routledge 2009). See also Arend Lijphart, 'Constitutional Design for Divided
Societies' (2004) 15 Journal of Democracy 96; John McGarry and Brendan
O'Leary, 'Introduction: Consociational Theory and Northern Ireland' in *The
Northern Ireland Conflict: Consociational Engagements* (Oxford: Oxford University
Press 2004); and Brendan O'Leary, Bernard Grofman, and Jorgen Elklit, 'Divisor
Methods for Sequential Portfolio Allocation in Multi-Party Executive Bodies:
Evidence from Northern Ireland and Denmark' (2005) 49 American Journal of
Political Science 198.

* * *

For assessments of the success of consociations, see all of the preceding
literature. In addition, Michaela Mattes and Burcu Savan have examined all peace
agreements between 1945 and 2005, and found that the presence of power-sharing
provisions (parity- or proportionally-based), in conjunction with appropriate security
arrangements, significantly reduces the likelihood of conflict recurrence: 'Fostering
Peace after Civil War: Commitment Problems and Agreement Design' (2009)
53 International Studies Quarterly 737. See also Pippa Norris, *Driving Democracy: Do
Power-Sharing Institutions Work?* (Cambridge: Cambridge University Press 2008), who
argues that power-sharing democracies outperform their alternatives.

Forthcoming work briefly surveys 'large N' studies from different authors, who
individually and jointly suggest that power-sharing works in (a) enhancing the
performance of democratic governments, (b) enhancing the performance of non-
democratic governments, (c) reducing the likelihood of political violence in
established democracies, and (d) reducing the likelihood of civil war or conflict-
recurrence in countries that have experienced such disorders: Brendan O'Leary,
'Power-Sharing in Deeply Divided Places: An Advocate's Introduction' in John
McEvoy and Brendan O'Leary (eds) *Power-Sharing in Deeply Divided Places* (Philadelphia, PA: University of Pennsylvania Press 2013).

* * *

On the antecedents of consociations: antecedents have been found in sources as
diverse as the political thought of the Protestant jurist Althusius and the early

twentieth-century Austro-Marxists. On Althusius, see Carl J. Friedrich (ed.) *Politica Methodice Digesta of Johannes Althusius (Althaus)* (Cambridge, MA: Harvard University Press 1932); Thomas O. Hueglin, 'Johannes Althusius: Medieval Constitutionalist or Modern Federalist?' (1979) 9 Publius 9; Patrick Riley, 'Three Seventeenth-Century German Theorists of Federalism: Althusius, Hugo and Leibniz' (1976) 6 Publius 7. On the Austro-Marxists, see, among others, Otto Bauer, *The Question of Nationalities and Social Democracy*, ed. Ephraim Nimni, trans. Joseph O'Donnell (Minneapolis, MN: University of Minnesota Press 2000); Ephraim Nimni, *Marxism and Nationalism: Theoretical Origins of the Present Crisis* (London: Pluto Press 1993).

* * *

On the European Union as a consociation, see Oliver Costa and Paul Magnette, 'The European Union as a Consociation? A Methodological Assessment' (2003) 26 West European Politics 1; Florian Bieber, 'Lessons from the European Union for Institutional Design in Multinational States' in Astrid Epiney, Marcel Haag, and Andreas Heinemann (eds) *Challenging Boundaries: Essays in Honor of Roland Bieber* (Baden-Baden: Nomos DIKE 2007); Paul Taylor, 'The Lessons of the European Community: The Limits of European Integration—The Concepts of Consociation and Symbiosis' in *International Organization in the Modern World: The Regional and the Global Process* (London: Pinter 1993); Brendan O'Leary, 'An Iron Law of Federations? A (Neo-Diceyian) Theory of the Necessity of a Federal Staatsvolk, and of Consociational Rescue: The Fifth Ernest Gellner Memorial Lecture' (2001) 7 Nations and Nationalism 273.

* * *

On Belgium as a consociation, see Kris Deschouwer, *Ethnic Structure, Inequality and Governance of the Public Sector in Belgium* (Geneva: United Nations Research Institute for Social Development 2004), and 'And the Peace Goes on? Consociational Democracy and Belgian Politics in the Twenty-First Century' (2006) 29 West European Politics 895. See also Thomas Ertman, 'Liberalization, Democratization, and the Origins of a "Pillarized" Civil Society in Nineteenth-Century Belgium and the Netherlands' in Nancy Bermeo and Philip Nord (eds) *Civil Society before Democracy: Lessons from Nineteenth-Century Europe* (Lanham, MD: Rowman and Littlefield 2000); Arend Lijphart (ed.) *Conflict and Coexistence in Belgium: The Dynamics of a Culturally Divided Society* (Berkeley, CA: Institute of International Studies, University of California 1981).

For discussions in English of consociation and federation in Belgium among political scientists, see Andre Alen and Rusen Ergec, *Federal Belgium After the Fourth State Reform of 1993* (Brussels: Ministry of Foreign Affairs, External Trade and Development Cooperation 1994); Marijke Breuning, 'Ethnopolitical Parties and Development Cooperation: The Case of Belgium' (1999) 32 Comparative Political Studies 724; Kris Deschouwer, 'And the Peace Goes on? Consociational Democracy and Belgian politics in the Twenty-First Century' (2006) 29 West European Politics 895; James A. Dunn Jr, 'The Revision of the Constitution in Belgium:

A Study in the Institutionalization of Ethnic Conflict' (1974) 27 The Western Political Quarterly 143; John Fitzmaurice, *The Politics of Belgium: A Unique Federalism* (Boulder, CO: Westview 1996); Martin O. Heisler, 'Hyphenating Belgium: Changing State and Regime to Cope with Cultural Division' in Joseph V. Montville (ed.) *Conflict and Peacemaking in Multiethnic Societies* (Lexington, MA: Lexington Books 1989); Liesbet Hooghe, *A Leap in the Dark: Nationalist Conflict and Federal Reform in Belgium* (Ithaca, NY: Cornell University Press 1991); Liesbet Hooghe, 'Belgium: Hollowing the Center' in Ugo M. Amoretti and Nancy Bermeo (eds) *Federalism and Territorial Cleavages* (Baltimore, MD: Johns Hopkins University Press 2004); Steven L. Lamy, 'Policy Responses to Ethnonationalism: Consociational Engineering in Belgium' in John F. Stack (ed.) *The Primordial Challenge: Ethnicity in the Contemporary World* (Westport, CT: Greenwood Press 1986); Arend Lijphart (ed.) *Conflict and Coexistence in Belgium: The Dynamics of a Culturally Divided Society* (Berkeley, CA: Institute of International Studies, University of California 1981); Alexander Murphy, 'Belgium's Regional Divergence: Along the Road to Federalism' in Graham Smith (ed.) *Federalism: The Multiethnic Challenge* (London: Longman 1995); Brendan O'Leary, 'Belgium and its Thoughtful Electoral Engineers: In Response to Kris Deschouwer and Philippe van Parijs' in *Electoral Engineering for a Stalled Federation, Rethinking Belgium's Institutions in the European Context* (Brussels: Re-Bel e-book 2009); Paul Pennings, 'The Utility of Party and Institutional Indicators of Change in Consociational Democracies' in Kurt R. Luther and Kris Deschouwer (eds) *Party Elites in Divided Societies: Political Parties in Consociational Democracy* (London: Routledge 1999); Wilfried Swenden, Marleen Brans, and Lieven de Winter, 'The Politics of Belgium: Institutions and Policy under Bipolar and Centrifugal Federalism' (2006) 29 West European Politics 863; and Philippe van Parijs, 'Power-Sharing versus Border-Crossing in Ethnically Divided Societies' in Ian Shapiro and Stephen Macedo (eds) *Designing Democratic Institutions* (New York: New York University Press 2000).

* * *

On the Netherlands as a consociation, start with Arend Lijphart, *The Politics of Accommodation: Pluralism and Democracy in the Netherlands* (2nd edn, Berkeley, CA: University of California Press 1975); Jacob P. Krujit, 'The Netherlands: The Influence of Denominationalism on Social Life and Organizational Patterns' in Kenneth D. McRae (ed.) *Consociational Democracy: Political Accommodation in Segmented Societies* (Toronto, ON: McClelland and Stewart 1974); and Hans Daalder, 'On Building Consociational Nations: The Cases of the Netherlands and Switzerland' (1971) 23 International Social Science Journal 355. See also Kurt R. Luther and Kris Deschouwer (eds) *Party Elites in Divided Societies: Political Parties In Consociational Democracy* (London: Routledge 1999). For discussions of 'depillarization', start with special issues of *Acta Politica*, the Dutch political science journal, in 1984, 2002, and 2008; see also Paul Pennings, 'The Evolution of Dutch Consociationalism, 1917–1997' (1997) 33 Netherlands Journal of Social Sciences 9.

* * *

On Switzerland as a consociation, start with Hans Daalder, 'On Building Consociational Nations: The Cases of the Netherlands and Switzerland' (1971) 23 International Social Science Journal 35; Jürg Steiner, 'Switzerland: "Magic Formula" Coalitions' in Eric Browne and John Dreijmanis (eds) *Government Coalitions in Western Democracies* (New York: Longman 1982); David Altman, 'Collegiate Executives and Direct Democracy in Switzerland and Uruguay: Similar Institutions, Opposite Political Goals, Distinct Results' (2008) 14 Swiss Political Science Review 483. See also Klaus Armingeon, 'The Stability of the Swiss Federal Government Coalition in Comparative Perspective' (1999) 28 Osterreichische Zeitschrift fur Politikwissenschaft 463, 'Consociationalism and Economic Performance in Switzerland 1968–1998: The Conditions of Muddling through Successfully' (2002) 37 Acta Politica 121, and 'The Effects of Negotiation Democracy: A Comparative Analysis' (2002) 41 European Journal of Political Research 81; Arend Lijphart, 'Negotiation Democracy versus Consensus Democracy: Parallel Conclusions and Recommendations' (2002) 41 European Journal of Political Research 107.

* * *

On consociation in Austria: in the 1970s, see Gerhard Lehmbruch, 'A Non-Competitive Pattern of Conflict Management in Liberal Democracies: The Case of Switzerland, Austria and Lebanon', Alfred Diamant, 'Austria: The Three Lager and the First Republic', and Peter Pulzer, 'Austria: The Legitimizing Role of Political Parties', all in Kenneth D. McRae (ed.) *Consociational Democracy: Political Accommodation in Segmented Societies* (Toronto, ON: McClelland and Stewart 1974).

For evaluations from the 1970s onward, see Anton Pelinka, 'Consociational Democracy in Austria' (2002) 37 Acta Politica 139; Kurt. R Luther and Wolfgang C. Müller (eds) *Politics in Austria: Still A Case of Consociationalism?* (London: Frank Cass 1992); Peter Pulzer, 'Politics in Austria: Still a Case of Consociationalism?' (1993) 22 Osterreichische Zeitschrift fur Politikwissenschaft 105.

* * *

On consociational aspects of Cyprus and negotiations over Cyprus, see Thomas W. Adams, 'The First Republic of Cyprus: A Review of an Unworkable Constitution' (1966) 19 Western Political Quarterly 475; Claire Palley, *An International Relations Debacle: The UN Secretary-General's Mission of Good Offices in Cyprus, 1999–2004* (Oxford: Hart 2005); United Nations, *Basis for the Comprehensive Settlement of the Cyprus Problem (The Annan Plan)* (Geneva: United Nations 2004). See also Arend Lijphart, 'Proportionality by Non-PR Methods: Ethnic Representation in Belgium, Cyprus, Lebanon, New Zealand, West Germany and Zimbabwe' in Arend Lijphart and Bernard Grofman (eds) *Choosing an Electoral System: Issues and Alternatives* (New York: Praeger 1986).

There is also work on power-sharing and Cyprus forthcoming from Neo Loizides, *Cyprus: Federal and Consociational Failures and Prospects* (Philadelphia, PA: University of Pennsylvania Press forthcoming) and John McGarry.

* * *

On Burundi and its consociational arrangements, see René Lemarchand, 'Burundi 1972: A Forgotten Genocide' and 'Burundi's Endangered Transition', both in René Lemarchand, *The Dynamics of Violence in Central Africa* (Philadelphia, PA: University of Pennsylvania Press 2009); René Lemarchand, 'Burundi 1972: Genocide Denied, Revised, and Remembered' in René Lemarchand (ed.) *Forgotten Genocides: Oblivion, Denial, and Memory* (Philadelphia, PA: University of Pennsylvania Press 2011); Daniel P. Sullivan, 'The Missing Pillars: A Look at the Failure of Peace in Burundi through the Lens of Arend Lijphart's Theory of Consociational Democracy' (2005) 43 The Journal of Modern African Studies 75.

* * *

On the Interim Constitution in South Africa as a consociation, see the exchange between Arend Lijphart and Michael Kelly Conners: Michael Kelly Conners, 'The Eclipse of Consociationalism in South Africa's Democratic Transition' (1996) 3 Democratization 420; Arend Lijphart, 'South African Democracy: Majoritarian or Consociational?' (1998) 5 Democratization 144. See also Courtney Jung and Ian Shapiro, 'South Africa's Negotiated Transition: Democracy, Opposition, and the New Constitutional Order' (1995) 23 Politics and Society 269 and 'South Africa Revisited: A Reply to Koelble and Reynolds' (1996) 24 Politics and Society 238; cf. Thomas A. Koelble and Andrew Reynolds, 'Power-Sharing Democracy in the New South Africa' (1996) 24 Politics and Society 221.

* * *

On the Northern Ireland Good Friday Agreement as a consociation, start with Brendan O'Leary, 'The Nature of the Agreement' in John McGarry and Brendan O'Leary, *The Northern Ireland Conflict: Consociational Engagements* (Oxford: Oxford University Press 2004); John McGarry and Brendan O'Leary, 'Consociational Theory, Northern Ireland's Conflict, and its Agreement, Part One: What Consociationalists Can Learn from Northern Ireland' (2006) 41 Government and Opposition 43, 'Consociational Theory, Northern Ireland's Conflict, and its Agreement, Part Two: What Anti-Consociationalists Can Learn from Northern Ireland' (2006) 41 Government and Opposition 249, and 'Part I: Argument—Power Shared after the Deaths of Thousands' and 'Part III: Response—Under Friendly and Less-Friendly Fire' in Rupert Taylor (ed.) *Consociational Theory: McGarry and O'Leary and the Northern Ireland Conflict* (London: Routledge 2009).

For legal assessments of consociationalism in Northern Ireland and its relationship to the British constitution, see Christopher McCrudden, 'Northern Ireland and the British Constitution since the Belfast Agreement', in Jeffrey Jowell and Dawn Oliver (eds) *The Changing Constitution* (6th edn, Oxford: Oxford University Press 2007) and 'Northern Ireland, the Belfast Agreement, and the British Constitution' in Jeffrey Jowell and Dawn Oliver (eds) *The Changing Constitution* (5th edn, Oxford: Oxford University Press 2004).

For a discussion of the relationship between the Framework Convention on National Minorities and Northern Ireland consociational arrangements, see Christopher McCrudden, 'Consociationalism, Equality, and Minorities in the Northern

Ireland Bill of Rights Debate: The Role of the OSCE High Commissioner on National Minorities' in John Morison, Kieran McEvoy, and Gordon Anthony (eds) *Judges, Transition and Human Rights* (Oxford: Oxford University Press 2007).

* * *

On Trentino, Alto Adige, South Tyrol, see the Special Statute for Trentino Alto Adige; for detailed discussions, see Stefan Wolff, *Disputed Territories: The Transnational Dynamics of Ethnic Conflict Settlement* (New York/Oxford: Berghahn Books 2003) and Antony Alcock, 'From Conflict to Agreement in Northern Ireland: Lessons from Europe in Northern Ireland and the Divided World' in John McGarry (ed.) *The Northern Ireland Agreement in Comparative Perspective* (Oxford: Oxford University Press 2001).

* * *

On the literature in English on the Bosnian war and its aftermath, start with Sabrina P. Ramet, *Thinking about Yugoslavia: Scholarly Debates about the Yugoslav Breakup and the Wars in Bosnia and Kosovo* (Cambridge: Cambridge University Press 2005). Follow with Sumantra Bose, *Bosnia after Dayton: Nationalist Partition and International Intervention* (New York: Oxford University Press 2002); Steven L. Burg and Paul S. Shoup, *The War in Bosnia-Herzegovina: Ethnic Conflict and International Intervention* (Armonk, NY/London: M.E. Sharpe 1999); David Chandler, *Bosnia: Faking Democracy after Dayton* (2nd edn, London: Pluto Press 2000); Norman Cigar, *Genocide in Bosnia: The Policy of 'Ethnic Cleansing* (College Station, TX: Texas A&M University Press 1995); Cynthia Cockburn, 'The Anti-Essentialist Choice: Nationalism and Feminism in the Interaction between Two Women's Projects' (2001) 6 Nations and Nationalism 611; Kimberley Coles, *Democratic Designs: International Intervention and Electoral Practices in Postwar Bosnia-Herzegovina* (Ann Arbor, MI: University of Michigan Press 2007); Robert J. Donia and John V.A. Fine Jr, *Bosnia and Hercegovina: A Tradition Betrayed* (London: Hurst 1994); Robert M. Hayden, *Blueprints for a House Divided: The Constitutional Logic of the Yugoslav Conflict* (Ann Arbor, MI: University of Michigan Press 1999) and '"Democracy" without a Demos? The Bosnian Constitutional Experiment and the Intentional Construction of Nonfunctioning States' (2005) 19 East European Politics and Societies 226; Attila Hoare, 'The Croatian Project to Partition Bosnia-Hercegovina, 1990–94' (1997) 31 East European Quarterly 121; Noel Malcolm, *Bosnia: A Short History* (London: Macmillan 1994); Joseph Marko, '"Unity in Diversity"? Problems of State- and Nation-Building in Post-Conflict Situations: The Case of Bosnia-Herzegovina' (2006) 30 Vermont Law Review 503; Indraneel Sircar, 'Transnational Consociation in Northern Ireland and in Bosnia-Hercegovina: The Role of Reference States in Post-Settlement Power-Sharing' (Unpublished PhD Thesis, London School of Economics and Political Science, University of London, London, 2006); Marc Weller and Stefan Wolff, 'Bosnia and Herzegovina Ten Years after Dayton: Lessons for Internationalized State-Building' (2006) 5 Ethnopolitics 1.

* * *

On the European Convention on Human Rights, the best history of its drafting is AW Brian Simpson, *Human Rights and the End of Empire: Britain and the Genesis of the European Convention* (Oxford: Oxford University Press 2004).

Standard accounts of jurisprudence of the European Court of Human Rights and its methods may be found in: Alastair Mowbray, *Cases and Materials on the European Convention on Human Rights* (3rd edn, Oxford: Oxford University Press 2012); Robin C.A. White and Clare Ovey, *Jacobs, White and Ovey: The European Convention on Human Rights* (5th edn, Oxford: Oxford University Press 2010); David Harris, Michael O'Boyle, Edward Bates, and Carla Buckley, *Harris, O'Boyle and Warbrick: Law of the European Convention on Human Rights* (2nd edn, Oxford: Oxford University Press 2009); Pieter van Dijk, Fried van Hoof, Arjen van Rijn, and Leo Zwaak, *Theory and Practice of the European Convention on Human Rights* (4th rev. edn, Intersentia Publishers 2006). Broader assessments of the Convention are given in Marie-Bénédicte Dembour, *Who Believes in Human Rights? Reflections on the European Convention* (Cambridge: Cambridge University Press 2006); Conor Gearty, *Can Human Rights Survive?* (Cambridge: Cambridge University Press 2006).

Bibliography

This bibliography includes books, chapters and articles cited in the main text. It does not include items in the bibliographical guide. References to legal documents and cases are found following this bibliography.

Adams, T.W., 'The First Republic of Cyprus: A Review of an Unworkable Constitution' (1966) 19 Western Political Quarterly 475

Al-Ali, Z., 'Constitutional Drafting and External Influence' in T. Ginsburg and R. Dixon (eds) *Comparative Constitutional Law* (Cheltenham: Edward Elgar 2011)

Althusius, J., *Politica* (tr. F.S. Carney, Liberty Classics edn, Indianapolis, IN: Liberty Fund 1995)

Amar, A.R., *America's Constitution: A Biography* (London: Random House 2005)

Andeweg, R.B., 'Consociational Democracy' (2000) 3 Annual Review of Political Science 509

Anonymous (ed.) 'Special Issue: Analysis of the Northern Ireland Peace Agreement' (1999) 22 Fordham Journal of International Law

Anthony, G., 'Public Law Litigation and the Belfast Agreement' (2002) 8 European Public Law 401

——and Morison, J., 'The Judicial Role in the New Northern Ireland: Constitutional Litigation and Devolution Disputes' (2009) 21 European Review of Public Law 1219

Apter, D., 'Political Religion in the New Nations' in C. Geertz (ed.) *Old Societies and New States: The Quest for Modernity in Asia and Africa* (New York: Free Press 1963)

Balkin, J.M., 'The Constitution of Status' (1997) 106 Yale Law Journal 2313

Ball, P., Tabeau, E., and Verwimp, P., *The Bosnian Book of the Dead: Assessment of the Database (Full Report)*, Households in Conflict Network Research Design Note 5. Available online at <https://www.hrdag.org/resources/publications.shtml>

Bardutzky, S., 'The Strasbourg Court on the Dayton Constitution: Judgment in the case of *Sejdić and Finci v. Bosnia and Herzegovina*, 22 December 2009' (2009) 6 European Constitutional Law Review 309

Bell, C., *Peace Agreements and Human Rights* (Oxford: Oxford University Press 2000)

——, 'Peace Agreements: Their Nature and Legal Status' (2006) 100 American Journal of International Law 373

Benhabib, S., *The Claims of Culture: Equality and Diversity in the Global Era* (Princeton, NJ: Princeton University Press 2002)

Bentley, K. A. and Southall, R., *An African Peace Process: Mandela, South Africa and Burundi* (Cape Town: Nelson Mandela Foundation HSRC Press 2005)

Bickel, A.M., 'The Supreme Court, 1960 Term: Foreword—The Passive Virtues' (1961) 75 Harvard Law Review 40

——, *The Least Dangerous Branch: The Supreme Court at the Bar of Politics* (Indianapolis, IN: Bobbs-Merrill 1962)

Bieber, F., 'The Balkans: The Promotion of Power-Sharing by Outsiders' in J. McEvoy and B. O'Leary (eds) *Power-Sharing in Deeply Divided Places* (Philadelphia, PA: University of Pennsylvania Press 2013)

Bogaards, M. and Crepaz, M.M.L., 'Consociational Interpretations of the European Union' (2002) 3 European Union Politics 357

Bose, S., *Bosnia after Dayton: Nationalist Partition and International Intervention* (Oxford: Oxford University Press 2002)

Brams, S.J., *Mathematics and Democracy: Designing Better Voting and Fair-Division Procedures* (Princeton, NJ: Princeton University Press 2008)

Braude, B. and Lewis, B. (eds) *Christians and Jews in the Ottoman Empire: The Functioning of a Plural Society, Vol. II—The Arabic-Speaking Lands* (Teaneck, NJ: Holmes and Meier 1982)

Brusis, M., 'The European Union and Interethnic Power-Sharing Arrangements in Accession Countries' (2003) 1 Journal on Ethnopolitics and Minority Issues in Europe 1

Burri, T., 'The Rigidity of Structures to Protect Minorities: Hidden Facets of the Strasbourg Court's Judgment in *Sejdić* and the Banjul Commission's Decision in *Endorois*' in D. Thürer (ed.) *The Rigidity of Structures to Protect Minorities, Vol. 3* (Zurich: Schulthess forthcoming)

Chandler, D., *Bosnia: Faking Democracy after Dayton* (2nd edn, London: Pluto Press 2000)

Cheeseman, N. and Blessing-Miles, T., 'Power-Sharing in Comparative Perspective: The Dynamics of "Unity Government" in Kenya and Zimbabwe' (2010) 48 Journal of Modern African Studies 203

Choudhry, S., 'Bridging Comparative Politics and Comparative Constitutional Law: Constitutional Design in Divided Societies' in S. Choudhry (ed.) *Constitutional Design for Divided Societies: Integration or Accommodation?* (Oxford: Oxford University Press 2008)

——, 'After the Rights Revolution: Bills of Right in the Post-Conflict State' (2010) 6 Annual Review of Law and Social Science 301

——and Stacey, R., 'Independent or Dependent? Constitutional Courts in Divided Societies' in C. Harvey and A. Schwartz (eds) *Rights in Divided Societies* (Oxford: Hart 2012)

Chryssochoou, D.N., 'Democracy and Symbiosis in the European Union: Towards a Confederal Consociation?' (1994) 17 West European Politics 1

Connor, W., *The National Question in Marxist-Leninist Theory and Strategy* (Princeton, NJ: Princeton University Press 1984)

Cornford, F.M., *Microcosmographia Academica: Being a Guide for the Young Academic Politician* (Cambridge: MainSale Press 1993 [1908])

Council of Europe, *A General Legal Reference Framework to Facilitate the Settlement of Ethno-political conflicts in Europe*, CDL-INF(2000)16 (Strasbourg: Venice Commission 2000). Available online at <http://www.venice.coe.int/docs/2000/CDL-INF(2000)016-e.asp>

Curran, D.L., Sebenius, J.K., and Watkins, M., 'Two Paths to Peace: Contrasting George Mitchell in Northern Ireland with Richard Holbrooke in Bosnia-Herzegovina' (2004) 20 Negotiation Journal 513

Deeks, A.S. and Burton, M.D., 'Iraq's Constitution: A Drafting History' (2007) 40 Cornell International Law Journal 1

Deloria Jr, V. and Lytle, C.M., *The Nations Within: The Past and Future of American Indian Sovereignty* (New York: Pantheon Books 1984)

de Renzy Channer, A., 'Defeat and Resurrection: A Political History of the Pan-Albanian Revolutionary Movement, 1912–2010' (Unpublished PhD thesis, University of Pennsylvania 2012)

Deschouwer, K., *Ethnic Structure, Inequality and Governance of the Public Sector in Belgium* (Geneva: United Nations Research Institute for Social Development 2004)

Dickson, B., 'The House of Lords and the Northern Ireland Conflict: A Sequel' (2006) 69 The Modern Law Review 383

Dunlap, C.J.J., 'Law and Military Interventions: Preserving Humanitarian Values in 21st Century Conflicts' (Humanitarian Challenges in Military Intervention Conference, Carr Center for Human Rights Policy, Kennedy School of Government, Harvard University 2001)

Dzehtsiarou, K., 'Does Consensus Matter? Legitimacy of European Consensus in the Case Law of the European Court of Human Rights' [2011] Public Law 534

Ekland, K., O'Leary, B., and Williams, P.R., 'Negotiating a Federation in Iraq' in B. O'Leary, J. McGarry, and K. Salih (eds) *The Future of Kurdistan in Iraq* (Philadelphia, PA: University of Pennsylvania Press 2005)

Embree, A.T., *Utopias in Conflict: Religion and Nationalism in Modern India* (ed. Mark Juergensmeyer, Berkeley, CA: University of California Press 1990)

Engelhart, K., 'Bosnia's Three-Headed Beast: *Sejdić and Finci v. Bosnia and Herzegovina* and the Case for "Reasonable" Discrimination'. Available online at <http://www.sant.ox.ac.uk/esc/docs/Dahrendorf_k.engelhart.doc>

Farry, S. and Neeson, S., 'Beyond the Band-Aid Approach: An Alliance Party Perspective upon the Belfast Agreement' (1999) 22 Fordham Journal of International Law 1221

Fearon, K. and McWilliams, M., 'The Good Friday Agreement: A Triumph of Substance over Style' (1999) 22 Fordham Journal of International Law 1250

Feldman, D., 'Renaming Cities in Bosnia and Herzegovina' (2005) 3 International Journal of Constitutional Law 649

——, 'Constitutionalism, Deliberative Democracy, and Human Rights' in J. Morison and K. McEvoy (eds) *Judges, Transition, and Human Rights* (Oxford: Oxford University Press 2007)

Finlay, A., *Governing Ethnic Conflict: Consociation, Identity and the Price of Peace* (London: Routledge 2011)

Fraenkel, J. and Firth, S., *The 2006 Military Takeover in Fiji: A Coup to End All Coups?* (Canberra: Australia National University, E Press 2009)

Fredman, S., *Discrimination Law* (2nd edn, Oxford: Oxford University Press 2011)

Gallagher, M., 'Comparing Proportional Representation Electoral Systems: Quotas, Thresholds, Paradoxes and Majorities' (1992) 22 British Journal of Political Science 469

Gould, C.C., 'Diversity and Democracy: Representing Differences' in S. Benhabib (ed.) *Democracy and Difference* (Princeton, NJ: Princeton University Press 2005)

Grewe, C., 'Making Minorities More Influential in Public Life: Opportunities Provided by Existing Constitutional Arrangements and Their Limitations' in Venice Commission, *The Participation of Minorities in Public Life, Science and Technique of Democracy* (Strasbourg: Council of Europe 2011)

Hanf, T., *Coexistence in Wartime Lebanon: Decline of a State and Rise of a Nation* (tr. J. Richardson, London: I.B. Tauris & Co 1993)

——, 'Conflict Regulation and Crises in Multi-Communal States: The Proliferation of Multi-Communal States in the Twentieth Century' in *Coexistence in Wartime Lebanon: Decline of a State and Rise of a Nation* (London: I.B. Tauris & Co 1993)

Harris, P. and Reilly, B., *Democracy and Deep-Rooted Conflict: Options for Negotiators* (Stockholm: International Institute for Democracy and Electoral Assistance 1998)

Hartzell, C. and Hoddie, M., 'Institutionalizing Peace: Power Sharing and Post-Civil War Conflict Management' (2003) 47 American Journal of Political Science 318

—— and ——, *Crafting Peace: Power-Sharing Institutions and the Negotiated Settlement of Civil Wars* (University Park, PA: Penn State University Press 2007)

Hayden, R.M., *Blueprints for a House Divided: The Constitutional Logic of the Yugoslav Conflict* (Ann Arbor, MI: University of Michigan Press 1999)

Hitchner, B.R., 'From Dayton to Brussels: The Story behind the Constitutional and Governmental Reform Process in Bosnia and Herzegovina' (2006) 30 The Fletcher Forum of World Affairs 125

Hoare, A., 'The Croatian Project to Partition Bosnia-Hercegovina, 1990–94' (1997) 31 East European Quarterly 121

Hodžić, E. and Stojanović, N., *New/Old Constitutional Engineering? Challenges and Implications of the European Court of Human Rights Decision in the Case of Sejdić and Finci v BiH* (Sarajevo: Analitika 2011)

Holbrooke, R., *To End a War* (London: Random House 1998)

Hueglin, T.O., *Early Modern Concepts for a Late Modern World: Althusius on Commu-nity and Federalism* (Waterloo, ON: Wilfrid Laurier University Press 1999)

International Crisis Group, *Bosnia's Gordian Knot: Constitutional Reform*, Europe Briefing No. 68 (2012). Available online at <http://www.crisisgroup.org/en/regions/europe/balkans/bosnia-herzegovina.aspx>

Issacharoff, S., 'Constitutionalizing Democracy in Fractured Societies' (2004) 82 Texas Law Review 1861

——, 'Democracy and Collective Decision-Making' (2008) 6 International Journal of Comparative Law 231

——, 'Courts, Constitutions, and the Limits of Majoritarianism' in J. McEvoy and B. O'Leary (eds) *Power-Sharing in Deeply Divided Places* (Philadelphia, PA: University of Pennsylvania Press 2013)

Iyer, V., 'Enforced Consociationalism and Deeply Divided Societies: Some Reflec-tions on Recent Developments in Fiji' (2007) 3 International Journal of Law in Context 127

Kennedy, D., *The Dark Side of Virtue: Reassessing International Humanitarianism* (Princeton, NJ: Princeton University Press 2004)

Klug, H., *South Africa's Experience in Constitution-Building*, University of Wisconsin Legal Studies Research Paper No. 1157 (2011). Available online at <http://papers.ssrn.com/sol3/papers.cfm?abstract_id=1808168>

Knaus, G. and Martin, F., 'Lessons from Bosnia and Herzegovina: Travails of the European Raj' (2003) 14 Journal of Democracy 60

Kocjančič, R., 'Bosnia and Herzgovina between Dayton and Brussels' (2011) 4 Journal of Comparative Politics 67

Krook, M.L. and O'Brien, D.Z., 'The Politics of Group Representation: Quotas for Women and Minorities Worldwide' (2010) 42 Comparative Politics 253

——, Lovenduski, J., and Squires, J., 'Gender Quotas and Models of Political Citizenship' (2009) 39 British Journal of Political Science 781

Kurland, P.B. and Lerner, R., *The Founders' Constitution* (Chicago, IL: University of Chicago Press 1987)

Kymlicka, W., *Multicultural Odysseys: Navigating the New International Politics of Diversity* (Oxford: Oxford University Press 2007)

——, 'The Internationalization of Minority Rights' in S. Choudhry (ed.) *Consti-tutional Design for Divided Societies: Integration or Accommodation?* (Oxford: Oxford University Press 2008)

Lantschner, E. and Poggeschi, G., 'Quota System, Census and Declaration of Affiliation to a Linguistic Group' in J. Woelk, F. Palermo, and J. Marko (eds) *Tolerance through Law: Self-Governance and Group Rights in South Tyrol* (The Hague: Martinus Nijhoff 2008)

Lemarchand, R., 'Burundi 1972: A Forgotten Genocide' in R. Lemarchand, *The Dynamics of Violence in Central Africa* (Philadelphia, PA: University of Pennsylva-nia Press 2009)

Lemarchand, R., 'Burundi's Endangered Transition' in R. Lemarchand, *The Dynamics of Violence in Central Africa* (Philadelphia, PA: University of Pennsylvania Press 2009)

——, 'Burundi 1972: Genocide Denied, Revised, and Remembered' in R. Lemarchand (ed.) *Forgotten Genocides: Oblivion, Denial, and Memory* (Philadelphia, PA: University of Pennsylvania Press 2011)

Lerner, H., *Making Constitutions in Deeply Divided Societies* (Cambridge: Cambridge University Press 2011)

Levenson, S., *Our Undemocratic Constitution: Where the Constitution Goes Wrong (and How We Can Fix It)* (Oxford: Oxford University Press 2006)

Lijphart, A., *The Politics of Accommodation: Pluralism and Democracy in the Netherlands* (2nd edn, Berkeley, CA: University of California Press 1975)

——, *Democracy in Plural Societies: A Comparative Exploration* (New Haven, CT: Yale University Press 1977)

——, 'Foreword: One Basic Problem, Many Theoretical Options—and a Practical Solution?' in J. McGarry and B. O'Leary (eds) *The Future of Northern Ireland* (Oxford: Clarendon Press 1990)

——, 'Self-Determination versus Pre-Determination of Ethnic Minorities in Power-Sharing Systems' in W. Kymlicka (ed.) *The Rights of Minority Cultures* (Oxford: Oxford University Press 1995)

——, *Patterns of Democracy: Government Forms and Performance in Thirty-Six Countries* (New Haven, CT: Yale University Press 1999)

——, *Thinking about Democracy: Power Sharing and Majority Rule in Theory and Practice* (London: Routledge 2008)

Lynch, M., '*Robinson v Secretary of State for Northern Ireland*: Interpreting Constitutional Legislation' [2003] Public Law 640

Mansfield, A.M., 'Ethnic but Equal: The Quest for a New Democratic Order in Bosnia and Herzegovina' (2003) 103 Columbia Law Review 2052

Mattes, M. and Savun, B., 'Fostering Peace after Civil War: Commitment Problems and Agreement Design' (2009) 53 International Studies Quarterly 737

McCrudden, C., 'Mainstreaming Equality in the Governance of Northern Ireland' (1998) 22 Fordham International Law Journal 1696

——, 'Consociationalism, Equality, and Minorities in the Northern Ireland Bill of Rights Debate: The Role of the OSCE High Commissioner on National Minorities' in J. Morison, K. McEvoy, and G. Anthony (eds) *Judges, Transition and Human Rights* (Oxford: Oxford University Press 2007)

——, 'Post-Multiculturalism, Freedom of Religion, and Antidiscrimination Law: The *JFS* Case Considered' (2011) 9 International Journal of Constitutional Law 200

——, 'Religion and Education in Northern Ireland', in M. Hunter-Henin (ed.) *Law, Religious Freedom and Education in Europe* (Aldershot: Ashgate 2012)

McCulloch, A., 'The Track Record of Centripetalism in Deeply Divided Places' in J. McEvoy and B. O'Leary (eds) *Power-Sharing in Deeply Divided Places* (Philadelphia, PA: University of Pennsylvania Press 2013)

McEvoy, J., '"We Forbid!" The Mutual Veto and Power-Sharing Democracy' in J. McEvoy and B. O'Leary (eds) *Power-Sharing in Deeply Divided Places* (Philadelphia, PA: University of Pennsylvania Press 2013)

McGarry, J. and O'Leary, B., 'Introduction: Consociational Theory and Northern Ireland' in J. McEvoy and B. O'Leary (eds) *Essays on the Northern Ireland Conflict: Consociational Engagements* (Oxford: Oxford University Press 2004)

——and ——, 'Stabilising Northern Ireland's Agreement' (2004) 75 Political Quarterly 213

——and ——, *The Northern Ireland Conflict: Consociational Engagements* (Oxford: Oxford University Press 2004)

——and ——, 'Iraq's Constitution of 2005: Liberal Consociation as Political Prescription' (2007) 5 International Journal of Constitutional Law 670

——and ——, 'Stabilising Northern Ireland's Agreement' in P. Carmichael and C. Knox (eds) *Devolution and Constitutional Change in Northern Ireland* (Manchester: Manchester University Press 2007)

——and ——, 'Consociation and its Critics: Northern Ireland after the Belfast Agreement' in S. Choudhry (ed.) *Constitutional Design for Divided Societies: Integration or Accommodation?* (Oxford: Oxford University Press 2008)

McRae, K.D., *Conflict and Compromise in Multilingual Society, Vol. 2: Belgium* (Waterloo, ON: Wilfrid Laurier University Press 1986)

Mearsheimer, J.J. and Pape, R.A., 'The Answer: A Three-Way Partition Plan for Bosnia and How the US Can Enforce It' *The New Republic*, 14 June 1993

Mehler, A., 'Not Always in the People's Interest: Power-Sharing Arrangements in African Peace Agreements' German Institute of Global and Areas Studies (GIGA) Working Papers (Hamburg: GIGA 2008). Available online at <http://repec.giga-hamburg.de/pdf/giga_08_wp83_mehler.pdf>

Milanovic, M., '*Sejdić & Finci v. Bosnia and Herzegovina*' (2010) 104 American Journal of International Law 636

Mill, J.S., 'Considerations on Representative Government' in H.B. Acton (ed.) *Utilitarianism: On Liberty and Considerations on Representative Government* (London: Dent 1988)

Morison, J., 'Ways of Seeing? Consociationalism and Constitutional Law Theory' in R. Taylor (ed.) *Consociational Theory: McGarry and O'Leary and the Northern Ireland Conflict* (London: Routledge 2009)

Mullender, R., 'Lawfare and the International Human Rights Movement' in R. Dickinson, E. Katselli, C. Murray, and O.W. Pederson (eds) *Examining Critical Perspectives on Human Rights* (Cambridge: Cambridge University Press 2012)

Neussl, P., 'Implementation of the Constitutional Court Decision on the "Constituent Peoples" in Bosnia and Herzegovina' (2003) 24 Human Rights Law Journal 309

Ní Aoláin, F., 'The Fractured Soul of the Dayton Peace Agreement: A Legal Analysis' (1998) 19 Michigan Journal of International Law 957

Nystuen, G., *Achieving Peace or Protecting Human Rights? Conflicts between Norms Regarding Ethnic Discrimination in the Dayton Peace Agreement* (The Hague: Martinus Nijhoff 2005)

O'Boyle, M., 'Electoral Disputes and the ECHR: An Overview' (2009–10) 30 Human Rights Law Journal 1

O'Brien, J.C., 'The Dayton Agreement in Bosnia: Durable Ceasefire, Permanent Negotiation' in I.W. Zartman and V.A. Kremenyuk (eds) *Peace versus Justice: Negotiating Forward- and Backward-Looking Outcomes* (Lanham, MD: Rowman and Littlefield 2005)

O'Leary, B., 'Gellner's Diagnoses of Nationalism: A Critical Overview—or What is Living and What is Dead in Gellner's Philosophy of Nationalism?' in J.A. Hall (ed.) *The State of the Nation: Ernest Gellner and the Theory of Nationalism* (Cambridge: Cambridge University Press 1998)

——, 'The Nature of the Agreement' (1999) 22 Fordham Journal of International Law 1628

——, 'The Protection of Human Rights under the Belfast Agreement' (2002) 72 Political Quarterly 353

——, 'Debating Consociational Politics: Normative and Explanatory Arguments' in S.J.R. Noel (ed.) *From Power-Sharing to Democracy: Post-Conflict Institutions in Ethnically Divided Societies* (Montreal, QC: McGill-Queens University Press 2005)

——, 'Power-Sharing, Pluralist Federation and Federacy' in B. O'Leary, J. McGarry, and K. Salih (eds) *The Future of Kurdistan in Iraq* (Philadelphia, PA: University of Pennsylvania Press 2005)

——, *How to Get out of Iraq with Integrity* (Philadelphia, PA: University of Pennsylvania Press 2009)

——, 'Power-Sharing in Deeply Divided Places: An Advocate's Conclusion' in J. McEvoy and B. O'Leary (eds) *Power-Sharing in Deeply Divided Places* (Philadelphia, PA: University of Pennsylvania Press 2013)

——, 'Power-Sharing in Deeply Divided Places: An Advocate's Introduction' in J. McEvoy and B. O'Leary (eds) *Power-Sharing in Deeply Divided Places* (Philadelphia, PA: University of Pennsylvania Press 2013)

——, Grofman, B., and Elklit, J., 'Divisor Methods for Sequential Portfolio Allocation in Multi-Party Executive Bodies: Evidence from Northern Ireland and Denmark' (2005) 49 American Journal of Political Science 198

——and McGarry, J., 'The Politics of Accommodation and Integration in Democratic States' in A. Guelke and J. Tournon (eds) *The Study of Politics and Ethnicity: Recent Analytical Developments* (Leverkusen: Barbara Budrich 2012)

Office of the High Representative, *The General Framework Agreement for Peace in Bosnia and Herzegovina*, 'Annex 7: Agreement on Refugees and Displaced Persons' (Sarajevo: OHR 1995)

Oraá, J., *Human Rights in States of Emergency in International Law* (Oxford: Oxford University Press 1992)

Palley, C., *An International Relations Debacle: The UN Secretary-General's Mission of Good Offices in Cyprus, 1999–2004* (Oxford: Hart 2005)

Peeters, P., 'Expanding Constitutional Review by the Belgian "Court of Arbitration"' (2005) 11 European Public Law 475

Phillips, A., *The Politics of Presence* (Oxford: Oxford University Press 2005)

Pildes, R.H., 'Foreword: The Constitutionalization of Democratic Politics' (2004) 118 Harvard Law Review 25

——, 'Ethnic Identity and Democratic Institutions: A Dynamic Perspective' in S. Choudhry (ed.) *Constitutional Design for Divided Societies: Integration or Accommodation?* (Oxford: Oxford University Press 2008)

Ramet, S.P., *Thinking about Yugoslavia: Scholarly Debates about the Yugoslav Breakup and the Wars in Bosnia and Kosovo* (Cambridge: Cambridge University Press 2005)

Reynolds, A., 'Reserved Seats in National Legislatures' (2005) 30 Legislative Studies Quarterly 301

——and Reilly, B., *The International IDEA Handbook of Electoral Design* (Stockholm: International Institute for Democracy and Electoral Assistance 1997)

Rosenberg, S.P., 'Promoting Equality after Genocide' (2007) 16 Tulane Journal of International and Comparative Law 329

Sadurski, W., *Equality and Legitimacy* (Oxford: Oxford University Press 2008)

——, *Constitutional Courts in Transition Processes: Legitimacy and Democratization*, Sydney Law School Research Paper No 11/53 (Sydney: University of Sydney, Faculty of Law 2011). Available online at <http://papers.ssrn.com/sol3/papers.cfm?abstract_id=1919363>

Sarajlić, E., 'Bosnian Elections and Recurring Ethnonationalisms: The Ghost of the Nation State' (2010) 9 Journal on Ethnopolitics and Minority Issues in Europe 66

Schneckener, U., 'Making Power-Sharing Work: Lessons from Successes and Failures in Ethnic Conflict Regulation' (2002) 39 Journal of Peace Research 203

Schwartz, A., 'How Unfair is Cross-Community Consent? Voting Power in the Northern Ireland Assembly' (2010) 61 Northern Ireland Legal Quarterly 349

Shahabuddinas, M., *A Normative Analysis of International Law Compatibility with Ethnic Conflicts*. Available online at <http://www.inter-disciplinary.net/ati/els/els2/Shahabuddin%20paper.pdf>

Sibona, N., 'BiH from Dayton to the European Union' (2010) 1 International Journal of Rule of Law, Transitional Justice and Human Rights 150

Sisk, T.D., *Democratization in South Africa: The Elusive Social Contract* (Princeton, NJ: Princeton University Press 1995)

——, *Power Sharing and International Mediation in Ethnic Conflicts* (Washington, DC: United States Institute of Peace 1996)

Šoštarić, M., 'Waiting for Godot: Efficiency of the BiH Judicial System in the Protection of Political Rights of Minorities' in A. Šehić, E. Demir, I. Stipanović, J. Jašarević, M. Sahadžić, M. Šoštarić, M. Savić, and R. Kotlo (eds) *Access to Justice on Bosnia and Herzegovina: Collection of Public Policy Analyses in the Field of Judiciary* (Sarajevo: Justice Network in Bosnia and Herzegovina 2011)

Steiner, H.J., 'Ideals and Counter-Ideals in the Struggle over Autonomy Regimes for Minorities' (1991) 66 Notre Dame Law Review 1539

Sweeney, J., 'Freedom of Religion and Democratic Transition' in A. Buyse and H. Michael (eds) *Transitional Jurisprudence and the ECHR: Justice, Politics and Rights* (Cambridge: Cambridge University Press 2011)

Taagepera, R. and Shugart, M.S., *Seats and Votes: The Effects and Determinants of Electoral Systems* (New Haven, CT: Yale University Press 1989)

Tansey, O., *Regime-Building, Democratization and International Administration* (Oxford: Oxford University Press 2009)

Taylor, A., 'Electoral Systems and the Promotion of "Consociationalism" in a Multiethnic Society: The Kosovo Assembly Elections of November 2001' (2005) 24 Electoral Studies 435

Taylor, P., 'The Lessons of the European Community: The Limits of European Integration—The Concepts of Consociation and Symbiosis' in P. Taylor (ed.) *International Organization in the Modern World: The Regional and the Global Process* (London: Pinter 1993)

Taylor, R. (ed.) *Consociational Theory: McGarry and O'Leary and the Northern Ireland Conflict* (London: Routledge 2009)

——, 'Introduction: The Promise of Consociational Theory' in R. Taylor (ed.) *Consociational Theory: McGarry and O'Leary and the Northern Ireland Conflict* (London: Routledge 2009)

Teitel, R., 'Transitional Justice and the Transformation of Constitutionalism' in T. Ginsburg and R. Dixon (eds) *Comparative Constitutional Law* (Cheltenham: Edward Elgar 2011)

Toal, G. and Dahlman, C.T., *Bosnia Remade: Ethnic Cleansing and its Reversal* (Oxford: Oxford University Press 2011)

Tran, C, 'Striking a Balance between Human Rights and Peace and Stability: A Review of the European Court of Human Rights Decision *Sejdić and Finci v. Bosnia and Herzgovina*' (2011) 18 Human Rights Brief 3

Tribe, L.H., 'The Puzzling Persistence of Process-Based Constitutional Theories' (1980) 89 Yale Law Journal 1063

Tull, D. and Mehler, A., 'The Hidden Costs of Power-Sharing: Reproducing Insurgent Violence in Africa' (2005) 104 African Affairs 375

US Central Intelligence Agency (CIA), *The World Factbook* (2000), available online at <https://www.cia.gov/library/publications/the-world-factbook/index.html>

Verougstraete, I., 'Judicial Politics in Belgium' in M.L. Volcansek (ed.) *Judicial Politics and Policy-Making in Western Europe* (London: Frank Cass 1992)

Wakeley, L.E., 'From Constituent Peoples to Constituents: Europe Solidifies Fundamental Political Rights for Minority Groups in *Sejdić v. Bosnia*' (2010) 36 North Carolina Journal of International Law and Commercial Regulation 233

Weller, M. and Nobbs, K. (eds) *Political Participation of Minorities: A Commentary on International Standards and Practice* (Oxford: Oxford University Press 2010)

——and Wolff, S., 'Bosnia and Herzegovina Ten Years after Dayton: Lessons for Internationalized State-Building' (2006) 5 Ethnopolitics 1

——, Metzger, B. and Johnson, N. (eds) *Settling Self-Determination Disputes: Complex Power-Sharing in Theory and Practice* (The Hague: Martinus Nijhoff 2008)

Wheatley, S., *Democracy, Minorities, and International Law* (Cambridge: Cambridge University Press 2005)

——, 'The Construction of the Constitutional Essentials of Democratic Politics by the European Court of Human Rights Following *Sejdić and Finci*' in R. Dickinson, E. Katselli, C. Murray, and O.W. Pederson (eds) *Examining Critical Perspectives on Human Rights* (Cambridge: Cambridge University Press 2012)

Wieman, A.M., 'Consociationalism with an External Actor in Bosnia: Blueprint for Success or Instability' (Unpublished MA dissertation, Rijksuniversiteit Groningen 2010)

Wippman, D., 'Practical and Legal Constraints on Internal Power-Sharing' in D. Wippman (ed.) *International Law and Ethnic Conflict* (Ithaca, NY: Cornell University Press 1998)

Wolff, S., 'Complex Power Sharing as Conflict Resolution: South Tyrol in Comparative Perspective' in J. Woelk, F. Palermo, and J. Marko (eds) *Tolerance through Law: Self-Governance and Group Rights in South Tyrol* (The Hague: Martinus Nijhoff 2008)

Yakinthou, C., *Political Settlements in Divided Societies: Consociationalism and Cyprus* (Basingstoke: Palgrave Macmillan 2009)

Ye'or, B., *The Dhimmi: Jews and Christians under Islam* (trs D. Maisel, P. Fenton, and D. Littman, Madison, NJ: Fairleigh Dickinson University Press 1985)

Table of Cases

INTER-AMERICAN COURT OF HUMAN RIGHTS

ITALIAN SUPREME COURT

UNITED KINGDOM

Table of State Constitutions and Legislation

UNITED KINGDOM

UNITED STATES

Table of International and Regional Treaties and Instruments

Table of Opinions, Reports, and Resolutions

Parliamentary Assembly

Venice Commission

See Council of Europe, European Commission for Democracy through Law

UNITED NATIONS

Human Rights Committee

Index